THE RELUCTANT ACTIVIST

Cover Photo Mark Mennie Photography
Helicopter Association of Canada Photos Paul Dixon
St. Louis AMTC photos Mark Mennie Photography
Seattle AMTC photos Mark Mennie Photography

You may order online at www.randymains.com

ISBN-13: 978-1725952003
ISBN-10: 1725952009

Typeset at SpicaBookDesign in Plantin
Printed and bound with www.createspace.com

For Kaye, my safe harbor…

Acknowledgments

*"If you see a turtle sitting on a fencepost
you can bet he didn't get up there by himself."*

My message would have never been heard without the effort and support of like-minded people. I want to thank those people here, alphabetically, for without them I would just be a guy with a very important message locked inside, with no way to get it 'out there'.

Alison DeGroot Associate Publisher HELICOPTERS Magazine.

Ammey McNalley

Bill Winn, General Manager National EMS Pilots Association.

Brig Bearden, Publisher at ECOCitySolutions Rotorcraft Pro Magazine.

Byron Edgington, Twenty-year veteran HEMS pilot, Author, Journalist.

Cam McCulloch, Manuscript editor and proof reader extraordinaire.

Christine Negroni, Freelance writer, aviation journalist, author.

Dana Maxfield, Creative Director at Oak Mountain Media, *Rotorcraft Pro* Magazine.

Dr. Andrew Berry, State Medical Director, NETS, New South Wales Australia.

Dr. Dan Hankins, Past President Association of Air Medical Services Emergency Medicine Staff Physician, Mayo Clinic.

Dr. David Claypool, Medical Director Mayo Clinic Medical Transport.

Dr. Graeme Field, President of the Aeromedical Society Australasia.

Dr. Kevin Hutton, CEO MedEvac Foundation International, CEO Golden Hour Data Systems.

Elizabeth Wegner, Project Manager, Oregon Aero.

Fred Jones, President, Helicopter Association of Canada.

Gail Mellegard, Business Development Manager Oregon Aero.

Glenn Lyden, Director, Medical Transport Public Affairs Mayo Clinic.

Jack Todaro, Marketing, Sales, Business Planner Oregon Aero.

Jeannie Krieger, Social manager/marketing coordinator, Oregon Aero.

Jon Bell, Jon Bell freelance writer Jon Bell Ink.

John Burton Design.

Jonathan Godfrey, Co-founder the Survivor's Network.

Kent Johnson, former President National EMS Pilot's Association.

Krysta Haugen, Co-founder the Survivor's Network.

Lisa Tofil, Partner in Holland and Knight firm fighting for patient's rights.

Lyn Burks, Editor In Chief at Rotorcraft Pro Media Network.

Marjorie Kramer, Oregon Aero.

Mark Mennie, Mark Mennie photography.

Matt Nicholls, Editor Wings and Helicopters magazine.

Matt Rigsby, FAA accident investigator.

Michael Burke, co-founder National EMS Pilot's Association.

Mike Dennis, President, CEO Founder, Oregon Aero.

Natasha Ross, Director of Education and Events Association of Air Medical Services.

Paul Dixon, Columnist at Wings / Helicopters Magazines, Photographer.

Paul Drucker, Director of Operations, Mayo Clinic.

Rex Alexander, former President National EMS Pilot's Association.

Rick Sherlock, President & CEO at Association of Air Medical Services (AAMS).

Ron Fergie, former President National EMS Pilot's Association.

Ron Whitney, former editor *Rotorcraft Pro* magazine.

Sandra Kinkade Hutton, President at Kinkaid International, also 23-year flight nurse.

Stu Cunningham, former President National EMS Pilot's Association.

Terry Palmer, Director of Training, Metro Aviation.

Tomas Judge, Executive Director at LifeFlight of Maine.

Tony Erickson, CEO Oregon Aero.

Treg Manning, Vice President, Commercial Sales and Marketing at American Eurocopter.

///

I also want to give special thanks to Linda Hanway. Linda, although we've never met in person, you have never failed to remind me whenever and where ever I speak to imagine you're sitting at the back of the room smiling, lending support and rooting for my cause.

Author's Note

When it comes to safely operating a helicopter air ambulance (HEMS), the Australians have it right.

My wife and I recently returned from Australia where I delivered two keynote safety speeches at their HEMS conference in Melbourne. What I learned there strengthened my argument for operating HEMS more safely in America.

On August 30, 2013, Phillip Hogan announced in his speech, "Civil Aviation Safety Authority regulations for the future of the Aeromedical Industry," that legislation is being proposed to make it *mandatory* for all air ambulance programs in Australia – helicopter and fixed-wing – to conform to part 121 airline standards of operation. That means mandating the use of twin-engine, two flight crew, fully instrument flight rules (IFR) category A, Performance Class 1 helicopters.

Performance Class 1 means an operation that, in the event of an engine failure in a helicopter with two engines, the helicopter is able to land within the rejected take-off distance available or safely continue the flight to an appropriate landing area on the remaining engine, depending on when the failure occurs. Performance Class 1 is the highest standard of "flyaway" capability during takeoff and landing any twin-engine helicopter can have.

Enacting similar legislation in the States would most certainly stem the terrible accident rate that has plagued the industry for the past 34 years.

As Hogan said in his speech, *"A patient does not have a choice to decide if they want to 'buy a ticket' to accept a certain level of risk by being transported on a HEMS helicopter so those patients who cannot choose for themselves, must be given the highest level of safety that can be afforded to them."*

The reality is 90 percent of the HEMS programs in Australia already voluntarily comply with the high airline standard. The operators do so for safety reasons. This new law will force those operators *not* already operating at the higher standard to comply.

The observations I make in this book to solve the safety issues in American HEMS that I have observed and practiced while living and flying abroad, are not unique. The same standards and practices have been recommended for quite a few years by the head of the Federal Aviation Administration (FAA), and representatives of the National Transportation Safety Board (NTSB), but for some unexplained reason here in America, their recommendations have not been made into law.

It is my hope that a day will come when laws similar to those soon to be enacted in Australia are embraced and followed back home. By doing so, those who fly on a HEMS helicopter can know they, too, have the highest level of safety that can be afforded to them.

I hope you enjoy my story detailing the last 29 years of my 13,000-hour international flying career. It is an adventure that has given me a gift that I am excited to offer you here: a much safer way to operate a HEMS helicopter that, if adopted in America, will surely save lives.

R.M.

Contents

THE RELUCTANT ACTIVIST

A Solution to Stop the Carnage Plaguing the Helicopter Air Medical Industry in America

Randolph P. Mains

car•nage /ˈkärnij/
Noun: The killing of a large number of people.
Synonyms: Mass murder, massacre, slaughter.

CHAPTER 1

August 8, 1988

Life Unraveling

I'm standing next to the helicopter's tail plane, looking up in disbelief at the massive damage I'd done. The accident was entirely my fault. I knew I shouldn't have been anywhere near a cockpit this morning. My mind wasn't focused on flight training, but I decided to fly anyway. It was a stupid mistake. The reality of knowing how badly I screwed up sickened me. As well as losing my wife to another man recently, it seemed likely I could now lose my job. This was not turning out to be one of my better mornings.

Omar, the junior Omani officer I'd been training, already saw the damage and was lying on the bench seat inside the cabin of the Bell 205 with his eyes closed – *resting* – waiting for the accident investigation team to arrive.

Omar loves to sleep. I once asked him, "Omar, why do you sleep so much?" and he replied, "Because it's so much better than real life."

What a character.

I wish I were outside "real life" right now.

I checked my watch: 0932. We were waiting for the accident investigation team to fly out from Seeb Airport to interview us. Ops said on the radio they'd arrive in about 45 minutes. That was 20 minutes ago.

I shielded my eyes against the morning desert sun looking up again at the tail rotor, still unable to believe the damage I'd caused. The 90-degree gearbox and the tail rotor were lying in a tangled mess, drooped on the opposite side of the pylon from where they should have been. The blades didn't really look that badly damaged considering they'd slammed into the dirt. If this had happened on a harder surface, like over tarmac at the airport, I would have gotten away with it because the stinger – the piece of tubular metal that sticks out from the end of the tailboom like a bee stinger – would have prevented the tail rotor from striking the ground. But we were flying over parched desert earth when it happened so the stinger dug in, which allowed the tail-rotor blades to strike the ground and caused one hellacious vibration through the airframe and my flight controls.

While we were skidding to a halt, decelerating through 30 knots, the vibration suddenly ceased. That had to be the point when the 90-degree gearbox, with its now out-of-balance tail rotor, sheared the four bolts holding it onto the top of the tail rotor pylon.

I looked away from the damage I'd caused and shook my head because I knew our fate could have been a whole lot worse.

I shouldn't have been flying because my mind wasn't on the job. Instead, I'd been thinking about my disintegrating marriage. It was over; I knew that. But I didn't want to admit it. I was an emotional wreck – not mentally fit. I had no business being in the cockpit but I flew anyway and ended up paying the price.

Four months before getting on an airplane in Los Angeles to begin this job nearly four years ago, my future wife and I had had a whirlwind summer romance. I'd invited her to join me on my annual two-week vacation to sail with me on my beloved 35-foot sloop *Moali*, my home for the five years I worked in San Diego. We'd planned to go scuba diving off the islands of San Clemente and Catalina, both situated off the Southern California coast.

I'd only known her for a few months prior to asking her to marry me. She'd been a flight nurse on the Life Flight team, hired as one of six new flight nurses to staff the third helicopter the hospital had added to its fleet. Soon after meeting her, going on two dinner dates and taking her out on only one day sail, I was quickly smitten and immediately drawn to her.

During our one-and-only sailing date she told me she was saving money to buy a sailboat of her own. She seemed to be everything I was looking for in a woman – smart, sporty, fun, pretty as well as being a top-notch nurse. We shared a common spirit of adventure too.

On the morning of our third day after sailing out of San Diego, while anchored off San Clemente Island, I was making preparations for our onward sail to Catalina. I'd just come out of the water from retrieving the anchor that had become snagged on a rock. While drying off in the dinghy next to the boat's cockpit, I asked her to marry me. She accepted and to seal the proposal she leaned over the aft lifeline to give me a kiss, accidentally bumped the stern-mounted barbecue and spilled several months of grey charcoal ash over my head and shoulders.

After a short civil ceremony in Catalina – wearing shorts and flip-flops and sporting great suntans – we made plans for our future. We'd live on *Moali* while working at Life Flight together until we could save enough money to quit our jobs, untie the dock lines and sail off to foreign ports. Then the job in Oman came along, which allowed us to quickly make some real money – "freedom chips" – the term cruising sailors use for cash. Our plan was to leave Oman one day to return to San Diego, put *Moali* back into the water, outfit her properly for blue-water sailing and takeoff on one huge adventure.

Thinking back on it now, I should have taken that incident with the barbecue as an omen of things to come.

Before the very recent and sudden collapse of my marriage I was very optimistic about the bright prospects for the two of us. At work I'd been asked by the chief pilot to be an instructor pilot and flight examiner for the helicopter side of the Police Air Wing. It was one of the highest compliments I had ever been paid in my professional career. I felt I was living a charmed life – a life that appeared promising on all fronts. Unfortunately, considering what I'd just done, it looked like my good fortune wouldn't last.

CHAPTER 2

Recalling Better Times

The accident happened when I was demonstrating an autorotation to Omar. An autorotation is an emergency procedure where you bring the machine down like an autogyro with no engine power being delivered to the rotor system, simulating losing an engine in a single-engine helicopter. The aircraft comes down very fast: about 2,200 to 2,500 feet per minute like an autogyro. When you are about 50 feet above the ground you flare the aircraft, which pulls the nose up to wash off the airspeed; then you level the aircraft and – using the inertia in the main rotor – you "cushion" the landing.

I was trying to teach Omar the importance of having at least 60 knots of airspeed prior to initiating the flare; otherwise, the rate of descent will not decrease when you do so. I demonstrated it to him once but I sensed that he didn't really understand what I was trying to teach him, so I showed him again. This time I flew well below the 60 knots and exaggerated the flare. Big mistake.

I over-pitched the aircraft in the flare, pulled back too abruptly on the cyclic stick and lifted the nose of the helicopter too high. Because the airspeed was so low our rate of descent wasn't adequately arrested, which caused us to fall through the flare and allowed the stinger on the tail – put there to guard the tail rotor – to strike the ground and dig into the soft dirt. That allowed the tail rotor to slam into the ground and caused an immediate and terrible vibration to rumble throughout the airframe. I managed to do a run-on landing with the skids sliding along the dirt like skis as we touched down on the parched desert earth doing about 40 knots.

Before the machine came to rest the vibration suddenly ceased. That's when the bolts must have sheared off the 90-degree gearbox and caused the gearbox and the tail rotor to flop onto the opposite side of the vertical tail plane.

When we exited the helicopter and we both saw the damage I'd done, I told Omar to remember what had happened because it was a lesson he could learn from. I was also thinking it was a lesson that could cost me my job.

To be a competent pilot you must have the utmost confidence in your ability. A good pilot knows his limitations and doesn't exceed them. I had exceeded mine. That realization shook my confidence to the core.

With a crumbling marriage, and the possibility of getting fired, my spirits fell into a huge black hole of despair. It sickened me to think this incident could end my short four-year career with the Royal Oman Police Air Wing because it was without doubt the best flying job I'd ever had.

My fate was totally out of my hands. The consequence of my bad judgment would rest in the hands of three pilots who would be assigned to sit on the panel of the accident investigation board. Then, after the verdict was in – which would most certainly uncover that I'd screwed up – they would send the final report to headquarters for senior officers to decide whether I would be allowed to stay in the country or sent packing.

I started to walk away from the tail of the ship while staring at the two deep ruts in the desert, caused by the skids when we made our unscheduled running landing. Unable to shake the feeling that this incident might signal the end of my flying career in Oman, I couldn't help reminiscing about how excited my wife and I had been when I was hired to become a uniformed major with the task of setting up a country-wide helicopter air ambulance (HEMS).

I was ecstatic when I was offered the job because I felt I

was being rescued from a HEMS industry back home that was dangerous and woefully underpaid relative to the responsibility and great risks involved. By accepting the job I knew I wouldn't have to deal with hospital administrators, company managers and the politics any longer. I was also relieved that I wouldn't be exposed to the dangers of flying a medical helicopter because in the six years I did it, I nearly lost my life on five occasions: three times due to bad weather when I inadvertently flew into the clouds at night; and twice – also at night – when I nearly flew into wires that crisscrossed a landing zone that had been perfectly set up on a highway by well-meaning first responders at the scene.

By taking the job I knew I wouldn't be flying single pilot in marginal weather or racing to pick up trauma patients on a life-or-death mission. There were times when I was so dog-tired from working my two-day shift at the hospital that I couldn't remember taking off from the hospital helipad.

I was grateful knowing that I would no longer receive those ungodly 2 a.m. phone calls from the hospital flight dispatcher that would jolt me out of a deep sleep and cause my heart to race because I knew the clock had started running – timing me and the medical crew – to make the five-minute lift-off time required by the hospital while we were launched into someone else's nightmare.

While in Oman, I was able to complete my first book, *The Golden Hour*. I wrote it to expose the dangerous attitudes and practices I had witnessed in helicopter EMS back home. It was my way to try to bring about change. It took more than a year to write and over another year to find a publisher for it after sending off countless queries via snail-mail.

I wrote *The Golden Hour* to highlight the fact that helicopter EMS was becoming deadly. Each crash seemed to be a repeat of the last: pilots pushing the weather going inadvertently IMC (instrument meteorological conditions), flying into fog or into a cloud or flying on a dark-moonless night with no visual horizon, not being prepared for or not trained to fly on instruments (or not being current or proficient to fly on instruments), losing spatial orientation and crashing. There is a term for it: "controlled flight into terrain", (CFIT), a way to describe pilots flying a perfectly serviceable aircraft into the ground killing themselves and everyone on board.

The problem with the helicopter air ambulance concept in America is that medical helicopter crews are still dying. The irony is that the medical people dedicated to saving the lives of others are needlessly dying in the line of duty. So I wrote *The Golden Hour* to expose the lunacy of what was – and still is – occurring in the industry. It was my way of trying to stop these crashes from happening.

It was an unexpected but very pleasant surprise to live and work in Oman: a country geographically close to Iran yet so vastly different. I'd fled Iran on the last charter flight out of the country at the beginning of the Islamic Revolution in 1979 when I worked for Bell Helicopter, so I'd had serious doubts about taking the job in Oman. I worried that life would be like what I'd experienced in Iran.

David Sutcliffe, the former British Royal Navy pilot whom I'd met at Flight Safety in 1982, while on the Bell 222 course, had been living and working in Oman. He assured me the country was nothing like Iran and he was right. My fears had been unfounded.

Since leaving the US Army in February 1971, my civilian flying career had taken me to the Australian Outback, where I herded cattle by helicopter like an aerial cowboy, and delivered meat by a small, single-engine fixed-wing aircraft to Aboriginal settlements in the Northern Territory. I'd flown seismic survey and heli-rig operations over the sweltering jungles of Papua New Guinea. I left the job in New Guinea to take a job with Bell Helicopter International in Iran as a senior instructor pilot. My job there had been to teach Western and Iranian pilots the art of flight instruction – that is, until we were forced to flee the country on the last charter flight out during the beginning of the Islamic Revolution.

I'd barely been back to the States for two hours when my best friend and army buddy, Joe Sulak, called to offer me a job flying a medical helicopter in Houston, Texas. I took the job and flew out of Hermann Hospital for one year.

I found piloting a helicopter air ambulance to be exhilarating, rewarding and sometimes scary because of the marginal weather and the pressure exerted on us by hospital administrators and my company bosses, who demanded we get the job done no matter what.

I was one of six former Vietnam pilots flying on the Hermann contract – each one of us eager to prove to the American public and the medical community that helicopters could save lives in America as we'd seen them do so effectively in South-East Asia.

I left Houston a year later for San Diego, California, where I set up the UCSD Medical Center Life Flight program working for Evergreen Helicopters.

I'd been in San Diego for just under two years when the hospital replaced its single-engine Bell Long Ranger III and acquired a fully IFR (instrument flight rules), twin-engine Bell 222 through Evergreen. I was sent to Flight Safety in Fort Worth, Texas, to do the ground school and flight simulator courses there. The Royal Oman Police Air Wing had acquired two Bell 222s of their own and sent its pilots to Flight Safety as well. That is how I met David Sutcliffe.

The job in Oman wouldn't have transpired had I not met David at Flight Safety. He was a Brit and had done his flight training in the British Royal Navy. When he left the navy he flew helicopters in Portugal prior to being hired by the police in Oman. David and I ended up in the same Bell 222 transition course and became fast friends.

About seven months later, David and his good friend, Richard Shuttleworth – who was then the chief pilot for the Police Air Wing – came to visit me in San Diego. David and Richard had gone through their naval officer training together at the Royal Naval Academy in Portsmouth, England. To save them money on a hotel I offered to put them up in the pilots' quarters apartment across the street from the medical center where I was working. As luck would have it, what they saw while staying in that apartment would land me the job in Oman.

After spending that first night in the pilots' quarters, David and Richard told me they were shocked at how many times I'd been called out in the middle of the night to go fly single pilot in marginal weather. At the end of their visit they told me that if a pilot opening ever came up at the Police Air Wing they would ask me to submit my CV to get me out of such a – in their words – "dangerous" situation flying in San Diego. True to their word, about eight months later, David called me to say the police were recruiting three more pilots and asked me to send him my CV.

There were 122 applicants for the three job openings. Oh how I wanted the job because I could see that flying a helicopter air ambulance in the States was fast becoming a very dangerous segment of commercial aviation. I saw no real future in it.

In the six years that I flew HEMS in the States, before being asked to apply for the flying job in Oman, there had been 15 fatal HEMS crashes across the country, killing 36 flight crews and a few patients as well. I saw the job in Oman as my way out – my escape – before I, too, became a statistic.

Before accepting the job, I told my wife about my experience with Bell Helicopter International in Iran and voiced concern about taking another job in the Middle East. I wasn't eager to be forced to catch the last charter flight out of another country. She needed to know the dangers before making a decision to embark on this adventure.

I told her how we expatriates in Iran had watched as the country slid into chaos as the populace rallied behind Ayatollah Ruhollah Khomeini, who was then living in exile in France and issuing orders to Iranian Loyalists, asking them to overthrow the Shah.

I told her it only took six months before the situation became untenable. She and I agreed that if there were ever any hint of a similar coup or civil unrest in Oman, we wouldn't wait until the last minute to get out of the country.

I told her that David Sutcliffe had assured me that Oman was a stable country – nothing like Iran. He said that the people were totally different, that it was a safe place to live and work and that we would like living here.

I had my doubts, but the job paid a much better wage than I could earn working for Life Flight in San Diego. Plus, it would be a great way to save money for the day we'd take that big sailing trip we'd dreamed about. As it turned out, David had been spot-on. Living and working in Oman was the shining star in my aviation career.

When I flew to England from San Diego to interview for the job, I was prepared to say or do anything to ensure I got it. I had no idea what I was going to be asked in that interview. As it turned out, one particular question shocked the hell out of me.

CHAPTER 3
The Interview

I remember sitting patiently in the waiting area at The Royal Albert Hall where the interview was to take place, having arrived that morning by London taxi a good 20 minutes early, eager to avoid being late.

David Sutcliffe had briefed me earlier, telling me that the police were interviewing three candidates per day for three days, making up a total of nine finalists vying for the three positions the police were offering. I was the third and last candidate to be interviewed that day.

A very distinguished English gentleman impeccably dressed in a dark suit entered the waiting room and said, "Mr. Mains, if you will please follow me."

He led me into the large conference room – heavily ornate with polished wood carving and white trim – and had me take a seat at a heavy wooden table with highly polished top. My chair was positioned opposite three men, immaculately dressed in dark business suits.

The man in the middle with a ruddy complexion spoke first with a flawlessly crafted English accent, "Welcome to England, Randy. My name is John Ilbert. I'm the commanding officer for the Police Air Wing." He offered his hand. I stood, leaned across the wide table and shook it.

"It's good to be here, sir."

He suddenly looked a little flustered in an understated, British sort of way. "I *can* call you Randy, can't I? You do know what 'Randy' means over here, don't you?"

I let out a small laugh, "Yes, I'm afraid I do. It means 'horny.' I found out the hard way when I went to Australia to find my first civilian flying job and said 'Hi there, I'm Randy,' to a guy named Clive staying at the Bankstown Aero Club. He soon sorted me out."

My comment brought a smile to his face; then he continued. "Richard Shuttleworth here has told me a little about you, Randy. So has David Sutcliffe, who I understand has flown with you in the Bell 222 flight simulator in Fort Worth."

"That's right, sir."

He looked down at a stack of papers lying on the highly polished tabletop in front of him and continued. "Your CV is quite impressive. I see you're involved with helicopter EMS back in the States."

"Yes, sir, I am. I've been doing it for six years now. I find it very rewarding."

"Hmmm ... and you've won some sort of award in America I see, for your contribution to helicopter EMS?"

"Yes, sir."

"It appears you're well involved with helicopter EMS in the States then?"

"Yes, sir. I'm afraid it's gotten into my blood. While it can tax one's ability at times and can be tiring, I find it the most rewarding flying I've ever done."

"Hmmm ... The Sultan of Oman has given the Police Air Wing two, $1-million EMS kits that he's purchased from the States. He wants them to be fitted into two of our new Bell 214STs, of which we have six. The Inspector General of Police and Customs has given us the task of supporting the Sultan using our newly configured EMS helicopters. To be totally honest, we don't know much about helicopter EMS. It's a pretty new field to us here in the U.K."

He then changed his direction of thought and read from a sheet of paper that he held in front of him. The first question he asked me caught me totally off guard.

"Randy, if we were to offer you a job working for the Royal Oman Police would you be willing to fly using night vision goggles, across the border into a neighboring country to Oman, with the equivalent of the SAS on board, to rescue diplomats from the rooftop of a foreign embassy?" He switched his gaze from the paper to look at me.

My mind raced. Wow, what was I getting into here? I knew the SAS, or Special Air Services, were some of the best trained Special Forces soldiers on the planet. Then I thought about David Sutcliffe and Richard Shuttleworth. They didn't strike me as Rambo types. I *really* needed this job. My wife and I had agreed that I would say or do anything to get this job. But this?

I thought about the geography. Let's see, there's Yemen to the southwest, Saudi Arabia to the west, the United Arab Emirates to the northwest and flying north across the Strait of Hormuz there's Iran. West of Iran there's Iraq, or maybe Bahrain, perhaps Kuwait. Would I do it? Let me get the job first; then I would make the decision on whether to fly a rescue mission, if asked. But here's what I was thinking: Hell no!

I was trying hard to conceal what was going through my mind at the time – struggling to maintain my composure – my best poker face.

I answered firmly in the affirmative, "Yes sir, I'd be willing to do that if asked," all the while holding his gaze, looking squarely back at the man, trying hard not to flinch. My insides felt like the proverbial duck in water – its body still and calm on the surface but its little feet going like crazy underneath him. I hoped I was carrying the unflustered conviction on my face as well as in my voice.

He broke his stare, then looked back down at the paper he held in his hand. "Hmmm ... would you be willing, if asked, to do the same scenario in Oman, to rescue people from a foreign embassy in the country?" He looked up at me again and waited for an answer.

"Yes sir, I would," I said without hesitation.

He paused to study me for a moment and then continued. "In your CV it says you flew in Vietnam. Did you do anything like that in Vietnam?"

"No, sir, not exactly. I did extract Special Forces teams

from the jungle in a bordering country to Vietnam using 150-foot ropes and flew them sixty miles to safety, setting them down on a friendly airstrip. The ropes we used were called McGuire Rigs."

"Sounds interesting."

I let out a little laugh. "Yeah, well, it depends on what you call interesting. If you mean 'scary,' it could be that too if you're getting shot at."

"Yes, well, I must admit that is something I have never experienced. Tell me Randy: If we were to offer you a position with the Royal Oman Police, when could you be ready to start?"

"My company only requires that I give a two-week notice."

"How about your wife? How does she feel about all of this?"

I glanced over at Richard Shuttleworth. "Well, Richard here says we'd like it. And David Sutcliffe assures me we'd like it there. Both men have told me that they and their respective family members love living in Oman. I trust their judgment, so I suppose I should listen to them. They've been there long enough to know. Sounds pretty good to my wife and me."

"Well, thank you for your time, Randy. We'll let you know our decision in a few weeks' time. I wish you the best of luck."

I shook my head, recalling the memory of that interview as I approached the beginning of the tracks in the dirt that were caused by the helicopter's skids where we'd touched down. I stopped and turned to look back at the aircraft sitting about 40 yards away. The two deep ruts in the dirt were remarkably straight considering I'd lost all tail-rotor thrust halfway through the running landing. From where I stood, the tail rotor didn't look too badly damaged, although seeing it resting on the opposite side of the tail rotor pylon did look odd.

I thought back again to that interview in London and the question about flying with the SAS. Since coming to Oman I had trained with them many times. They were training the

Omanis who worked in the Sultan's Special Forces (SSF) and the Sultan's Task Force (STF) to do fast roping and abseiling exercises from our Bell 205s to mock "killing houses" they had set up to practice landing on embassy buildings. So far we hadn't done any real training with night vision goggles (NVGs), and more importantly the Air Wing hadn't been asked to fly over the border to rescue diplomats. I secretly hoped *that* was something I would never have to do.

When I first met David Sutcliffe at Flight Safety and he told me he lived and worked in Oman, I looked it up in a world atlas and noticed that the Strait of Hormuz, the entrance to the Arabian Gulf separating the two countries, measured only 21 miles between the tip of Oman and the coast of Iran. I couldn't fathom how there could possibly be such a vast difference in the people and culture when they were separated by only 21 short miles. But there is a world of difference.

When I was asked to interview for the job, my wife and I did some reading about the country to educate ourselves. Being a sailor, Oman's history as a seafaring nation intrigued me.

In 200 B.C., ships from Oman traded with India and Mesopotamia (think Iraq, the northeastern section of Syria, southeastern Turkey and parts of southwestern Iran) carrying marble and copper taken from Oman's high mountains and later traded frankincense – a treasure the country became famous for.

In later years, the Omani traders sailed as far as China and other countries in the Far East. The coastal town of Sohar, located 120 miles north of the capital city, Muscat, was reputed to be home to the legendary Sinbad the Sailor.

The guide books talked about stark, craggy mountains in a mountain range called the Jebel Akdar in the north of the country not far from Muscat, where we'd be living. The mountains reached lofty heights of nearly 10,000 feet. Further south, spreading inland, were the sweeping sand dunes of the Wahiba Sands. The pictures taken of those dunes reminded us of what we imagined Arabia to look like with shifting sand dunes, some reaching heights of 700 or 800 feet in places.

There were wadis (dry river beds) to explore, beautiful waterfalls, and fertile oases that stretched down to lush green mountains in the south of the country. An old remnant of a palace situated just north of the southern town of Salalah was, according to legend, used by the Queen of Sheba.

The guide books touted pristine beaches stretching a thousand miles. In my nearly four years in Oman, I flew over many of them. "Unspoiled" and "stunning" are two words that come to mind to describe them.

The events that led up to Oman joining the twentieth century can be attributed to the monarch – Sultan Qaboos bin Said – and his strong affinity to England. He had been sent to attend school there at the age of 16 by his father, Said bin Taimur. At 20, Qaboos (pronounced "kaboose") entered the Royal Military Academy, Sandhurst. After graduating, he joined a British Infantry regiment, The Cameronians, and was posted in Germany for a year.

When Qaboos finished his military service, he studied local government subjects in England and returned home to Salalah, which was then a small town on the south coast of Oman not far from the northern border of Yemen. Sultan Qaboos spent the next six years in the royal palace under virtual house arrest by his strict father.

In July 1970, with help from friends whom he'd met in the British military, Qaboos overthrew his father in a bloodless coup and named the country the Sultanate of Oman, becoming its head of state.

His father had not invested the oil wealth back into the country but instead kept it for himself. This kept Oman in the dark ages. Qaboos, after deposing his father, used the oil revenue to launch his country into the twentieth century both economically and socially. To this day, Oman's oil revenue has been consistently invested in national infrastructure, particularly roads, schools, hospitals and utilities, making Sultan Qaboos much loved and respected by his people.

What we found intriguing in our reading was that the

sultan did not allow tourists to enter the country. The only Westerners or "outsiders" allowed into the country were those invited to work and live there.

My wife and I found living in Oman, a country totally unspoiled by the influences of the "outside world" and yet working to fully join the twentieth century, to be like living in our own exclusive, unspoiled playground, with no other visitors to share it with, other than expatriates like ourselves. It didn't take us long to come to the conclusion that Oman was the best kept secret in the Middle East.

As part of my employment package, I was given a fully furnished two-story, two-bedroom villa and a company car – a white Peugeot 504 – with unlimited free fuel. When I first arrived I thought it really couldn't get much better than that. But I was wrong. The social life would turn out to be on a scale neither of us had ever experienced.

The day we arrived in the country, David Sutcliffe had arranged for us to join him and some friends at their table at a gala New Year's Eve dinner to be held at the Intercontinental Hotel. All the men, mainly British, wore tuxedos ("DJs" or "dinner jackets," as they are called by the Brits), the women (also mainly British) wore elegant ball gowns. It was the most lavish affair I had ever attended. I didn't own a tux so I wore the only suit I had: the one I had purchased to wear to Washington and the same suit I had worn for the job interview at the Royal Albert Hall in London nearly four years prior.

The splendor of that evening showed me that life in Oman was unlike anything I'd experienced in Iran. Expatriate life in Oman was more than civilized. I would call it "opulent." I knew that if that first night was any indication of what was to come, my time in Oman would be the complete antithesis to what I had experienced living and working in Iran.

There are – by far – more Brits living and working in Oman than any other foreign nationality except, perhaps, for the East Indians who work as clerks and shopkeepers. It made sense to me that the Brits would have a significant presence in

Oman because of the strong ties and deep affinity the sultan has with Britain.

As a "Yank" I felt grateful and privileged to have been asked to join the expatriate workforce as a non-Brit. I had David Sutcliffe and Richard Shuttleworth to thank for that. They'd thrown me a lifeline after witnessing the dangerous environment I'd been flying in back home.

David and his Portuguese wife, Theresa, introduced us to expatriate life in Oman when, on my first weekend off from work, they invited us to join them and some friends on an Omani dhow they had chartered. We were headed to one of many secluded beaches in a remote area called Bandar Khayran.

We loaded up a boat with barbecues and cool boxes filled with smoked salmon, hamburgers, hot dogs, soft drinks, champagne and beer purchased from the Police Club. There were about 12 of us that day.

We left the dhow and fired up barbecues on the soft, sand beach while the children from the various families splashed and swam in the warm, gentle waters of a stunning azure-blue Arabian Sea. Kids and adults all gathered in friendly camaraderie, with lots of talking and laughter – everyone enjoying the sun, sand and warm water. I climbed up a nearby hill and took a picture of the dhow at anchor in our secluded anchorage.

My wife and I knew after that first day at the beach, and talking with those whom we met, that we were extremely lucky to be living in such a very special place: a beautiful, unspoiled country free of tourists. We knew something else – we knew David Sutcliffe *had* been right. Oman was unique. But the details of the job would keep getting better.

When I left Vietnam I thought I would never fly my favorite helicopter again – the Bell 205 (nicknamed the "Huey") – but I would be wrong. In my book *Dear Mom I'm Alive – Letters Home from Black Widow 25* – detailing my one-year tour as a young Army combat helicopter pilot in Vietnam – I mention going out to the Widow Web, our flight line, where Charlie Company's aircraft were parked. I walked out there with two friends from flight school, Joe Sulak and Tom Shonehour, just days before we were to leave Vietnam for good to return to "The World" as we called the States back then. We went to the Widow Web to say a final goodbye to the much-loved and reliable Bell 205 "Huey" helicopter that each of us had flown for over 1,000 combat hours in that year. We wanted to see the Huey one last time because we knew we would miss her and thought we would never fly that wonderful old bird again. But I *would* fly the Huey again because, as it turned out, the Police Air Wing had six of them. Who would have thought that 15 years after flying my last combat mission in Vietnam, I would have the opportunity to fly my favorite helicopter again? I'd also fly the new, state-of-the-art, extremely powerful, twin-engine, twenty-place Bell 214ST.

Vacation time would be another huge perk that came with the job. When I was about to leave the army, a colonel at the Fort Wolters training base gave a room of warrant officers our final debriefing in an effort to convince us to stay in the service, with one of his arguments being: *"Where else but the United States Army could you ever hope to get one-month's paid vacation a year?"* Well, I had found such a job working for the Royal Oman Police. I would have *two* months paid vacation a year, such a stark contrast from the meager two-week vacations I was given when I worked in the States.

Once my flight training and theatre conversion in the Bell 205 and the Bell 214ST was complete, I set about the task of setting up a countrywide helicopter EMS program, something that I had originally been hired to do. I met with a doctor by the name of Waheed al Karusi, an eminent and amiable Omani doctor who was extremely keen and very excited about the prospect of setting up a helicopter EMS system for his country. After a short meeting with him, I quickly determined a countrywide helicopter EMS program was going to be a non-starter for the simple fact that Oman had no ambulance system in place. None. The only ambulance in the country was operated by the police in the capital area plus one ambulance stationed at the airport.

I learned, to my great surprise, that the ambulance attendants had no first aid training.

Doctor Karusi was deeply disappointed and terribly saddened when I told him that he had to put together an ambulance system first, complete with radio dispatch center and *trained* ambulance personnel before he could consider implementing a helicopter air ambulance program.

The HEMS experience I brought with me from the States was not totally wasted, however. I was able to set up a HEMS program in support of the sultan. Whenever he travels by road in any part of the country the police fly a medically configured Bell 214ST overhead with a doctor and respiratory therapist on board if the need should arise. The sultan's Royal Flight fly one of their Puma helicopters ahead of where the sultan is driving to do a reconnaissance as one Puma helicopter flies back and forth over the entourage flying top cover. The Royal Flight pilots are British nationals, most of them former Royal Air Force pilots.

The police employ 18 helicopter pilots and 10 fixed-wing pilots. While being a para-military organization, with all the pilots having flown in the military, all the pilots agree the Police Air Wing has a flying club feel about it.

The fixed-wing aircraft used by the Police Air Wing included one Boeing 727, a Lear Jet, two twin turboprop Dornier 228s, and two larger twin turboprop De Havilland Buffalos used like aerial trucks by the police.

While doing our operational tasks our *real* job was to train the Omani pilots so they could one day take over our job. Nearly all of the Omanis are junior lieutenants like Omar. They didn't yet have much experience or flight time so it would be quite a few years before they could take over the role themselves.

The variety of tasks we were asked to perform kept the job fresh and interesting. The police use their helicopters to do just about everything a helicopter can do.

The first job I was tasked to do, after I had finished my initial flight training, was to fly supplies and equipment up to workers who were restoring fifteenth-century Portuguese watchtowers that dotted the hills surrounding Muscat. The Brits called that particular task the "*Fawlty Towers*" load lift after the name of the popular British television series starring John Cleese. The operations officer would mark it as such on the daily flight program board in operations.

If the weather was good, and it usually was, and we had a job for the Bell 205 that was inside the capital area, we would usually fly single pilot. When flying the Bell 205 single pilot on the *Fawlty Towers* load lift, which was literally in downtown Muscat not far from the sultan's palace, I would sling cement and aggregate material under my helicopter on a 20-foot strop up to the men working on the watchtowers. It was satisfying for all of us involved to think we were taking part in restoring some of the historic relics in the country.

The police also did radio repeater site maintenance, flying men and equipment to repeaters situated in the high mountains of the Jebel Akhdar south of the capital, 40 miles west of Muscat, with some peaks reaching as high as 10,000 feet.

What made my experience in Oman so special wasn't the varied flying jobs and tasks. It wasn't the two-month vacations where I had the time and money to visit any country in the world. It wasn't the opulent lifestyle that elevated me, in my mind anyway, way above my station in life. Nor was it the truly wonderful friends I met while living in a country unspoiled by tourism, where I could enjoy all the beauty and splendor Oman had to offer.

The true value of the job was my exposure to a new paradigm, a new way of doing things in helicopter aviation. What I learned in Oman could be a lifesaving gift – knowledge that I could take back with me to America to share with those in dire need of it.

The HEMS accident rate back home had remained deadly. I cringed every time I heard of another air-medical helicopter crash. The statistics remained shocking and, in my mind, totally unacceptable. In the nearly four years I'd been in Oman, there were 20 fatal air medical crashes, killing 53 medical crew members back home. I kept wondering, "When will it ever stop?"

CHAPTER 4
The Jewel in the Crown

I checked my watch again noting that 20 minutes had passed. I figured the accident investigation team would arrive soon.

I began walking slowly back to the damaged aircraft where I knew Omar would probably still be sleeping in the back. I walked between the two ruts carved in the parched earth caused by the aircraft's skids when we did our running landing. Thinking that I may lose my job because of the damage I'd caused to the aircraft, I thought about the lessons I might take back with me to America if I had to return home.

Without doubt, the most valuable lesson I learned during my conversion training into the 17,500-pound all-up weight, twin-engine, twenty-place, Bell 214ST that we flew using two-flight crew was in that first month in Oman that I began to learn how to fly as one of two-crew (pilot and copilot) like the airlines do it, and came to realize how much safer it is rather than the way I'd done it when I flew single pilot back in the States.

With the possibility that I might be forced to leave Oman if I lost my job, I thought back on some of the tasks I'd miss. My job interview in London referred to exciting (and potentially hairy) missions in support of the SSF (the Sultan's Special Forces) and STF (the Sultan's Task Force). SSF is a unit that trains for international terrorist operations; STF is a separate unit dedicated to domestic operations. SSF trains to storm an embassy outside of Oman. STF is like a SWAT team trained to storm buildings within the country in the event of a hostage or terrorist situation. As mentioned, both units are trained to do their jobs by former members of the British SAS (Special Air Services), some of the best trained and highly disciplined special-forces soldiers in the world. They are a highly disciplined, professional and rigorously trained great bunch of guys commanding my highest respect.

Another rewarding task occurs during the rainy season – usually in January or February. I would usually fly as captain or copilot in a Bell 214ST. We would fly over normally dry riverbeds (wadis) that had become flooded in the winter rains. We'd be sent to rescue people whose cars had been overcome by a rushing torrent of water – often the result of a flash flood. When we arrived on scene we usually found people standing on their upside-down cars and we'd winch them up into our helicopter to safety. One such mission stands out in my mind because it was a mission where we saved lives.

It had rained heavily through the night. The following morning a call came in to the Police Air Wing dispatch center from the police station in Nizwa reporting that several cars were stuck in a flowing wadi in the Sumail Gap.

As previously mentioned, we flew our Bell 214ST with pilot and copilot. This day we had two crewmen in back, one to operate the winch and one to be lowered down on the winch wire to assist the person being rescued.

When we arrived over the flowing wadi near Nizwa we could see a long line of cars on each side waiting to cross. We could also see up ahead, two overturned cars in the middle of the wadi. The water level was so high they were nearly covered.

Sitting on each overturned car was an Omani man waiting to be rescued. We noticed a third car that hadn't flipped over, with water rushing over it to a level just under the driver's window. We couldn't tell if there was anyone inside so we decided to first rescue the two men standing on their cars.

It was an easy matter to hover 30 feet over the two vehicles although, with the water rushing at a good clip below us, I had to concentrate my hover by looking out the side window at the bank of the wadi while my copilot read out the engine power instruments for me.

Once settled in a stable hover, winchman Sgt. Moosa

lowered crewman Cpl Ali down on the winch wire to the stranded cars. It didn't take long for Ali to secure the two men off their respective vehicles and pull them up into our hovering helicopter. With both men safely secured on board, we landed on the road next to the rushing wadi where Police were waiting to look after the rescued men.

Moosa suddenly said over the intercom, "Sir, there're people in the other car."

I could see people's arms waving to us for help from an open window, the water only inches from spilling into the car.

I took off and flew the machine over the vehicle. Once in a stable hover I said, "OK Moosa, Ali, you guys ready?"

"Ready sir."

Moosa lowered Ali down on the wire, placing him on top of the vehicle. Ali got on his hands and knees as we hovered there. He tried to peer into the open window on the driver's side. Suddenly, a small baby, that couldn't have been more than a few days old, was thrust out of the window into his arms. Moosa winched Ali and the baby up to the safety of our helicopter, took the baby from Ali's arms and sent him down again.

This time a young Omani girl climbed out the window. Ali brought her up to the car's roof and clipped her on to his harness. Then, Moosa winched them both up. There were a total of five people in the car, including the baby.

The nerve-wracking thing about the rescue was that the car naturally became lighter as each person was winched up to the safety of our helicopter. At one stage when Ali was clipping on the third person – a young boy – the car lurched and began to bounce sideways downstream. Ali held the boy, trying to keep him from falling off the top of the car as the car skidded and bumped downstream. One of the car's tires must have caught on something underwater which stopped it from being swept away.

When Ali had the last person – a man in his late 40s – out of the car and secured and began his ascent toward the helicopter, the car suddenly broke free and began to tumble. It rolled sideways over and over as Moosa continued to winch Ali and the man up and into our helicopter. Had we not been there to winch those people to safety they all would have died. It was a very rewarding day for us all.

This same scenario occurs every year during Oman's rainy season. There are always those who think they can cross a flowing wadi in their car, which sometimes results in tragic – even fatal – outcomes.

One February night, the town of Sohar, situated 120 miles north of Muscat, became totally flooded. We were called out to rescue people who were stranded.

Using a Bell 214ST with two pilots, a winch operator and a crewman in the back, we flew nine hours through the night until the early hours of the morning. Our only stop was to refuel from barrels of jet fuel positioned at the Sohar police station. We ended up winching 97 people to safety from rooftops, cars and trees in what would turn out to be a very satisfying mission.

The most bizarre helicopter rescue mission I've ever flown occurred while flying a police Bell 205 single pilot when I had to winch three workmen off a stadium light pole at night.

The call came in to our dispatch center around 9 p.m. reporting that three workmen, who had been working on a tower changing light bulbs at the police soccer stadium, had become stranded. The scaffolding they were using had come adrift because of a broken steel cable. I'd been told I could use either a Bell 205 or the much larger Bell 214ST. I thought the smaller Bell 205 would be more suitable for the task, being that the rescue would be conducted in such close quarters. So, along with Sgt. Moosa as the winchman and Cpl Ali again as the man who would be on the wire, we flew into the capital area to pick up the stranded workers.

There was an empty parking lot nearby where rescue vehicles had marked out a safe landing area, so we landed there and shut down. A police general was there to meet us and he quickly brought us up to speed on what had happened.

A cable had parted on one side, causing the scaffolding to

fall away. Looking up at the tower, I could see three men hanging on to the upward part of the scaffolding guard railing, with the bottom end of the scaffolding nearly pointing straight down.

The general told us that there wasn't a fire truck with a ladder long enough to reach the three men, who I estimate were 150 to 200 feet in the air, which is why he called us. I told the general we could get them down using the winch in the helicopter. I briefed Moosa and Ali. Then we got airborne.

The night was like black ink, with no moon. There was nothing for me to make reference to out of my side of the aircraft except the very top of the light tower. I could see the parking lot below me through the helicopter's chin bubble but I couldn't make out anything beyond the soccer stadium.

While working hard to hover the machine, trying to keep it perfectly still in relation to the top of the light tower off my right side, I told Moosa he could send Ali down on the winch wire to begin the rescue. That's when something really odd happened.

I was managing to hover about 200 feet above the parking lot, and I was able to keep the top of the light tower out my window rock-steady, but I was really over-controlling the cyclic, the control stick I held in my right hand to maintain the hover. It was really weird, and totally threw me, because something like this had never happened to me before.

Normally, in a no-wind situation, to maintain a hover I would only need to move the cyclic in the space of a quarter. But for some reason, I was moving the cyclic all over the place, nearly bumping it against my knees. I couldn't understand what was happening even though the tower next to me out my window appeared not to be moving.

I said over the intercom, "Moosa, is everything alright? I seem to be moving the controls all over the place up here."

"Yes, sir, everything is OK. The tower is moving back and forth from the rotor downwash that's all, but Ali has the first man and I'm winching them both up now."

It made sense to me now. The tower was swaying from the

rotor wash and without being conscious of it I was keeping the aircraft stable relative to the swaying pole. Because I couldn't see the terrain behind the tower to use as reference I couldn't tell the tower was moving. It was something I had never experienced before.

Moosa and Ali managed to winch the three men to safety, bringing them into the helicopter. I remember, as I was hovering there during the rescue, glancing occasionally down through the chin bubble to the parking lot below, I could see the general jumping up and down waving his arms in excitement, reacting to the drama he was witnessing above.

Once the three workers were safely aboard the helicopter, I landed back on the parking lot and shut down. The general was ecstatic, relieved that we were able to rescue the three men. He went up to each of us, shaking our hands, speaking very quickly. I think he was more excited about the rescue than we were.

One week later three Oris watches arrived at the Police Air Wing. Sent from police headquarters, each watch had a blue Royal Oman Police crest on its face. One was meant for Sgt. Moosa, one for Cpl Ali and one for me. Each watch had an individual letter of appreciation personally addressed to each of us from the general who had been in the parking lot that night.

///

The faint sound of a Bell 205's familiar whop-whop-whop created by its main rotor-gently cutting into my reverie – brings me back. The distinctive sound of a Huey can usually be heard before you can see it.

I shielded my eyes from the sun, scanning the sky to the north above the desert landscape – landscape that looks very much like the topography around Palm Springs or Las Vegas: parched, rugged, waterless, craggy and barren.

I continue searching the sky. Soon the familiar outline of a Bell Huey comes into view. Squinting, I see by the camouflage paint scheme it belongs to the Police Air Wing. On board will be the head of the Director General of Civil Aviation, Greg Rodriguez, to take my statement.

"The clock starts now," I think to myself. In several weeks I should know whether I will be asked to leave Oman for good, or whether I will be allowed to stay.

CHAPTER 5
The Verdict

I wasn't going to play a game of cat-and-mouse with the accident investigation team, hoping that by doing so I might get off lightly. I think the lead investigator was very surprised at my candor when he asked me point blank, "What happened?"

And I said, "I screwed up,"

My honesty was worth seeing the wide-eyed reaction on his face.

Naturally, I couldn't fly until the investigation was over and a verdict came down from headquarters. The investigation lasted two weeks and the findings were sent up to headquarters for consideration.

Another week passed until I was called in to the CO's office. John Ilbert knew I was going through a real tough patch dealing with a marriage that was falling apart under the public scrutiny of a very small expat community. I think he had some compassion for my plight. He seemed genuinely pleased when he delivered the news, "You've been exonerated, Randy."

He could sense my great relief. "Thank you sir."

He continued, "These things happen in training. They know that up at HQ. We've had a few training incidents in the past and we know it's a risk we take. They've just sent a cautionary letter saying, 'Do not let it happen again.'"

"It won't, Sir, I can assure you. And I want to thank you for whatever part you've had in all this."

"The Omanis like you, Randy. Omar went to bat for you saying you're a patient teacher and that it would be a shame to lose you."

"I owe both of you, Sir. Thank you."

"That's all. I'll tell Ops that they are free to put you back on the flying schedule."

I was elated.

%

Four new Omani pilots arrived to the Air Wing a month later for me to train as copilots in the Bell 214ST. They were terrific guys, about 21 years old. Their names were Ibrahim, Ahmed, Dera and Zayed. They had just returned to Oman from doing their flight training in New Zealand having received their commercial helicopter licenses there. They were smart, polite, keen and eager to get started. The police had recruited them a year earlier from the local college.

I began my first day of training with them like I did with all the Omanis I trained. I began by telling them a little story about positive and negative motivation. Positive motivation means a student *wants* to be a pilot and is positively motivated to become one. A pilot who is positively motivated will do his lessons, study and won't have to be hounded by me.

A negatively motivated pilot, on the other hand, is lazy. He doesn't study his lessons or bothers to learn his emergency procedures. He isn't prepared for the next day's lesson. To motivate him I would need to force him to learn each lesson, which is not the way I like to do things.

To illustrate my meaning, I told them the story that I told all the Omani pilots I flew with. I told them about two students I'd had in Iran, when I worked for Bell Helicopter. That story always served to let them know where we stood. I wanted them to know that I was determined to make competent, safe pilots out of them one way or the other, positively or negatively. They could either do it like Dadashan did (positively), or they could do it like Karbasi did (negatively).

I would tell them, "The decision is yours."

Dadashan and Karbasi were lieutenants in the Iranian army, about 24 years old when I got them. They had already gone through flight school and had been awarded their wings, so they knew how to fly. But because there had been very little operational flying in their squadron, they were being sent through flight school again to build up their flight hours. They needed 500 hours in order to be sent to Methods of Instruction to learn how to become flight instructors.

Dadashan had a great attitude. He was highly motivated. He did his homework and he was always prepared. He retained what he had been taught and performed well. He was positively motivated; that is, he *wanted* to be a pilot and did what he had to do to achieve that goal. He was a dream student and gave me no problems at all.

Karbasi, on the other hand, was not a dream student. He was an underachiever. He didn't want to work to get through his flying training. In fact, he wanted to do as little work as possible and to be carried through the program. He was negatively motivated; that is, to motivate him, I would need to hit him over the head with a brick.

I knew Karbasi was going to be difficult the first flight I had with him when, walking across the flight line toward our aircraft on that first day, he tried to offer me candy. It was a nice gesture to be sure, but it didn't take me long to see he was trying to butter me up. It wasn't going to work.

On our first flight together he didn't know his lesson. Because I was a new instructor for him, I gently quizzed him to find out what he knew and what he didn't know. I quickly assessed him to be a below-average pilot. I told him he needed to study and be prepared for future flights.

A student was graded after each flight so I told him, "I'm giving you a satisfactory grade this flight, Karbasi, only because it's your first one with me and I want the two of us to get off on the right foot. So tomorrow, please know your lesson, know your emergency procedures and know the aircraft limitations; otherwise, you'll get a marginal grade for your flight. Understand?"

"Yes, sir."

The next day, as we walked across the flight line to our

assigned helicopter, Karbasi tried to offer me candy again. He didn't know his lesson. He didn't know his emergency procedures. He didn't know the aircraft limitations. As promised, I gave him a marginal grade for the flight and warned him again.

Karbasi finally earned what is called a pink slip, signifying an unsatisfactory flight. He earned it because he had demonstrated two more days of poor performance. He received another pink slip the following day, too.

I finally told him, "Karbasi, I'm going to make a pilot out of you one way or the other. We can either do it the easy way, where you get *positively* motivated to become a pilot and do your homework, and learn your emergency procedures and the aircraft limitations on your own, or I will make you learn them. The decision is yours."

The following day he wasn't prepared so he received another pink slip.

"OK, Karbasi, I can see the only way you're going to learn is to have a talk to your major and explain to him why you're not doing what you are supposed to." His face went white. I'd warned him it might come to this, but I think he thought I was bluffing. I wasn't.

At the end of that flying day I marched him down to the Iranian major's office and we discussed the problem with him. "Leave Mister Karbasi with me," the major told me. "I will ensure he learns his lesson. You should see a marked improvement in his performance after the weekend."

The next working day, two days after I left Karbasi with the major, he turned up with a shaved head. "What happened to you?" I asked.

"The major took me to jail. In jail they always shave your head. Then they hung me upside down on a pole."

"They did what?" I said, shocked.

"Hung me upside down on a pole," he repeated, not appearing to be fazed about what had happened to him.

That was harsh treatment to be sure, but I didn't have any trouble with Karbasi after that. He always had the next lesson learned, his limitations and emergency procedures memorized. What had happened to Mr. Karbasi was a classic example of negative motivation, Iranian-style.

Once I told that story to my young Omani flight officers, if I felt they were getting a bit slack in their studies, all I had to say was, "Remember Karbasi?" and their bookwork would improve exponentially.

Another important message I wanted the young Omanis to bear in mind was on the subject of *Wasata* (pronounced *wasta*). Wasata is an Arabic word that means getting something through favoritism rather than merit.

Wasata is endemic in the Middle East and has no place in the cockpit of an aircraft. I told the Omani pilots that an aircraft doesn't care how important you are. An aircraft doesn't care how influential you are. An aircraft doesn't care what your background is or what station you hold in life. An aircraft doesn't care if you were born a Bedouin or if you are the ruler of a country. All that is important to the operation of an aircraft is how safely the pilot operates it. That is the only thing of importance to any aircraft and something they needed to keep in mind if they wanted to live to see the next day.

The Omanis understood what I was saying and they "got it." They understood the important safety concept of working hard to be knowledgeable and, more importantly, knowing their own personal limitations as pilots and knowing not to push them.

Unfortunately, a time would come in my aviation career years later when, while flying in another Muslim country not too far away from Oman, I would witness several of the local pilots relying on wasata rather than skill, merit and humility to further their aviation careers; pilots who believed that their own sense of self-importance – rather than hard work and sound judgment – would make them safe and competent pilots.

One pilot in particular would fall into this deadly way of thinking. Combined with a pumped-up opinion of himself, a lack of meaningful checks and balances in the company by those instructors, examiners and corporate managers who knew he was weak in critical areas of his training, and a series of preventable links in the error chain, combined one night and cost the lives of seven people in what would be termed, "the crash that didn't happen."

///

My wife managed to get a job working as a nurse at the American Embassy. A byproduct of that job was that I would be drawn into the embassy crowd; with it would come a proposition made to me by one of the embassy employees that I am very glad I refused, for it would have probably supplied me with way more excitement than I could have handled.

My wife had been working for the embassy for about eight months as their health nurse when, at an embassy function, a member of the CIA tried to recruit me to supply information to him on an ongoing basis. He wanted to be my "case worker" and I would be his "asset."

I told him, "You can find out more of what's going on in the country by reading the local newspapers than anything I can tell you." I meant it too.

I respectfully declined his offer, not wanting to create a conflict of interest with my employer. I was unwilling to take an unnecessary risk by becoming a "spy" in a foreign country. In my mind, Oman was a stable country, the sultan being very pro-Western, with his strong affinity with Britain and the USA. Sultan Qaboos was a peace-loving leader and wanted nothing to do with radical Islamic principles. His aim was to provide a stable, quiet life for his country and his people. He had proven that he would do whatever it took to ensure that happened. Oman, after all, was considered the "Switzerland of the Middle East" so I figured things would tick along just fine without me going undercover, clandestinely working for the United States government.

I thought about the ramifications if I got caught supplying

information to a spy agency even though we were supposedly on the same side. How would that sit with my employer, the Royal Oman Police? I could spend time in an Omani jail. I politely told the CIA case worker, "no thanks," and never heard another word about it.

Being approached to supply information to the CIA caused me to remember a childhood incident when my best friend at the time, Glen Ryan, and I managed to catch a real live spy.

Where I grew up in the San Fernando Valley, the Southern Pacific railroad track ran about a half-mile from the back of our house in Northridge, California. It was along those railroad tracks near the Van Nuys airport and the RCA plant that Glen and I first spotted our spy. I was 12. Glen was 10.

Glen and I caught the spy quite by accident. We were two young boys walking along the railroad tracks on our way to the Van Nuys airport to watch planes land when we spotted him lying in the bushes. We didn't think much of him at first but as we got closer we thought he looked suspicious, so we hid and watched him.

He was wearing green military fatigues and a green fatigue baseball-style hat. He looked like he was in the military. We crept closer for a better look, lying low in the tall grass while trying not to be seen. Closer now, we could see he had two air force stripes on his sleeves. What was suspicious about the man was that he was lying next to a tree on his stomach looking through binoculars at the RCA plant. We knew, even at our young age, that the RCA plant made more than TV sets and radios. The RCA plant had contracts with the government too.

We slowly slipped away from where the man was lying; making our way to the railway trestle so we could talk without being heard.

"What's that guy doing?" Glen asked me excitedly.

"Don't know, but *whatever* he's doing looks suspicious to me."

"Yeah, me too. Do you think he's a spy?

"Maybe. What do you think we should do?"

Glen looked back in the man's direction. "Don't know. Let's keep watching him. See what he's up to. See what he does next."

"OK, but we can't let him see us."

We made our way back to where we had first seen him and to our shock, he'd vanished.

"What are you boys doin' watching me?" came a gruff voice from behind us, causing me to nearly wet my pants.

We wheeled around. The man was standing over us, face full of stubble, lip upturned in a snarl. The really distressing thing, and we both saw it at the same time, was the big knife he held in his right hand.

"Well?"

Our hearts were really pounding now. I wanted to spring up and run away but thought, "What if Glen got caught?" The man was too close to us to get away from him. He would have us if we tried to bolt. What if he used his knife? We were trapped. Our eyes were fixed on that knife.

"You two come with me," he said, motioning with his knife. "Let's talk."

Glen and I looked at one another. I'm sure my face looked as ashen as his.

I said, "Look, mister, we're just on our way to the airport, that's all. We just want to watch the ...."

"Be quiet, kid, and do what I say," he said, gruffly cutting me off.

I hadn't noticed it before but one of his front teeth was a gray color like it was dead. This was getting serious but, for the time being, we decided to comply because we felt we had no other option.

He led us over to a clump of high bushes under a willow tree and had us sit down. "Now, why were you two watching me, huh?" He sat down cross-legged in the grass across from us, picked up a branch and began to whittle. That really made me nervous, Glen too.

"Well?" he said, glaring at us, waiting for an answer.

I tried to explain, "Look, we came to watch the airplanes land, that's all. We saw you lying over there and we kept going. Honest, mister, that's all. Just let us go, please?"

"Don't know. Why should I?" He kept whittling.

"Because we want to watch the airplanes come in. Honest, that's all."

He kept us there, looking at us as he whittled on that branch, asking us over and over why we were spying on him. We kept giving him the same answer.

Finally, to our great relief, after about five minutes he finally said, "OK, you two can go. But don't let me catch you two spying on me again or else," as he drew the knife across his throat, demonstrating how he would slit ours if we disobeyed him. It was at that point I thought I really was going to wet my pants.

"No, sir, we just want to watch the airplanes come in, that's all." We sprung up and ran away from him as fast as our young legs could carry us, not looking back until we knew we were well clear.

Once we were far enough away from him we stopped to catch our breath. I knew there was a National Guard Air Force base at the Van Nuys airport. I said to Glen between heavy gasps, "Let's go to the base and report him. He may be a spy. He looks like one to me. What do you think?"

"Yeah, it wouldn't hurt to tell them about that guy. He scared the shit out of me."

"Me, too. Let's go."

We walked to the main gate on Balboa Boulevard and told the guard at the gate what had happened. He listened to our story then went to the guard shed and made a phone call. In a few minutes a captain arrived at the gate driving a jeep.

"Hello, boys. Hear you have a story to tell. Hop in." I noticed he was wearing a pistol on his hip in a black spit-shined holster.

He drove us to the main hangar, a huge building big enough to hold several of the huge Boeing C-124 four-engine prop-driven Globemaster Transport planes they flew there. He ushered us into a meeting room and had us sit down. In 10 minutes we were telling our tale to eight senior air force officers, answering questions, giving a description of the man. A stenographer was taking down our every word. Glen and I were quite amazed at how seriously they took us.

One of the officers, a full colonel, sitting at the head of the table asked us, "Would you recognize this man again if you saw him?"

"You bet we would."

"OK then ..." He spoke to the captain who drove us in. "Jim, drive these men around the base. Show them around the places where this guy might work. It's worth a try."

"Yes, sir," The captain said. Then to us, "Come with me boys."

The captain drove us around the base. Fifteen minutes into our search, Glen and I both spotted the man walking on the expansive flight line towards the big aircraft hangar. We both pointed and said excitedly, "There he is!"

The captain stepped on the accelerator, causing the jeep to speed up. Hearing the approaching jeep, the man spun around. Yep, it was him. When he saw the two of us with the captain and the jeep bearing down on him, he quickly turned and began to run. He made it to the hangar and disappeared inside.

The captain stopped the jeep short of the hangar in a screech of brakes and a boil of dust. "Come on. Let's get him."

We followed the captain, who was now running in hot pursuit. He drew his gun as he ran and hollered, "Halt." It was like watching a movie ... except this was real and it was happening to us!

The captain was a faster runner than the "spy" and he quickly had the man cornered.

When we got to him, the captain had the man turned around against the hangar wall and was handcuffing him.

The "spy" turned, looking at us over his shoulder. His eyes narrowed and he said, "You two."

The captain made a call and had the man taken away by the MPs. Then he drove us to the main gate. Once there he said, and I will never forget this, "If there would have been more men like you two at Pearl Harbor, it wouldn't have happened." Then he actually saluted us, thanked us, and we were on our way.

We were on a high for a week after that. It took us about six months though to get over wondering whether the "spy" would come get us. Luckily we never saw him again.

Six weeks later we each got a letter thanking us, along with an explanation of what our "spy" had been doing. He was spying alright, but not on the RCA plant. He was spying on his wife, who he thought was seeing someone else, and he was gathering evidence for a divorce.

That probably explains why the man was so grumpy.

CHAPTER 6

Oman — Life Continues

One of the more unusual tasks the Police Air Wing performed was to supply HEMS cover for the sultan whenever he would leave the capital area on a road convoy, a task that sometimes lasted months. One of our medically configured Bell 214STs would be tasked to fly overhead the sultan's road convoy supplying medical cover. There were also three Royal Flight Puma helicopters that provided top-cover security for the road convoy.

What made the task unique was where we would have to stay when we followed the sultan and his entourage during his yearly "Meet the People Tour."

The sultan would take many of his ministers with him on his "Meet the People Tour," which could last for up to four months at a time. He would travel the length and breadth of the country, traveling from north to south, always finishing up the "Tour" in the southern town of Salalah.

His convoy would leave the capital area and snake its way through small towns and villages in the country. Omanis would line the streets shouting and waving and throwing flowers as the sultan would lead the procession, driving his Land Rover, often tossing money out of his open window to his people.

He would end each day camping in a big tent that had been set up for him in advance, usually in the desert where he would meet with his people face-to-face to listen to their needs. The sultan insisted his ministers travel with him so that if there was a complaint about – for example – housing, he could instruct his minister of housing to "fix" the problem immediately.

The majority of the locations where we stopped for any length of time were in remote desert areas. To accompany the sultan and his entourage was like becoming a desert nomad, but instead of using camels to travel across the dunes and the desert, we got around by air conditioned helicopter.

It was an adventure unlike anything I had ever experienced in my life before or since. I suppose the closest I came was when I was seven years old and used to sleep in a small tent in my backyard during the summer when I lived in the San Fernando Valley; or similarly, when I slept under the stars in my swag (sleeping bag) in the Australian outback – on my first flying job after leaving the military, when I lived and worked on a 1,369-square-mile cattle ranch – prior to doing a cattle muster the next day.

The sultan would have an entourage of around 400 support staff accompany him on his tour. That included the royal guard, several tanks, armored personnel carriers, and a portable guided-missile system. All of this defense hardware was collectively referred to as "the ring of steel" that would surround his encampment in the desert like covered wagons would encircle an encampment in the early days of the Wild West in America.

The crew makeup of the medical helicopter would include the captain, copilot, Omani helicopter crewman, respiratory therapist and trauma doctor. Although our helicopter was normally configured to carry 18 passengers and two pilots, it was medically configured to carry four people in the back plus the sultan on a stretcher if the need arose.

The helicopter contingent in the convoy consisted of the Royal Flight pilots, their support staff, and the crew from the Police Air Wing who flew in the EMS helicopter.

Once we made camp, we set up our own one-man tents that we arranged under a large camouflaged tarp, which offered some semblance of shade for our encampment. There was one larger green canvas army-type tent that served as the mess tent for our little camp which was run very efficiently by East Indian cooks.

The Royal Flight pilots had a large flatbed truck with a cabin on the back that acted as a communications van and general meeting place for the pilots and engineers (helicopter mechanics) to hang out and socialize when not flying. We could expect to stay in any particular campsite for as long as a month, sometimes longer.

Water would be brought in to us by tanker truck for our washing and drinking needs. Our shower was a canvas tarp held by four metal stakes that held the tarp to about waist level. To take a shower we would fill a specially made bag full of water that had a shower head attached to the bottom of it, allowing the water to pour over us via gravity. With the temperatures in the desert sometimes reaching 120° F in summer, if we wanted a cold shower we needed to take it in the very early morning hours.

When we had to camp in the desert during the summer months, I could never get to sleep until past midnight as it was just too hot in my tent in those temperatures. Luckily, the sultan didn't normally travel in summer but it did happen on occasion and when it did, everyone dreaded it.

Another thing we all dreaded were the camel spiders. The rumor was that a camel spider, being nocturnal, would inject you with an anesthetic while you slept, then would proceed to gnaw on your face. Many of the stories of the camel spider were folklore but scary to imagine nonetheless. In the 13 years I spent in Oman, and the countless times I slept in my tent while living in the desert, I only saw two camel spiders. They were ugly and scary looking to be sure, but none of them ever tried to chew my face off.

The logistics of flying out food, mail, and the changeover of personnel and supplies to the desert encampment would be handled by the police De Havilland Buffalo fixed-wing aircraft. The Buffalos are rugged aircraft that reminded me of an aerial truck.

There were the classic sand dunes in the desert near our camp, similar to the Wahiba sands, but there were also endless miles of flat, hard-packed desert where the plane could easily land to deliver its daily cargo.

When we were given an ETA (estimated time of arrival)

for the Buffalo fixed-wing, one of us would drive the sand-colored police Land Rover to anyplace on the desert near our camp that looked suitable to land an airplane. We would talk to the pilot via the VHF radio that was fitted to the police Land Rover. Once we saw the aircraft on the horizon we would pop two smoke grenades at the threshold of where we wanted the pilot to make his approach. And that's where he would land.

The sultan would slowly work his way south down the country and end his "Meet the People Tour" in Salalah where he would typically spend the summer months in his southern palace.

Between the months of June and September, Salalah is blessed with a unique meteorological phenomenon called the *Khareef* (pronounced: *hareef*) caused by the southeast monsoon. Blessed because the Khareef brings with it cool, misty weather during what is the hottest time of the year elsewhere in the country.

The Khareef brings in a low overcast, which forms in an area about 25 miles across, with a frequent fine drizzle offering very cool temperatures as a respite from the heat. The occurrence of the Khareef every summer makes Salalah a popular destination for visitors from the Gulf states.

Salalah during the Khareef was a perfect place for us to practice our instrument flying because the clouds would extend up to about 4,000 feet with a ceiling at the bottom of clouds of about 800 feet, so in a country usually bathed in sunshine year-round we could get some good practice flying in real clouds.

Once the sultan arrived in Salalah at the end of his "Meet the People Tour," the police would station their HEMS-configured Bell 214ST on a helipad at the police club located several miles from the sultan's palace, where we would do one-week rotations on EMS standby for the Sultan for as long as he stayed down there. It was a relaxing break from our normal operational flying duties up north.

Whenever I was back up north, and had time off, my wife and I would take the opportunity to go on camping trips with friends on beaches and in the dry wadis. Many of the wadis had small waterfalls and deep running pools of cool water where we could swim.

At night, we'd all sit around a campfire under a spectacular blanket of stars in an impossibly dark but temperate night and give thanks for the opportunity to be working and living in such a safe, serene and unspoiled country.

We became members of the Royal Flight Club, situated a five-minute drive from the Police Air Wing housing complex. The Royal Flight was mainly made up of British expats. It was the home to those pilots and engineers (flight mechanics) and support staff who worked for the sultan's Royal Flight.

The Royal Flight Club had all the amenities. To enter the club at night the men were required to wear a long sleeve shirt and tie. The long, fully stocked bar was manned by East Indian bartenders. The first-class restaurant was staffed by East Indian waiters.

The club had two tennis courts, a squash court, a gym, and a large swimming pool. If, during the day, you wanted to relax by the pool an East Indian waiter with starched long-sleeve shirt, black bow tie, black pants and shined black shoes was always on duty to politely take your order and then bring it to you on a tray. If a waiter was not immediately available, there was a buzzer to summon him to take your order. It felt like an echo of The British Raj, alive and well in the Sultanate of Oman.

The helicopter side of the Royal Flight had six, twin-engine Puma helicopters that supported the sultan and visiting dignitaries when traveling by road. On the fixed-wing side, there was the sultan's personal 747, a DC-8, and two Grumman Gulfstream IV business jets for use by his ministers.

The police had their own club too. There was the Police Officers' Club in the suburb of Ruwi, outside Muscat, built in the theme of an ancient Omani dhow, a sailing ship not unlike what Sinbad the Sailor had sailed in. Everything about the Police Officers' Club was first class. The Omanis, in native dress, long white dish-dash and the Indian waiters wearing white long-sleeve shirts, black trousers and bow ties, would tend to your every need.

The opulence around us wasn't taken for granted. On more than one occasion I thought back to how different my life had become since leaving my HEMS flying days back in the States when I lived on a 35-foot sailboat, living from paycheck to paycheck, not even in possession of a suit or tie.

One would expect it would be difficult to obtain alcohol in a Muslim country. The Omanis are very tolerant in that regard as they are tolerant in just about everything in life. As we were members of the Royal Flight Club and the Police Officers' Club we had no trouble obtaining booze. We could purchase everything from Australian beer to the best French wine or champagne because each club had its own fully stocked bottle shop that we, as members, could access. Barbecues and picnics on the beach – or wadi bashes as they were called – usually always included a well-stocked cold box filled with beer, wine or champagne for the occasion.

Because I worked for the police, another perk we enjoyed was being eligible to join the SAF (Sultan's Armed Forces) Beach Club. The beach club, while not very fancy, was more than adequate. It looked like a beach club one would imagine seeing in the Caribbean. It was very well run, with its own restaurant. Along with scuba diving facilities, there was a boat ramp, which made it easy to launch a personal ski boat or small sailboat into the Gulf of Oman.

I always felt like I was on vacation whenever I went there. With its stunningly beautiful azure-blue warm water and white sand beach, the club was a perfect place to go to relax after a week at work.

There was a restaurant and bar, again run by East Indian staff. Because the expatriate community working for the military was relatively small, you tended to know most of the club members.

The social life in Oman was opulent. There were endless dinner parties and usually four grand balls a year held at five-star hotels, necessitating my buying a personal tux or D.J. (dinner jacket) made for me by an Indian tailor.

One such ball was the Marine Ball held at the six-star Al Bustan Palace Hotel. A young woman I met at a scuba diving course shortly after my divorce asked me whether I would be her date for the 1989 Marine Ball. Neither of us could have known that night that I would eventually ask her to be my wife, but it wouldn't happen for another 15 years after that magical evening.

CHAPTER 7

October 1988

Meeting Kaye

My wife and I had been together for 3½ adventure-filled years when, thinking all was well for a bright and promising future, my life took an unexpected nosedive that launched me into immediate misery and despair.

It all began at an embassy function we were attending. He was a colonel in the U.S. Air Force serving over there. I liked him from the first moment I met him. He was a good officer, well liked and respected by all who knew him. He was very sporty, a good-looking guy, and fun to be around. I knew I was in trouble the first time he met my wife because I could see from the very moment they first laid eyes on one another the attraction was palpable.

As it transpired, there was nothing I could do to stop it. I talked to him in private about my concerns and, of course, I talked to her too. But the chemistry between them was too strong for either of them to stop.

I certainly couldn't understand what took place when it was happening because what occurred nearly mortally wounded my heart when I watched, seemingly powerless, as she fell in love with him. I will say that I do understand now but I certainly didn't understand it when it was happening.

I realize it's possible that when two people meet and are drawn so strongly to one another they almost cannot help themselves. I truly do "get it" now. True love occurs quite suddenly, striking two unsuspecting people like a random bolt of lightning, taking them both by surprise, transporting them on a ride they hadn't signed up for, as if passengers in their own lives.

Knowing I would probably be living and working in Oman for a few more years, I took a one-month leave to California to do two things: file for divorce from a woman I still loved but could never take back because of the annihilation of trust and after the hurt she'd caused me, and to put my sailboat, *Moali,* up for sale.

I had decided that when the time came to go sailing again I would search for a slightly bigger boat. That meant the time had come to say goodbye to that wonderful little boat that had given me so much joy and pleasure for the five years I lived aboard her and sailed her while working in San Diego.

She looked sad and forlorn sitting in that storage yard in Mission Valley, near the cement plant, collecting a thick layer of gray dust where she'd sat for several years ... waiting. It was time she found a new home: to go to someone who could bring her to life again. It was time to set her free; to put her into the hands of someone who could love her as much as I had.

After filing for divorce and leaving *Moali* with a yacht broker in San Diego, I flew back to Oman, returning to an empty house. The furniture was still there because it was police property, but my wife had moved out and into a place in town provided by the American embassy. All that was left on the now-bare walls were the nails where our pictures had once hung.

I had two choices for handling the deep funk I found myself in. I could turn to the bottle to solve my woes. But that just isn't me. Or I could exercise. I chose that option.

I went to the Royal Flight gym seven days a week. When I worked out I tried to wear myself out as a way to purge the frustration and anger I felt from the loss of my wife. I also played 2½ hours of tennis four times a week. I had no real appetite for food so I ate only one meal a day. Consequently I lost 15 pounds and firmed up.

In six months' time, at age 42, I had the strength and look and stamina of a much younger man. Although I still felt empty and hollow inside from the loss of my wife to another man and the consequent divorce, my friends said I looked really good … considering.

It was at that time in my life that I met Kaye, a classy young lady from London, England, who was working as a nurse at the Royal Hospital in Muscat.

I needed to distance myself from the embassy crowd where my wife and her new man were working so I joined the Muscat Divers and the British Sub Aqua Club to renew the scuba certification I had attained when living in Australia. I saw joining the club as an opportunity to find a new circle of friends and to do something I had not done before in Oman. Besides, I had told myself that, before leaving the country for good, I wanted to sample the world-class scuba diving I had heard so much about.

The first time I laid eyes on Kaye is an event I will never forget. It was early evening. I was a passenger sitting in the back seat of a friend's car, on the way to the Intercontinental Hotel to attend a dinner theater with friends.

Out my window, I saw this woman wearing an Omani ladies black *Abaya*, the material blowing wildly in the wind, trailing out the open door of the old, faded-red Suzuki Jeep she was driving. All I could see of her face were the sand goggles. What an improbable sight! Someone in our car waved. She waved back.

When we arrived at the hotel we took our places at a reserved table for 12. One of our party introduced us. We said our pleasantries but that would be the extent of our conversation that evening. Her name was Kaye, the woman I'd seen driving the faded red Suzuki Jeep 15 minutes earlier. She had removed her sand goggles and taken off her black Abaya revealing a very pretty, flowing, white-silk dress. I do remember thinking, though, that without the sand goggles she looked quite beautiful.

I especially noticed how she addressed everyone. She would call them "darling." I would later learn she found it easier to call them "darling" than to actually remember their names. No matter what the reason, I found it endearing. That is why those in the expat community who knew her referred to her as "Kaye Darling."

I saw Kaye again several months later in a scuba class I had enrolled in to get recertified. She had just broken up with her boyfriend and had two tickets for the American Marine Ball, the hottest ticket in town every year. She approached me and asked me if I would like to be her date. I told her about my circumstances and my recent divorce, only doing so because I knew that my wife and her new beau would be there and I didn't know if I wanted to put myself through the anguish of seeing them there together. She convinced me to go, so I accepted her kind invitation. Besides being very attractive, she was light-hearted, quick to laugh, enjoyable to be with, and a good listener, keeping me well-clear of becoming morose or maudlin. "Kaye Darling" was just what I needed.

The Marine Ball was a black-tie affair held at the breathtaking, newly built, six-star Bustan Palace Hotel overlooking the sea. Kaye wore a stunning, full-length, red ball gown that she told me she had ordered from the U.K. especially for the event. She looked amazingly elegant and stunningly beautiful. She was such a vision; I took a picture of her as she descended the marble steps of the hotel to greet me. I had someone take our picture standing together in the marbled foyer of the hotel.

At one point in the evening I saw my former wife and her new beau sitting together. When I told Kaye I'd seen them at a table near the dance floor she said, "Don't worry, Darling. You can take me on your arm, escort me to the dance floor and I will gaze up into your eyes admiringly as we pass by them."

I offered her my arm. "Well then, Miss Draper, in that case, would you like to dance?"

"Oh, Darling, yes, I'd love to."

We danced to the band's lively music into the early hours of the next morning, making a wonderful memory – a memory that we cherish to this day.

Following the disintegration of my marriage, I followed actions predictable of someone whose trust had been recently betrayed. I became leery of my own judgment of women. I adopted a defense mechanism to ensure I wouldn't be hurt again. I became commitment-a-phobic. I, like anyone whose trust has been shattered in a relationship, was not in a hurry to have it happen again. I felt I had to rebuild my confidence over time before I could offer my trust to someone again. Harboring that standoffish attitude is how I lost Kaye.

Kaye and I did become very good friends. We became diving buddies at the dive club. Whenever we went diving together we acted as safety person for the other as "dive buddies." We dated on and off, too.

At one point, Kaye spent the night with me at my villa at the Police Air Wing housing complex. In the morning I noticed she had left her washcloth and toothbrush in my bathroom. It was a subtle sign that she wanted to become a more regular fixture in my life. Without mentioning it, I neatly folded her washcloth and placed it along with her toothbrush in the back seat of her car. Nothing was said but my action didn't go unnoticed. It was my subtle way of saying I was not ready for her to begin moving in. After that incident, we did not see one another for three weeks.

After a time I began to date other women. In fact, once women found out I was single they began making a play for me. This sudden attention and affirmation that I was indeed desired by women again did wonders for my badly bruised ego.

Kaye phoned me one night in tears to tell me her job at the Royal Hospital was becoming untenable. She had been working there for over two years and the politics were wearing her down. She said she was working in a professional wasteland where she feared if she stayed, she would become unemployable anywhere else. She asked me what she should do. I told her if she felt that way perhaps she should go somewhere she was appreciated and where she could further her professional career as a nurse. So, after much thinking about it, she called me several weeks later to tell me that she had handed in her resignation and that she planned to return to England.

Kaye would tell me many years later that if I would have asked her to stay in Oman with me, that no matter how bad things were for her at the Royal Hospital, she would have stayed. I felt I was in no position mentally to make that kind of a commitment to her, so in the first week of December 1989, Kaye left Oman for good. We promised one another we would stay in touch. It was a promise neither of us would break.

CHAPTER 8
Claire

I'd been single for more than a year when I attended a black-tie New Year's Eve dinner at the Royal Flight Club, where I met Claire.

Claire was new to Oman and worked as the public relations and marketing rep at the Intercontinental Hotel. We enjoyed each other's company and got along extremely well; consequently, we began seeing one another.

We had only been dating a few weeks when she called me one evening, very distraught, to tell me she had been fired from her job at the Intercontinental Hotel. She had been told by the general manager that she had to be out of the country in 48 hours and that her visa would be canceled at that time.

I never really found out the reason for her being fired but, after speaking with Claire about it, she suspected she had made a client of the hotel angry and he put pressure on the general manager of the hotel to fire her. Unfortunately that's not an uncommon story in the Middle East.

This sudden turn of events threw our courting process into overdrive, causing us to shift gears into something resembling light speed. She only had hours left in the country and we were unable to take the normal amount of time to get to know each other. So we decided that before we made a decision on what she should do, we would each make a list of what we were looking for in a relationship. Once our respective lists were complete we would go to a secluded beach, open a bottle of champagne and read each other our lists. So that's what we did.

After going over our lists and polishing off a bottle of champagne, we decided we should try to give it a go. The plan was she would go to Dubai where, as she was British, she could easily get a one-month visa and stay with friends there. Then, through acquaintances she'd met in Oman, she would try to find a job back in Oman and, if successful, she would move in with me and we would take it from there. Whew! No pressure.

One of the items on my list that I had to make perfectly clear was that I still had the dream of one day going sailing. I said I needed a partner to go sailing with me. Claire said she had learned to sail as a girl and had been on a few boats but had not done any serious sailing. She said she was willing to give it a try.

Using the contacts she had made while working at the Intercontinental Hotel, she managed to find a job working for a British property company based in Muscat.

It was during this timeframe that the book I had written, *The Golden Hour*, had finally found a home with a small independent publisher. It made its debut in December 1989.

My good friend, Mike Burke, co-founder and then president of the National EMS Pilots Association, told me the organization wanted to display and sell copies of *The Golden Hour* at the upcoming Air Medical Transport Conference to be held in Nashville, Tennessee, that year.

I'd kept an eye on the HEMS industry back in the U.S. since I left it and the accident rate had not abated. In fact, there was growing concern by the National EMS Pilots Association, the FAA (Federal Aviation Administration) and the NTSB (National Transportation Safety Board) about the accident rate. Those organizations were desperately trying to do something to stop the alarming loss of life. I saw this as an excellent opportunity to take Claire to America for my one-month vacation and attend the conference.

It was good to see Mike Burke, Tom Einhorn and Don Wright again. The three men had founded the National EMS Pilots Association, NEMSPA, four years earlier. Each man had written a blurb for the back cover of my book and told me they were anxious to get it "out there" to help in their effort to try to stem the accident rate that, in their words, showed no signs of abating.

When I spoke to them I could see they were frustrated that their efforts so far had not borne fruit. Mike Burke had allowed himself to be interviewed on the investigative news program, *60 Minutes*, with his face in deep shadow and his voice altered, as he gave the reasons why there had been so many accidents.

He then testified before Congress, hoping they would make meaningful laws to stop the carnage. To his great disappointment and to those at NEMSPA, nothing whatsoever was done and as a consequence HEMS helicopters continued to crash at an unacceptable rate.

Six months later, on my next leave, I booked a two-week sailing vacation on a 30-foot sloop as a way to determine if Claire would take to sailing. I'd booked a boat for the two of us to sail in a flotilla along the south coast of Turkey with 10 other boats. Claire told me she loved it. She seemed to be a natural sailor and was a great cook to boot. More importantly, we got along well together while living in such a small, cramped space.

We'd only been living together less than a year when our time in Oman looked like it was going to come to an abrupt end when on Aug 2, 1990, the Iraqi leader, Saddam Hussein, invaded Kuwait. I remember we were at the SAF Beach club when someone hollered the news across the beach.

It was a nerve-wracking time for everyone working and living in the Middle East. In Oman, no one knew how the Omanis would react to Saddam's aggression and his threats that he wouldn't hesitate to fire scud missiles into Israel. We knew that if Israel were pulled into the war it could force the rest of the Arab countries to side with Saddam, which would cause real problems with the West and, by inference, we Westerners living in Oman.

When we first learned of the invasion, Claire and I laid out an aviation chart on our bed to determine if a Scud missile carrying chemical weapons could reach Oman. Luckily, as it turned out, we were well out of range.

Every pilot at the Air Wing was summoned into work to be on standby for any civil unrest that might occur. For three days we were made to stay at work, unable to leave, waiting to see what the local populace was going to do. Our meals were brought in. We had to sleep on mattresses on the marble floors in our offices. We were issued Browning 9mm pistols from the Air Wing armory and we waited.

Oman didn't have satellite television at that time so our only news came from what we saw on Oman television, which wasn't much. Being the peace-loving country Oman is, it took three days for the Omanis to admit on TV that Saddam Hussein had indeed invaded Kuwait. We expatriates were forced to get our news from short-wave radio. We would listen to the BBC to find out what was going on in the country. The scenario was too reminiscent for my liking to what had occurred to me in Iran. I wasn't going to wait to be evacuated on the last charter flight out of the country this time.

It looked as if Saddam didn't back down, the United States was going to war. The Police Air Wing was informed by the airport authorities that if war broke out, the airport in Muscat would be closed to all domestic aircraft. Armed with that information, we had to decide if family members should leave or stay because once the war started they would have to remain in Oman until it was over. Claire and I discussed this possibility. To her credit, she said she wasn't going to leave me and that she wanted to stay.

We watched with more than a little nervousness and anticipation as the buildup of troops and heated rhetoric quickly escalated. A 300-bed hospital was erected across the runway from the Police Air Wing. Huge air-to-air refueling tanker aircraft began arriving. Before long there were 22 of them parked on the police ramp outside operations. When I saw the stealth fighters and stealth bombers arrive, I knew the air war was about to begin.

Every day the tension built like gas pressure filling an ever expanding balloon. It became the main topic of conversation among the expats. We watched and listened anxiously to rumor and speculation, wondering what the future held for us. I could feel the tension building as I read the daily newspapers and listened to the BBC on shortwave radio, something that I carried with me everywhere. The world watched transfixed as the coalition built, each country sending troops to the Gulf. Days prior to the beginning of the war there were more than 1.6 million troops amassed ready to invade Iraq.

The air war finally began on January 17, 1991, with troops following in February after days of relentless pounding from the air. It actually came as a relief to wake up one morning and learn the ground war had finally begun.

Once the troops crossed over the border to retake Kuwait and pressed deep into Iraqi territory on the march toward Baghdad, it became a rout that ended just days after it had begun, with the coalition enjoying a quick and resounding victory.

With the Gulf War behind us, stability once again settled in the Middle East, causing life in Oman to return to normal, which meant attending dinner parties, going to at least two black-tie affairs a year, going to the beach, wadi bashes (driving in dry river beds) in our four-wheel drive, camping, playing tennis, working and going on sailing vacations every five months.

Two-and-a half years after Claire moved in with me I asked her to marry me one morning over pancakes. It was one of the least romantic things I have ever done in my life and was something I was reminded of on more than one occasion. She accepted my less-than-romantic proposal anyway and we were married at the British Embassy in Muscat on May 27, 1992.

We took our honeymoon in the Virgin Islands where I'd rented a 36-foot sloop for three weeks. We stopped in 40 different anchorages sailing in the warm, 15-knot trade winds through both the American and the British Virgin Islands. It was idyllic.

One of the more memorable expeditionary trips we took while living in Oman was to travel for three days through the Wahiba Sands south of Muscat.

The Wahiba Sands are a series of long, golden, windblown mountains of sand stretching out in meandering amber dunes. Seeing the perfection in the lines and the texture and soft appearance of the sweeping dunes reminded me of the sensual curves of a woman's body.

The Wahiba Sands extend 120 miles and are 60 miles wide, stretching to the Arabian Sea. The dunes can reach heights of 400 to 600 feet. While on that three-day trip, we saw nomadic Bedouin camps along sandy tracks and trails in the isolated desert. We brought a hand-held GPS. Without it, and without local knowledge, I'm certain we would have become lost.

There were eight of us in 4, four-wheel drive vehicles. We let the air out of our tires down to 10 pounds and struck off into the dunes. We carried enough food for a week and enough water for much longer. As a precaution, we had also told operations at the Air Wing to send out a search party in five days if we didn't turn up.

We felt like ancient explorers surrounded in a timeless Arab setting. We made it a point each day to set up camp several hours before the sun set below the last dune. We would eat our evening meal sitting around a crackling campfire where we'd tell stories and socialize under a shimmering mantle of stars set against an impossibly clear Arabian sky.

As mentioned earlier, when the Sultan stayed in his Salalah palace during the summer months we would base a Bell 214ST at the police officer's club in Salalah to support him in the HEMS role. Two pilots would do one-week rotations from their normal flying duties up north.

Salalah had a special attraction to me other than the Khareef, the cool weather in summer and supporting the Sultan in the EMS role. The port of Raysut in Salalah was a refuge for sailors usually in the middle of their circumnavigation. They would wait out the weather there until they could venture up the Red Sea to the Mediterranean. When I was stationed in Salalah on one of my one-week tours, I would often drive the police

Land Rover down to the port to see if I could meet some of these brave souls who were doing what I wanted to do one day.

The two most memorable people I met there were Lee and Mel. They were on their second circumnavigation, sailing a Swan 42 named *Affaire de'cour* (Affair of the heart). They were so memorable because of their ages considering what they were doing. Lee was a woman in her seventies. Mel was 79.

They were longtime friends and sailing companions. Lee was nearly blind. She had to read using a prism. Mel was nearly deaf and wore two hearing aids that were constantly squealing from the feedback one hearing aid received from the other.

Together this unlikely duo were sailing the world's oceans. They were both spritely and young at heart. When I asked them how long they thought they would continue sailing they looked at me like I had just asked them a question in Arabic. They told me they couldn't *ever* imagine *not* doing it.

Mel told me, "You know, I go home and I see friends my age and they're in rocking chairs and using canes and walkers to get around. That just isn't me. I can't relate to them at all."

We invited Lee and Mel up to Muscat to stay with us if they wished. They took us up on our offer and enjoyed a week's break from the boat.

We received a letter from Lee four months later. In the letter she said that they were at anchor in Thailand when Mel suddenly got up out of his berth and went to the radar, shouting orders as if they were at sea. He was taken to a hospital and died several days later.

Hearing of Mel's death shocked Claire and me. I wanted to go sailing while I still could. Meeting Mel and Lee was a testament that you can do it at any age; that is, as long as you don't die while you're waiting to go.

I had been taking a correspondence course from the National Marine Correspondence School based in Birkenhead, England, to obtain my Yacht master Offshore certification through the Royal Yachting Association. The school was run by two retired Royal Navy lieutenant commanders. It took me nearly two years and I had recently finished it. I was ready to finally go, so I tendered my two-month notice to the Police Air Wing.

An unexpected moment occurred several days before I was to leave Oman for good. Omar – whom I had seen rise up the ranks to become chief pilot of the helicopter section – asked me to stop by his office. When I knocked on his door he called out for me to enter. When I did, he was sitting at his desk and all eight of the other Omani pilots were sitting in the room as well.

"Hey, Omar, what's going on?" I asked.

"Mister Mains, please take a seat."

Omar had placed a chair in the middle of the room facing the other Omani pilots. Once settled, each man took a turn thanking me in his own special way for, in their words, "All that I had done for them as trainer examiner and mentor in the 13 years I had served in the Royal Oman Police Air Wing." Each man offered a personal anecdote of an incident that involved me that had touched him in some way.

Omar's anecdote was to recall how he would always remember to keep at least 60 knots of airspeed in autorotation so that the aircraft will respond in the flare. He, of course, was making reference to the incident that occurred nine years prior when I was demonstrating in the Bell 205 what would happen if he had less than 60 knots in the flare. That was the day I struck the tail rotor into the dirt.

Having seen those Omanis go from fledgling aviators to experienced pilots, and knowing I had made a difference in their lives by being their mentor, was a very special moment for me. It served to reinforce what kind, appreciative and humble people the Omanis are. Without doubt, that day in Omar's office was one of the most touching moments I've ever experienced in my aviation career.

So, on October 31, 1997, at the age of 51, the time had finally come for me to hang up my headset, find a sailboat, live aboard her and go sailing full time. What had begun as a two-year commitment to live and work in the Sultanate of Oman had stretched to 13. It was time at last to say a fond goodbye, *ma'a salama* in Arabic, to a country and its people that shall always hold a very special place in my heart.

In one of Kaye's Christmas letters she had written to me from England, saying that Oman was her "golden time." I could not have summed up my feelings for my time spent there any better than that.

%

From the time I left San Diego, in December 1984, to take the job in Oman, the HEMS accident rate back in the U.S. showed no signs of improving. Sixty accidents had occurred over 13 years I'd been in Oman causing 90 people to lose their lives. Some of those lives lost were patients being transported, while the majority of lives lost were flight crew members. New flight programs were springing up all across the country. HEMS in America was fast becoming a lucrative business. It was also gaining a darker, more sinister notoriety: it was gaining the reputation as the most deadly job in America.

Most of the crashes were the same preventable tragedy occurring over and over again: CFIT (controlled flight into terrain), where an aircraft with no mechanical problems is flown into the ground.

The book I'd written, *The Golden Hour* – my effort to stop the tragic loss of lives back home – had made no impact whatsoever to bring about safety changes in an industry that was out of control. I was sickened but not surprised every time I learned of yet another HEMS crash because meaningful measures had not been undertaken by the FAA, NTSB and Congress to make flying on a HEMS helicopter any safer than it was when I did it.

In subsequent years, flight crews and patients would continue to lose their lives. It was, from my perspective, the embodiment of Einstein's definition of insanity: doing the same thing over and over again and expecting a different result. It was well and truly nuts.

But I was leaving Oman – bringing one solution to the problem with me – a solution to reduce that accident rate by a minimum of 80 percent. It was an answer I knew they wouldn't buy back home because the cost to do so would need a paradigm shift and would adversely affect the bottom line.

If I could, I would ask the decision-makers: "How about doing it like we do it in Oman, using two pilots who are instrument rated, current and proficient?" First of all, it would take the fear out of flying in the clouds if you inadvertently happened to fly into instrument conditions because you'd have two pilots who were comfortable with instrument flying.

Because it has been statistically proven that inadvertently flying into instrument conditions has been the biggest single cause of HEMS accidents, why not outfit a helicopter so that if it does happen there's a fighting chance it won't crash? At the very minimum why not mandate that every HEMS helicopter be fitted with an autopilot?

HEMS operations in Europe and in Canada operate with a pilot and copilot. The Brits and Norwegians fly pilot and copilot on the North Sea. The oil companies wouldn't have it any other way. In fact, the oil companies abroad *demand* two pilots to ensure the safety of their people. Hospitals could demand the same of their HEMS helicopter providers: fly two pilots or you don't get the contract. Hospitals would be doing it for the same reason the oil companies demand it: for the safety of their people. Now there's a novel concept. But it hasn't come to that yet. I'm still waiting.

I knew in my heart the new paradigm I had been exposed to in Oman wouldn't be accepted back home. Hospital administrators would never spend the kind of money it would take to provide an aircraft with a two-pilot contingent and the additional training that would entail. There would always be a helicopter company that would undercut a bid and do it on the "cheap" and why? Because the federal regulations allow it – so who can blame them?

The engine for change in the HEMS industry will not

come from the hospitals or the companies who supply the helicopters to them. The change will only happen through strict government regulation like they did with the airlines. Perhaps one day they *will* get it. Perhaps someone in government will finally say, "Enough of this senseless loss of life. Too many people have died already. We tried to let the operators and hospitals self-regulate and it hasn't worked. It's time for *real* change so this is how it must be done. You either comply or you don't get into the game and you don't operate in American airspace."

I knew in my bones that until that time came more lives would be lost in HEMS accidents. It was a depressing thought. A fact I had absolutely no control over. Knowing that fact could cause me to go nuts, therefore it was time to fulfill a dream. The time had finally come to find a boat and go sailing ....

Moali, my home for 5 years while living and working at UCSD Medical Center's Life Flight program in San Diego, en-route to a storage facility in Mission Valley

One last cruise on my beloved sailboat Moali before going to take the new flying job in the Sultanate of Oman

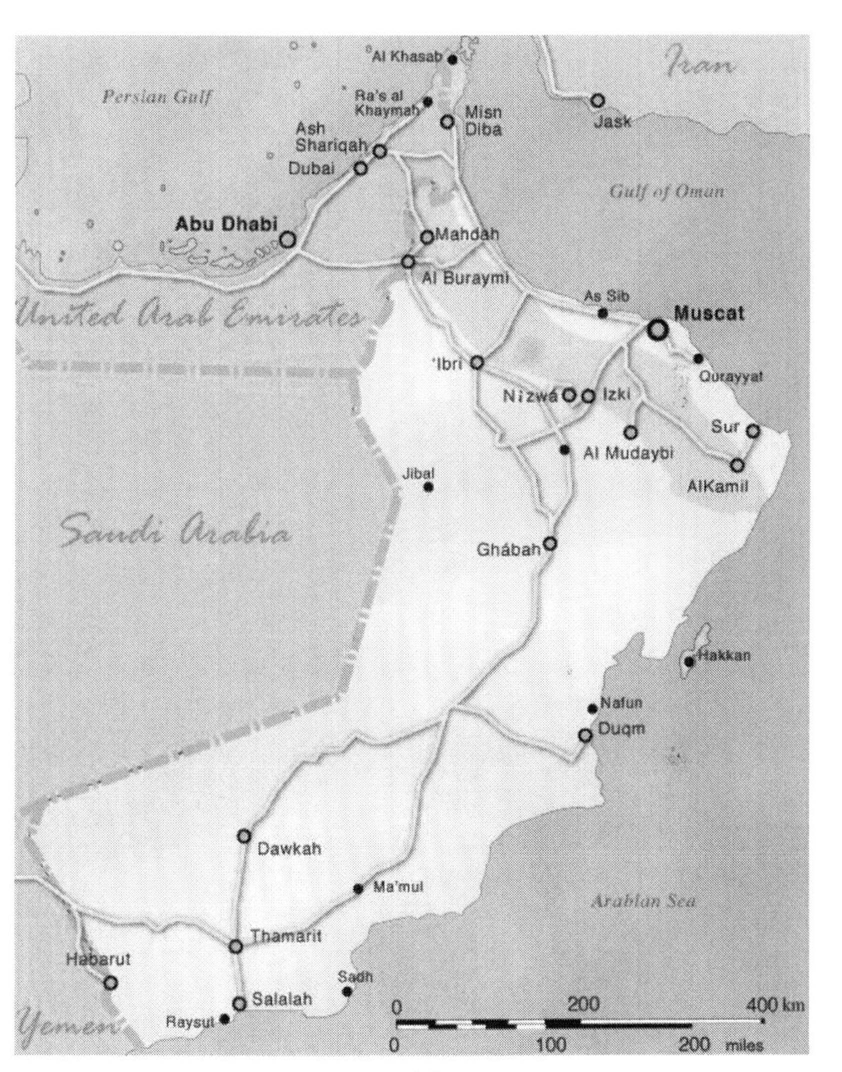

Map of the Sultanate of Oman

David and Theresa Sutcliffe New Year's Eve Oman

Toasting in the New Year of 1985 locking arms with David Sutcliffe and Richard Shuttleworth in celebration the day we arrived in Oman. Richard Shuttleworth is unfortunately hidden behind David's glass of champagne.

Enroute to Bandar Khayran on an Omani Dhow during our first weekend in Oman

Our two-bedroom villa on the Police Air Wing compound

15th Century watchtowers in the capital area of Muscat where we flew the 'Fawlty Towers Load Lift' slinging aggregate and materials to restore them using the police Bell 205s.

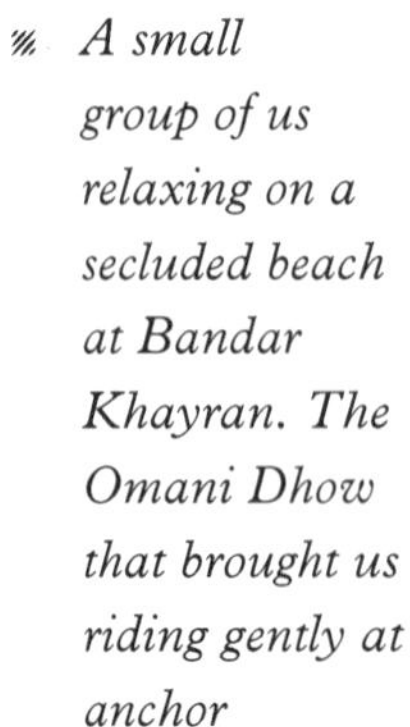

A small group of us relaxing on a secluded beach at Bandar Khayran. The Omani Dhow that brought us riding gently at anchor

Winching a man off his stalled truck from a flooded wadi near the town of Nizwa

Class A police uniform worn when flying HEMS cover for visiting VIPs

Pilots and Crewmen on the ramp in front of the Police Air Wing. Far left, John Ilbert the CO. I am standing behind him. Richard Shuttleworth is lying on the ground. Peter Allen is on one knee. David Sutcliffe is standing over Peter's left shoulder arms crossed.

Training with SSF and STF teams using the Bell 205. The Omani team members were trained by former members of the British SAS.

Friendly local kids from the village of Sur who came to inspect the police 214ST helicopter

Omani Girl

Omani Boy

Chilled-out Camel on the beach in Salalah Southern Oman near the Yemeni border.

Twenty-place twin-engine Bell 214ST near Kumzar village in the Musandam area in the far north of country — Omani dhows in the background blending the old with the new.

Practicing an EMS drill using the Bell 214ST.

Sultan of Oman's Yacht

Landing a Bell 214ST on the Sultan's Yacht

After landing a Bell 214ST on the Sultan's yacht.

Royal Flight campsite in support of the Sultan's convoy on the Harassis central Oman. Note the campsite to the left. On the right, the three Royal Flight Puma helicopters and the Police Bell 214ST HEMS aircraft.

Royal Flight Ops Van on convoy in the desert in support of the Sultan's 'Meet the People Tour'. Royal Flight pilot Peter Norton on duty manning the radio.

On convoy with the Sultan on his 'Meet the People Tour'

Camel Spider

SAF Beach Club

Royal Flight Club bar

At the controls of the Police Bell 214ST

Camping with fellow expats on Fins Beach

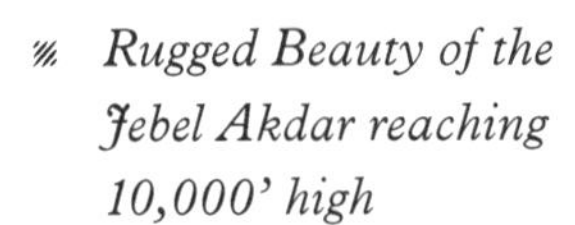

Rugged Beauty of the Jebel Akdar reaching 10,000' high

Hiking along a precipice in the rugged Jebel Akdar

Heading out for a dive with the Muscat Divers. Kaye is seated behind me wearing a black swimsuit.

My diving buddy Kaye Draper before going for a dive

Kaye descending the stairs to meet me at the Al Bustan Hotel

First date with Kaye at the Marine Ball at the Al Bustan Palace Hotel

Group of Omai men and boys outside the Nizwa souq

Young Omani women living in the jebel

Woman – Nizwa Souq

Flying low over the dunes in the Empty Quarter or MFN 'Middle of Fucking Nowhere' as we called it. MFN was the designation we would enter in the aircraft's GNS, Global Navigation System.

Setting shelter under a Bell 214ST to escape the Omani desert sun

Meeting with Omani elders at 6500' in the Jebel Akdar

In contrast—the green entrance to Wadi Shab on the Omani coast

Practicing police diver drops in the Bell 205 off the Omani coast near Muscat

After flying the diver drops off the coast

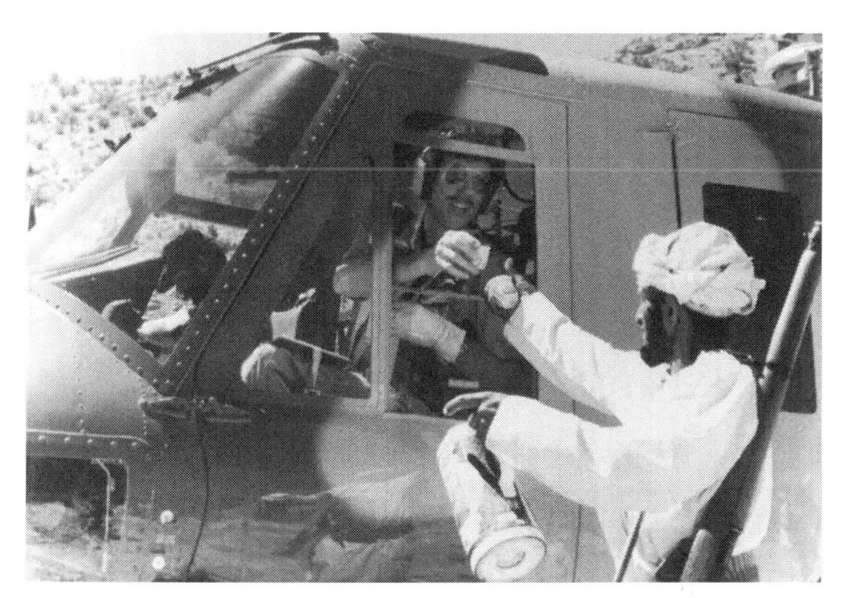

Omani hospitality even at 6000' in the mountains – being served Omani coffee.

I'm replacing a 5000 pound generator for the ship navigation light on the Strait of Hormuz

My last dive with Kaye before she left Oman to return to England

Wahiba Sands

Claire and I camping at 7000' in the mountains in the *Jebel Akdar*

First sailing vacation with Claire off the West coast of Turkey

Sailing past rock tombs Dalyan Turkey

Sailing to Kapi Creek Turkey with Claire

Landing a Bell 214ST at dusk on the Al Said, the Sultan of Oman's yacht

Returning home to the police Air Wing after a day's flying.

The following is a list of HEMS fatal accidents that occurred after I left San Diego and during the 13 years I lived and worked in the Sultanate of Oman.

(Source Air Medical Memorial Website
www.airmedicalmemorial.com)

1985		
St Mary's Air Life	Monument Valley, UT	Dec 24, 1985
Air Care	Ainsworth,NE	Dec 20, 1985
Life Flight	Adrian, MI	Dec 10, 1985
Providence Hospital	Juneau, AK	October 22, 1985
Metro Ambulance Services	Duluth, GA	May 20, 1985
unknown program	Tuba City, AZ	April 19, 1985
Mercy Flights	Central Point, OR	February 9, 1985
Lifeguard	Carson, NM	January 20, 1985
1986		
Life Guard	Pendleton, OR	December 3, 1986
SkyMed	Jamestown, TN	December 3, 1986
AirCare	Galax, VA	Sept 23, 1986
Baptist Medical Center	Peterson, AL	June 2, 1986
Maryland State Police	Baltimore, MD	January 19, 1986
1987		
Care Flight	Bridgeport, CA	June 21, 1987
FlightCare	Bay City, MI	June 7, 1987
North Central Mercy Flight	Choteau, MT	June 5, 1987
unknown program	Eagle, CO	March 27, 1987

Samaritan AirEvac	Flagstaff, AZ	February 20, 1987
EastCare	Pollockville, NC	January 8, 1987
	1988	
Air Evac Life Team	Cape Girardeau, Missouri	Dec 22, 1988
Medical Air Transport	Cajon, CA	April 17, 1988
	1989	
Acadian Air Med	Houma, LA	September 3, 1989
Heartflite	Blanchard, ID	August 27, 1989
Mercy Flights	Gold Beach, OR	August 21, 1989
HELP Flight	Big Timber, MT	June 1, 1989
Dare Medflight	Coinjock, NC	March 26, 1989
Flight For Life	Tyler, TX	February 13, 1989
	1990	
unknown program	Boulder, CO	April 1, 1990
Life Force	Sand Mountain, GA	October 3, 1990
Aeromedical Services	Rapid City, SD	February 9, 1990
	1991	
Southern Tier Air Rescue	De Ruyter, NY	December 9, 1991
Care Flight of Reno	Bridgeport, CA	November 27, 1991
unknown program	Bohemia Walton, Oregon	August 28, 1991
Guthrie One Helicopter	Sonestown, PA	January 26, 1991
	1992	
Medic Air	Herlong	Dec 31, 1992
Life Star 1	Middletown, CT	June 20, 1992
unknown program	Freeland, MI	March 5, 1992
unknown program	Ft. Grant, AZ	March 4, 1992

1993		
AirMed	Casco Bay, ME	Nov 19, 1993
Llifeguard	Agusta, GA	August 7, 1993
Spirit of Kansas City Life Flight	Cameron, MO	May 27, 1993
Life Flight	Casper, WY	April 6, 1993
Critical Air Medicine	Eagle Mountain, CA	March 11, 1993
1994		
Midwest MedFlight	Ann Arbor, MI	December 1, 1994
Life Flight	Perry, FL	November 4, 1994
Flight For Life Colorado	Huron Peak, CO	July 9, 1994
AirCare	Bluefield, West Virginia	April 22, 1994
Critical Air Medicine	San Antonio, TX	February 10, 1994
Augusta Aviation	Elizabethton, TN	April 7, 1994
1995		
AirLift Northwest	Bainbridge Island, WA	September 11, 1995
1996		
Mercy Flight Central	Penn Yan, NY	Dec 12, 1996
Guardian Air	San Francisco Peaks, AZ	January 31, 1996
Aeromed	Spokane, WA	January 8, 1996
1997		
AirLife Denver	Littleton, CO	December 14, 1997
Acadian Air Med	Lena, LA	March 14, 1997

CHAPTER 9

Hanging Up the Headset — First Try

Claire and I flew to Fort Lauderdale to begin our search for a boat. We could have, literally, gone anywhere to look for a boat but we chose Fort Lauderdale. We knew there were more reasonably priced used boats in acceptable condition there than anywhere else in the world.

We found a blue-water cruiser for a good price, a Tayana-42 in very good condition. We purchased her and named her, *Ocean Spirit*. We outfitted her, went for a few shake-down cruises and waited for the weather to improve so that we could sail across to the Bahamas.

Nineteen Ninety-Eight was an El Niño year. Named after the "first child" – a reference to Jesus because it usually occurs around Christmas – El Niño is a band of anomalously warm ocean temperatures that develops off the western coast of South America. Usually occurring every five to seven years, El Niño brings climatic changes across the Pacific Ocean that can cause extreme weather in many regions of the world.

The weather didn't look favorable for the Bahamas that year so we waited in Fort Lauderdale. However, with the hurricane season approaching we headed north to Boston. That ended up being a wise decision because 1998 would turn out to be one of the strongest El Niño years ever recorded.

A highlight of our trip was anchoring at the base of the Statue of Liberty in New York Harbor on August 2, 1998. It was thrilling to be anchored under the watchful gaze of such an historically famous lady. We watched the sun set over the stern of *Ocean Spirit* as the lights of Manhattan and the Statue of Liberty came to life. Of course, with the events of 9/11, I am certain a boat wouldn't be allowed to anchor off the Statue of Liberty now.

We logged over 2,200 miles, sometimes sailing in the Atlantic and sometimes following the Intercoastal Waterway. We enjoyed sailing up the Chesapeake Bay, exploring many of the historic anchorages there, then sailing down Delaware Bay to New York into Long Island Sound and on to Boston.

We decided that spending a year on the boat was enough of an adventure so we put the boat up for sale in Annapolis, Maryland. As we had kept her in such good condition we immediately had three buyers and sold her in 12 days for more money than we paid for her. In fact, the profit we made covered our expenses for the whole year.

The man who bought *Ocean Spirit* had his own unique story to tell. He was a lawyer from Delaware who had driven down to Annapolis to visit the grave of his son who had died two years earlier at the age of 10. He told us he had been in the market ever since for the "perfect sailboat." He told us that while at his son's gravesite that day he had a strong feeling that while in Annapolis he should look at boats to see what was for sale. He saw *Ocean Spirit* and immediately fell in love with her. He took possession within the week and sailed her up to his home in Baltimore, Maryland.

Now boat-less and having nowhere to live, Claire and I decided we would drive to Southern California to see if we could afford to live there. Claire flew back to England to pick up my pilot log books and to spend some time with her parents. In the meantime, I loaded our meager belongings from the boat into a rented van and began my five-day cross-country journey to the West Coast.

Once in San Diego I met with a realtor and in four days found a house in Carlsbad, north of San Diego, subject to Claire's liking. She did, so we bought it. We were now the proud owners of a 30-year mortgage.

I set about making myself busy. I went surfing. I golfed once every two weeks (I could only stand that much frustration). I joined Toastmasters as a way to meet interesting people who were keen to hone their public speaking skills. I had no idea then, but the training I would learn in that Toastmasters club would come in very handy in 10 years' time when I would deliver the speech of my life.

I volunteered at the local grammar school for what was called "The Rolling Reader Program," where volunteers met with kids in the classroom who were having trouble reading. As I had flunked the first grade for being a poor reader, I thought it was a worthwhile program and a way I could personally make a difference.

I played tennis four times a week and renewed my flight instructor certification dedicating two days a week to teach students how to fly helicopters at Palomar Airport. It was my way of giving back to an industry that had been very good to me.

My motto has always been "Have fun at work!" I suppose "fun at work" could be considered an oxymoron like the classic "military intelligence," or perhaps "business ethics," or how about "jumbo shrimp," or my favorite "crash landing"? The thing is if I'm not having fun at work there's something that needs changing and if it's something within my control, I change it.

An excellent example where I definitely was *not* having fun at work was the time I had to fly with a female freelance photographer in San Diego, a beautiful young woman in her early thirties by the name of Desiree.

Whenever I think of Desiree I have to punctuate her name with the visual of her tossing her head back with a simultaneous flip of the wrist throwing her thick mane of blonde hair over her shoulder like an affected actress.

My crewchief in Vietnam used to have the perfect saying to describe any woman he saw of unimaginable beauty like Desiree. He'd tell me, "Sir, I'd eat a thousand meters of commo wire just to hear her fart through a field phone."

Desiree was always impeccably turned out. One could easily fall in love with a woman like Desiree except for one very big character flaw: she had a reputation among the young flight instructors for being a bully. If you looked up the highly derogatory "B" word in the dictionary you'd see Desiree's picture.

I got to experience the full double barrels of Desiree's abrasive personality one morning when the boss asked me if I would fly Desiree on one of her photo missions over San Diego. I reminded him that I was retired and really only wanted to fly students twice a week as my way of personally giving back but I said, "OK, just this once to help you out."

We were going to fly in a Hughes 300 with the doors off. Desiree was half-an-hour late. She swanned over to me, gliding across the apron and with a flick of her hand through that impossibly thick blonde hair, tossed it back said, "Are you ready?"

"Yep, just show me on the sectional chart where you would like to photograph."

I circled the places she wanted to take pictures and of course nearly every spot was just off the active runway of nearly every airport in San Diego County. I told her, "We're going to need a little more fuel. It'll just be a minute."

I got the heave of the shoulders, the rolling back of her blue eyes and the long, exasperated low-pressure-inducing sigh. I didn't rise to her obvious displeasure. I just quickly topped up the tanks and we got in.

I began going over the short checklist as she adjusted her seat belt cradling her Nikon on the lap of her $200 jeans. Then she said something that served to make this a day immediately un-fun.

"I want to ask you something," she said.

I continued going over the checklist. "Yep, what is it?"

"Have you *ever* flown with a professional photographer before because it appears to me that you obviously have not?"

I'd flown numerous motion picture crews and photographers in my career. I had even won two first prizes with my own photography. All I said was, "Yes, I have."

"Well you should have been prepared then. The helicopter should have been fully fueled and ready to go before I got here. Now we're late. Can you tell me why you weren't prepared?"

I didn't remind her that she had been 30 minutes late but it was her tone that set me right off, speaking to me like she would to one of the young flight instructors whom she was used to bullying. I could immediately feel my earlobes throbbing with blood as my pulse rate shot up past disco level of 120 beats per minute. I had my hand on the key, ready to start the engine, when I looked over at her and after a short pause said, "Wasn't I married to you once?"

I am sure the air traffic controller in the tower heard her neck snap at being talked to like that.

I continued, "Young lady, I'm basically retired. I do this for fun and I can tell right now that flying with you today isn't going to be fun at all. Besides, do you really want to fly for 2½ hours in an aircraft with the doors off with a pilot who you've managed to totally piss off? I have your life in my hands right here." I tapped the cyclic. "So you know what? We're not going to do this today," I said and got out.

"But, but ... you have to," She stuttered in obvious shock.

"Actually ... I don't." I turned and began walking to the hangar.

"I'm going to call your boss, you know!"

I walked back over to her, taking the boss's card out of my wallet. "His number's right there," I pointed, then turned and walked back to the hangar.

I arranged for one of the other flight instructors to fly her that day. He was thankful for the flight time. When I told him what I'd done he did a fist pump. He'd flown with her too. I was a bit of a hero around the hangar for a week or so.

The boss? He just laughed. Turns out he'd flown with Miss Desiree once or twice before and had several un-fun days of his own.

///

On outward appearances anyone looking at Claire and me and our life together would say we had it made. But no one really knows for certain what goes on inside a marriage. Claire and I were a great team and terrific partners in a brother-and-sister sort of way. We had been a great team in Oman and as sailing companions. Claire had been a very competent first mate while on the boat and a wonderful cook too.

Our problem was that we both had trouble resolving differences so we never "went there" and consequently our differences were never addressed. Rather, they festered and grew into full-blown resentment.

I will not go into specifics because it takes two to make a marriage work and the details only serve to make things sound petty and unimportant. But I knew it was over when I could no longer find greeting cards with words that would not make me sound like a hypocrite if I gave them to her. It was over, dead in the water for both of us, and time to move on.

Consequently, I was about to run a bulldozer right through all of my hard work again, something I was becoming very good at doing. I was going to sabotage all that I had worked for over the previous 10 years because, deep down inside, I wasn't happy. I was going to allow myself to throw the switch in that deep dark place in my soul and do what I had to do to make myself happy again. And that is what I did. We filed for divorce on April 12, 2001.

When Claire and I decided to divorce we were determined it would be a civil undertaking because we were eager to keep the lawyers out of it. I guess you could say we disliked lawyers more than we disliked our situation.

In California you can receive a free half-hour consultation with a lawyer to discuss your case without charge so we both found three lawyers in the phone book, met with them, then sat down and reported to the other what we had learned. All six lawyers we talked to seemed to say the same thing so we agreed on a settlement dividing everything right down the middle. We used a paralegal to file the divorce so instead of costing thousands of dollars each, with the possibility of legal wrangling and further hard feelings, it cost us less than $600.

A divorce is, of course, the worst thing that can happen to one's net worth. I went from being retired and not needing to work to now needing to find a job very quickly.

I drove to Las Vegas in search of a job flying tours in the Grand Canyon. I met with the lead pilot at Papillon Helicopters and, after speaking with him for about 20 minutes, he told me I had a job if I wanted it. I told him there might be a slight possibility a good friend of mine would offer me a job flying in the Middle East and could I keep the option open for two weeks. He was very good about it and told me, "Sure, no problem."

As if following a well-constructed script I had a feeling at 4 o'clock the next morning that I should check my email so I did and there it was, a job offer from my good friend, Frank Pole, whom I had flown with in Oman. He was now chief pilot for an outfit that supplied a HEMS Bell 214ST to the king of Saudi Arabia. He wanted to know if I wanted a job. I told him "Yes" and called the chief pilot at Papillon Helicopters that morning to thank him for his kind job offer but that I had received a job offer in Saudi Arabia and I was going to take it. He thanked me for letting him know, wishing me good luck.

Frank had received his flying training in the British Royal Air Force and had flown as a captain for Bond Helicopters in the North Sea. Six months before Claire and I left Oman, Frank had left the country to take the job as chief pilot of SETE Technical Services, a Greek company owned by the powerful Latsis Group that supplied 2, twenty-place, twin-engine Bell 214STs for EMS standby for the king of Saudi Arabia and several of the royals there.

Frank told me that the job entailed working five months a year during the summer months when the royals went cruising on their yachts. I let him know how thankful I was to receive his timely offer and accepted the job with much gratitude.

I had learned an important lesson about being retired at such a relatively young age. I found retirement to be a lot like ditching school – there's no one your age to play with. I discovered that I missed flying and being around other pilots and the camaraderie I found working with such an interesting bunch of guys. I missed the challenges and the adventure that flying a helicopter offers.

I was excited to be on my way back to the Middle East again, this time to Saudi Arabia. I had heard much about the strictness in the kingdom and I was curious to see firsthand what it was like to live and work there.

With nearly all my worldly belongings packed away in a small storage locker in San Diego, I boarded a plane in Los Angeles bound for Jeddah, Saudi Arabia. I was very eager to begin my new job as a HEMS pilot flying the Royal 214ST helicopter for the king of Saudi Arabia operating off his 500-foot private yacht.

There is no way anyone could have known that five months after taking that job, 19 men of Middle Eastern descent – 15 of them of Saudi origin – would hijack four American airliners and execute the most heinous terrorist attack in U.S. history. Their acts of terrorism would change life as everyone once knew it and plunge America into two wars fought in two separate Middle Eastern countries.

CHAPTER 10

April 2001

Life in the Kingdom

As I descended the plane's steps on the evening of April 27, 2001 then stepped onto the hot tarmac in Jeddah, I could hear the familiar calls to prayer emanating from speakers at several of the local mosques dotted around the city. It seemed very familiar to be enveloped by the humidity, the searing heat and the sights, sounds and smells of the Middle East again.

Frank Pole, the chief pilot of the organization, and good friend since 1988 when we flew together in Oman, met me at the airport and gave me an enthusiastic embrace. He then drove me to the company compound to show me where I would be living.

SETE Technical Services, formally Petrol Air, supplied two pristine Bell 214STs, both fitted with medical EMS kits, one for King Faud and one for Prince Sultan, the No. 3 man in the country and head of the Saudi military.

I hadn't flown the Bell 214ST for 3½ years, since leaving Oman, but because I had flown it for so many years prior having been an instructor and examiner in it, flying it came back to me quickly.

My main job would be on EMS standby for the royals whenever they went cruising on their yachts. If they or any of their family members became sick or injured, we were to fly them to a pre-arranged hospital.

The job was a great cocktail-party piece; that is, if someone asked me what I did for a living I'd say, "Oh yes, well, I work five months a year flying an aeromedical helicopter for the king of Saudi Arabia and his step-brother, Prince Sultan, flying off their private yachts."

The reality of the job, like most VIP standby jobs, was that it was balls-achingly boring. It entailed waiting around the office at the hangar inside the palace grounds in Jeddah, to be called to reposition the helicopter on a three-minute flight to one of the yachts a half-mile away. We would then stand by on that yacht until the king or Prince Sultan disembarked. Once they were off the boat we would fly the helicopter back to the hangar where we would wait some more.

The king preferred weekend yacht cruises so that is when we would usually be asked to fly the helicopter onto his yacht. Once the king was wheeled on board in his wheelchair, the yacht would depart the palace berth and cruise up the Red Sea to another palace 40 miles north of Jeddah. Once there, the king would be wheeled off by his family and entourage and we, the flight crew and engineer (mechanic) would stand by on the yacht for three days. We'd then do the same thing in reverse cruising back to Jeddah and returning the king to his palace.

No expense was spared for our small aviation unit to buy Jeppesen instrument approach charts that covered half the world. But we never once practiced flying to the hospital at J-Base, the military base where we were told we would have to take the king in a real medical emergency.

My orientation to the hospital at J-Base was unusual, if not just plain bizarre. I wasn't taken over there to look at it. We didn't fly to it either. My first view of the helipad where we would have to take the king if the need arose – and my orientation to it – was from the bridge of the king's yacht, the *Abdul Azziz,* looking at it from a half-mile away through binoculars as Frank Pole explained the approach procedure to me.

"You'll fly to the edge of the wall at the far end of the palace grounds where it meets the sea. We have a waypoint in the GPS called "WALL." Once you reach it you'll follow it along, making a sharp dogleg left past the construction cranes, keeping them on your right and staying well clear of that big stadium over there on your left. See it?"

"Yep."

"Oh yes, that stadium is unlit at night so keep that in mind. You'll want to keep heading straight between the cranes and the stadium until you see those rockets on sticks. See them?"

He was referring to several rockets held up on long poles in the center of a roundabout on the other side of the wall.

"Yes, I see them."

"Well, if you go to them you've gone too far. The helipad is just before you reach them. To depart you'll have to take off toward those rockets on sticks and make an immediate hard-left turn before hitting them, aiming toward the coast, keeping a close eye on the towers and construction cranes on either side of your departure path."

I lowered the binoculars and looked at him. "Frank why don't we just go to the base and have a look at it or, better yet, how about arranging with whomever we need to talk to and get permission to land there; you know, a practice run?"

"Because I've been told that if we ask to practice landing there someone may think we're plotting a coup."

I was dumbfounded. "Are you serious?"

"Yep."

"Really?"

"That's just how it is. We've *always* done it this way."

I shook my head in disbelief and, raising the binoculars to my eyes once again, scanned the obstacle course we'd have to negotiate to get in there. Because I was new to the operation I didn't want to upset the status quo. My only reply was to say, "God help us if we're called to go in there at night in bad weather, having never been in there before." I was determined not to let this be the last Frank heard from me on the subject.

Frank's answer to the way we would practice for a medevac shocked me because we did everything *but* rehearse what we would have to do if we were called out. What we *needed* to practice was an actual approach and landing on the hospital helipad at J-Base. Instead, we would practice flying instrument approaches at the airport in Jeddah several miles away.

Another practice exercise someone had dreamed up, that had no relevance to the job we were expected to do, was to fly 20 miles offshore to a GPS waypoint we called "the reef" and practice flying non-precision approaches to an MDA (minimum descent altitude) from whatever approach chart we were flying that day.

Before doing this exercise, prior to going flying, we would grab a non-precision approach chart from one of the many Jeppesen instrument books of places in the world at or near sea level that had an NDB approach.

The NDB (non-directional beacon) approach at Stavanger, Norway, is one approach I remember, for example, because we would fly that approach off the coast of Jeddah as if flying it in Norway. That, of course, would come in *real* handy when and if we were trying to find the helipad at J-Base during a medevac; something we had *never* done before.

Because of my past HEMS background, I could see that we were just "playing" at supplying a viable EMS service for the royals. I vowed to myself that I would press for the opportunity to train properly. The break I was looking for would present itself the second year I was there.

On my days off in Jeddah I was able to get a feel for the local people. What I noticed right away was that, while I found the people congenial on a one-to-one basis, as far as the total ethos of the town I felt that the people in Jeddah were living life in a joyless society.

The wealth I saw going to the royals – earned from the country's vast oil reserves (one million dollars a year spent for flowers for the king's yacht for example) – and witnessing first-hand how their unimaginable wealth was squandered but not shared with the local people, unsettled me somewhat. I felt the city of Jeddah had no spark, no heart, no energy. The city appeared dusty and dirty like the whole place needed a good power wash, scrub and a fresh coat of paint.

For example, the area along the waterfront looked like it had been very beautiful at one time. It probably was stunning when it was first completed. But there didn't seem to be a maintenance plan to keep the city looking fresh. If there was an antithesis to what I saw in Oman, Jeddah was it.

After my first tour in Jeddah ended August 31, 2001, I flew back to San Diego to house-sit for friends who were on vacation for three weeks. I planned on driving up to Canada once they returned.

I had been back in the States from Saudi for 11 days when on the morning of September 11, I received a phone call from my good friend Bruce Hair.

He said, "Turn on the TV because it looks like World War III has begun."

I was stunned, shocked and deeply saddened by what I saw. Four airliners had been hijacked. Two of them had been flown into the World Trade Center. Another had been flown into the Pentagon. The fourth aircraft had crashed in Pennsylvania, stopped from completing its objective of flying into the White House by the brave passengers on board. When I learned that 15 of the 19 hijackers were from Saudi Arabia I thought, "That's it, my job there is finished."

I have learned from my travels that no matter what country I have been to, most people on the street are like me, just striving for a comfortable life, to have a roof over their head; raise their kids, and put food on the table. People are like people everywhere on the planet. They are not all bad guys no matter what country they come from. They are simply human like you and me.

Saying all Saudis share the same beliefs as those who flew the planes into the World Trade Center Twin Towers and the Pentagon, and took over United Airlines flight 93 that crashed in Pennsylvania, is like saying all Americans are like Timothy McVie, the man who planned and executed the bombing of the Murrah Federal Building in Oklahoma City in April 1995, killing 168 and injuring more than 800 people.

When I watched the carnage on TV that those Middle Eastern men caused in America I was enraged like everyone else. I wanted to take up arms against them. I wanted to rejoin the army. I wanted to do *something.*

I had to remind myself that Osama bin Laden represented a small minority who shared his radical views and skewed interpretation of Islam. I had to remember that he had been booted out of Saudi Arabia and other Islamic countries because he verbally attacked the rulers of those countries for not following his distorted interpretations of the Quran.

I am not defending anyone here. I am simply pointing out that it is very dangerous to tar the population of a country with the same brush, thinking all who live there share the same beliefs as a few radicals who happen to come from that country.

Once I arrived back in Jeddah to begin my second tour in April 2002, one of the very first things I did was to make a trip to the American Embassy. I wanted to offer my services if they needed me. I felt I might have been in a position to help in some small way. I wanted to do *something* to help bring anyone to justice who might want to harm America and Americans again.

A woman at the embassy took my details: name, date of birth, Social Security Number. She thanked me for coming in. I never received a call back so I assumed there were enough “information gatherers” and “assets” in their cadre to get the job done so my services were never required.

To give you a feel for the Kingdom of Saudi Arabia, I will describe some of my observations and things that happened to me while living in Jeddah.

While driving to the royal palace one morning – in response to a call to fly the king’s helicopter onto his ship because he wanted to go for a cruise – I noticed a policeman approaching me from behind at high speed. He didn't have his overhead lights on but when he came to within six inches of my back bumper I figured he probably wanted me to pull over, so I did.

I got out of my car and walked back to his police car. He didn't speak English. My Arabic is in the form of greetings and goodbyes only. He extended his hand, palm up, as if asking for my license. I went to my car to get my palace pass. It said in Arabic that I was the king's helicopter pilot. I handed it to him. He looked up at me with a look of surprise on his face after reading it and said, "King?"

I nodded and said, "Yes. King."

He studied me momentarily. Then he looked back at my palace pass. He looked back up at me and again said, "King?"

"Yes, King," I replied.

He looked back down at the palace pass and shifted his weight from left to right. He looked up at me again now with a puzzled look on his face, "King?"

"Yes, King," I answered.

More seconds passed. He rubbed his jaw, then he said, "King? King?"

"Yes, King .... King."

Now more of a statement than a question this time, "King! King!"

I answered in the same tone, "Yes, King!"

He pointed to his name tag and made a sign like he wanted to write something down. I went to my car again and retrieved a piece of paper from the glove compartment, brought it back, and handed it to him.

"Pen, pen," he said, holding out his hand.

I handed him my pen.

He placed the piece of paper on the hood of his police car, wrote something in Arabic and then handed it back to me. He gestured that I was supposed to give the paper to the king and he said, "King. King."

I took the note, folded it up and placed it in the top pocket of my shirt. I nodded in the affirmative, "OK, King. King."

We shook hands. He got back into his police car and I got into mine. He did a U-turn. I drove on to the palace.

Mohammed, our Pakistani cleaner was sweeping the hangar floor when I walked in. I told him what had happened and handed him the note asking him to translate it for me.

He took the piece of paper, read it and began to laugh. Then he told me, "The policeman wrote here that you were speeding and that he didn't take you to jail because he knew you were going to fly for the king."

Mohammad began to laugh again.

"What's so funny?" I asked.

"It says, because he didn't take you to jail he wants the king to give him a house."

///

One of the few joys I experienced in Jeddah when I had a day off was to go scuba diving in the Red Sea. The reef there is pristine with lots of sea life in the warm, clear water. In fact, it was some of the best scuba diving I have ever experienced. I had been in Jeddah for only one week when I witnessed an incident at the Al Nakeel Beach Club that was one of the most bizarre things I have ever seen.

I was sitting at a palm-thatched table sipping a soft drink and enjoying the lazy beach atmosphere. There were children splashing in the water, women sunbathing, men swimming or playing paddleball near the water, people eating food they'd purchased at the beach club restaurant. Activities you'd see on any Western beach.

Suddenly I heard the loud wail of a siren. The whole mood of the place instantly changed from calm to near panic. Most everyone began to run. The ladies ran from their loungers on the beach or by the pool into the cover of the ladies' changing room. Other ladies quickly threw on their black abayas to cover their bodies completely. The beach club staff, mostly East Indian, ran around handing out black abayas to the women who did not have them, urging the women to quickly cover up. It went from being a fun day at the beach to an atmosphere of ominous foreboding.

About two minutes after the siren sounded I saw three Saudi gentlemen in white robes and long head dresses each with near identical long beards, walking from the front entrance along the boardwalk. They walked slowly, one of the men fingering his worry beads.

They surveyed the beach club as they continued walking to the end of the pier and then back again. They left the premises about 7 to 10 minutes later. That's when the siren began to wail again. People slowly emerged out of hiding, went back to where they had been sitting, and continued doing what they'd been doing before the interruption. Abayas were flung off.

As quickly as the mood had changed when the religious police – the *Mutawwa*, – had arrived it returned back to "normal."

I never saw road rage while driving in Jeddah. I saw no malice. What I did see was bad driving in its purest form. Driving practices that would be a flagrant violation in the United States or any other Western country are perfectly legal in Jeddah. Driving in Jeddah is like watching a driver's education film on how *not* to drive, viewing situations you would never encounter in the States.

A typical driver's education film scenario in the States would be something like this: You are driving along a quiet neighborhood street. A ball suddenly bounces into the street in front of you from your right between two parked cars. You are asked, "What will happen next?" Pretty straightforward stuff. The way to avoid an accident in Jeddah is to expect the totally unexpected.

I will use the pronoun he or him in this description of the Saudi driving rules because in Saudi Arabia women are forbidden to drive. I have lived and driven in two counties where women were either forbidden to drive or – like in Iran in the '70s when I was there – where you *rarely* saw a female driver. I have therefore come to the conclusion, through observation only, that women must be better drivers than men. That's because the two places where I have witnessed the most appalling driving were places where women did not drive. So it stands to reason that if women were to take the wheel the driving would be more sane. That should answer that age-old question once and for all.

The Saudis have an odd way of determining who is at fault if there's an accident. If the accident involves *you* (a Westerner) and a Saudi, you will automatically be at fault. Their thinking? Well, the accident would not have occurred if you were not in their country. Using that logic it *had* to be your fault.

A word about the dotted lines on the road: In Saudi Arabia, dotted lines on the road – while spaced apart and appearing to define individual lanes – are purely advisory. They are primarily used for a driver to position his car to straddle over it.

The way this is done is to line up your hood ornament with the dotted lines like the sight of a gun, so if you could imagine the line as a buzz saw it would cut your car in half. In Jeddah it's perfectly OK to straddle the line as you drive down the highway. You will never be cited by a policeman. In fact, in many instances, you'll see a policeman driving this way.

A word of caution about passing a car that is straddling a dotted line. Because the car you are passing is effectively using both lanes you really never know which lane the driver will drift into if the mood takes him. So it's better to pass the car using one whole empty lane as a buffer between your car and his.

Another driving rule involved the traffic lights, which are positioned so high that the driver of any car stopped at the waiting line cannot see them. Whether this is by fault or design is neither here nor there. It is simply a fact of life. I suspect it is just a flaw the engineers who designed the traffic lights didn't consider.

So, if you see that the light has changed to green, you must immediately honk your horn at least one-half of one nanosecond after it turns green, to let the cars in front know it's time to go.

A rule about the horn: give it a practice beep before leaving your house or compound before the first drive of the day. Consider this a preflight safety check. If it doesn't work, consider your car unserviceable. You won't be able to communicate in roadway parlance if your car horn doesn't work and that can be dangerous.

Another thing to consider is the left-hand turn rule. The left-hand turn rule must state that it is OK to make a left hand turn from the far right-hand lane of a four-lane highway which, by doing so, will cut off six cars waiting for the light to change. I say six cars in a four-lane road because that will be how many cars there will be waiting abreast for the light to change.

Making a left-hand turn from the far-right lane is legal whether travelling along the road at 60 miles per hour or turning from a dead stop, for example, from a red light when the light turns to green and you have just been honked at. It is of no consequence that you are cutting off three other lanes of cars. This is something you can expect to see regularly.

A caveat to the rule: If you are exercising this rule you *must* look at the other drivers you are cutting off as if you are totally in the right and preferably offer them a little self-righteous look of indignation as if all six drivers you've just cut off are in the wrong.

A particularly tricky variation to the left-hand turn rule, which if performed well will give you great satisfaction, is to begin your turn from the left-hand turn lane. Where you would normally do a U-turn or a left-hand turn at the intersection from this lane you simply do a right-hand turn in front of the six cars jammed into the four lanes that are waiting at the light, remembering of course to incorporate the look of self-righteous indignation.

A natural follow-on to the left-hand turn rule is that you can also perform this maneuver from the far left-hand lane, which will then become the right-hand turn rule. The only stipulation is that if you are carrying a passenger it must be the passenger who offers the look of self-righteous indignation to the other drivers you are cutting off, as they may not be able to see the expression on *your* face from where they are sitting, especially as you will most likely be wearing a head dress that cuts your peripheral vision like blinkers to about a 30-degree forward field of vision.

Unlike the West where we have cut-and-dried rules for giving right-of-way there are degrees of right-of-way in Jeddah. For example, if you are driving a top-of-the-line Mercedes you have right-of-way over everyone but the king, Prince Abdulla or the No. 2 man, Prince Sultan. In short, the more expensive your vehicle relative to the car you are exercising your right-of-way over, then the more right-of-way you have over them.

This last rule does not take into consideration the Gross Tonnage Rule, however. If your vehicle is considerably larger or heavier than a vehicle of the same worth you are exercising your right-of-way over, then you have the right-of-way under this rule. That is because if he *doesn't* give you the right-of-way, you are going to squash the shit out of him with your heavier vehicle if he doesn't let you pass.

Another thing you might want to try is to drive as fast as you can, weaving through traffic, passing everyone you can overtake so that you make it to the next red light before anyone else. I've decided that it must give an almost euphoric sense of accomplishment to do this otherwise no one would do it.

I had never had anyone pay particular attention to my smile, that is, until I pulled up to the Royal Guard shed one day at the entrance to the king's palace.

I slowed the company car and stopped alongside the guard shed and handed my palace pass out the car window to the guard. This particular guard had a kind face and a pleasant smile. He gave a cursory glance at the piece of paper I handed him, then looked back at me, studying my face for a very long moment. He smiled. I smiled back. I noticed him studying my teeth. It was so obvious that I suddenly felt self-conscious and instinctively glanced in the rearview mirror thinking I had something stuck between my teeth. There wasn't. I looked back at the still-smiling Royal Guard soldier. He pointed at my teeth. "*Quais*," he said. "*Quais, Quais*!" Meaning "good, good, good."

I then noticed a very large gap between his two front teeth. I pointed at my mouth: "America," I said, indicating I had my teeth worked on in America.

"*Amreekee*?" he said (Arabic for America).

"Yes, America." I said, nodding.

He leaned forward, nearly putting his head through my open car window and studied my smile. Because of what my dental insurance company and I had paid to have my teeth done, I was more than willing to have someone admire Dr. Addleson's handiwork. I opened my mouth real wide for the guard's inspection and turned my head from side to side. I even tilted my head back, too, looking straight up at the headliner of my car. I wanted to give him a real good look.

The guard cocked his head back and forth giving my mouth an inspection with the same scrutiny I had only seen my dental hygienist give me. He finished, stood up, handed me back my palace pass and said "Quais. Quais!" He pointed at his teeth. "Amreekee?"

"Yes, America," I said, thinking "America, the land of the perfect smile."

"Quais," he said, giving me the thumbs up as he waived me through the palace gate.

The Arab toilet hasn't enjoyed much evolutionary change since man began doing his business in the wilds. I imagine that before toilets were invented, we used to squat behind a tree or a rock somewhere away from prying eyes. We in the West had Mr. Crapper to thank for developing the toilet we enjoy today. The Arabs, on the other hand, simply improved the hole in the ground that they have used for centuries by making it porcelain and putting some non-slip grooves on either side to give your feet traction as you squat down. That's so your feet don't slip out from under you and send your bottom plopping down into the hole.

Only in desperation have I had to use one of these Arab toilets. Every time I had to use one, it occurred when out shopping or out and about in the city where I couldn't find a tree or rock to hide behind to do my business.

If you're a man and you have to pee using one of these Arab toilets there's no real problem. Just take a big breath (to guard against a most certain brutal assault on your olfactory system) and hold it for as long as possible as you go in, do your business and leave. Oh yes, remember to exhale. If you have to do a bowel movement that's where real problems arise.

Having lived in several countries where these toilets are the norm and not the exception, I have concluded that the anatomies of the people who live in those countries are different from ours in the West. Their center of gravity must be further forward than ours. I think it has to be a genetic thing passed down through the millennia. As Darwin would probably describe, those who did not adapt would have just fallen backwards into the hole and disappeared, supporting his theory of natural selection. Only those with the forward-center-of-gravity gene survived.

It is all I can do to squat over one of the holes without my center of gravity shifting way too far aft, causing me to fall backward and plop my ass into the abyss. Luckily, this hasn't happened yet but I've had some very close calls. Before I commit myself to a full squat I always look for something to hang on to so that I can keep myself from falling in. A good idea would be to have a rope lanyard attached to the closed door in front of you that you could hang on to while you rocked back and aimed your butt over your intended target. Sort of like abseiling but with a difference.

There is another problem I've found with this kind of toilet. The predicament presents itself once you drop your trousers. Where do you put them? I have never found a toilet stall with hooks anywhere or found any ledges to hang my pants on.

To fully understand the problem I have to explain that there is no toilet paper in these toilets. There is always a hose or a container with water. Sometimes there's a hand-held sprayer similar to what you might find in your kitchen sink. It's located on the wall next to the hole in the ground. If you have not had the forethought to bring your own emergency supply of toilet paper you have two options to clean yourself: you can either blast your rear end with a stream of water from the hose and hope it cleans you well enough, or you do as the Arabs do and wipe yourself with your left hand and clean up after yourself with the help of water from the hose. If you didn't know it before, now you know why an Arab never eats with his left hand.

So, as you can imagine, when you enter the stall it looks like there's been the mother of all water fights going on, with water sprayed all over the floor and walls.

If you just imagine for a moment you can see how if you drop your pants and let them collect around your ankles, like you would in the West, they will fall on the floor and in this case you will end up with very soggy pants from the residual water on the floor.

My technique is this: With one hand I keep my pants off the floor and with the other hand I hang on to something with a death grip to keep from plonking my butt down into the hole. As I am trying to keep my pants off the wet floor I will probably not be able to get my pants out of the way from under my butt quickly enough to avoid shitting into them. If I am really lucky and I miss shitting into my pants I will probably not miss shitting into my underwear. If I do manage to shit into my pants or into my underwear it totally negates the whole exercise anyway so, knowing my chances of shitting into my pants anyway, I have seriously considered the option of just foregoing the whole experience and just shitting my pants while I am shopping and be done with it. That way I could avoid going through the hassle of using one of these dreadful toilets in the first place.

I would like to offer one word of warning about the water hose in one of these toilets. When you have finished doing your business, before taking aim with the water hose at a very sensitive part of your anatomy, give it a trial squirt first. Just a short burst will do. Squirt it down the hole and make sure it's aimed away from any sensitive parts of your body. This will allow you to determine the force of the spray.

I didn't do this once and quickly learned a very valuable lesson. I did my business, took the hose and sprayer, slipped it under my leg as I was crouching (trying not to fall in), took very close aim and pulled the trigger on the spray head while trying to keep my pants up off the wet floor with my other hand. The force of the stream that impacted my sphincter could be likened to falling off water skies naked, ass-first, at 60 miles an hour with both legs over my head! When I pressed the trigger on the hose the shock of the stream of water that hit me nearly caused me to jump five feet into the air and I am certain water spurted out my mouth, nose and both ears!

To say that the waterfront in the evenings in Jeddah in July is a very busy place is as understated as saying Los Angeles International airport is a "little" busy the week before Christmas.

The waterfront at night is buzzing with human activity. The evening is a time for Saudi families to flee the confines of their houses where many of them have been cooped up all day escaping the heat. It's a time when they can get outside and take advantage of the cooler temperatures now that the searing heat of the day has abated to a balmy 85 degrees and *only* 85-percent humidity. So they flock to the waterfront in hoards.

They assault the narrow corniche and set up carpets on the concrete where they sit themselves down and have a picnic. They eat boiled rice, samosas, corn on the cob, or whatever, and play very loud Arabic music that blares from boom boxes or open car doors from cars parked along the street only feet away from where they're sitting.

The groups are typically one man dressed in a white robe and head dress and about six women who are dressed from head to toe in black abayas. They're all sitting on their carpets set on the sidewalk with kids running amok like little rabbits. If a picture could be a definition of a word this scene is the definition of chaos!

When I left the nearby company camp where I was staying to take my walk, which was nearly every night around 8:30, I often felt I was negotiating an obstacle course because I had to continually dodge carpets, stretched out legs, cool boxes and moving objects such as small children. I would snake my way past old men, old women and hookah pipes, while dodging kids who were running here and there giggling or laughing, and often being chased by a brother or sister, while screaming at the top of their lungs. Add to that humanity the camels with bells clanging from bulging knees as they ambled along, led by their owners who touted camel rides to anyone interested.

I must not forget the Shetland ponies being led by their Indian or Pakistani owners, usually giving rides to children on the sidewalk along with everyone else vying for the cramped space. We're talking about a walkway maybe 15 feet wide from street to the water. Not much room to avoid the animal droppings lying in wait on the concrete like silent landmines, awaiting an unsuspecting sneaker or sandal to tread on them and unleash an explosion of foul odor.

Then there are the potholes. Every 200 yards or so, you can count on negotiating a pothole large enough to swallow a small camel. There were smaller ones too, but the larger ones were the size of bomb craters. The Saudis were good at building sidewalks; they just didn't do as well keeping them in repair.

Now throw in the fireworks going off everywhere. Because of the small area, it was like celebrating our 4th of July in a Bedouin tent. The vendors who sell the pyrotechnics are teenage or younger Saudi girls who are dressed from head to toe in their black abayas, spending their evening walking up and down the corniche from carpet to carpet, family to family, selling sparklers or Roman candles to anyone who has the Saudi rials to buy them.

I winced every time I saw very young children, and I have seen kids barely able to stand, holding the fireworks clutched in their small hands unsupervised by their parents who, at the time, were seemingly oblivious of the potential for blowing off an appendage or shooting out an eye or nailing a passerby like me! I had not seen such a grand pyrotechnic display since I was stationed at LZ Sally during New Year's Eve 1969 in Vietnam! At least in Vietnam I was armed and could defend myself.

Anyway, one particular night I was trying to keep up a good pace on my nightly walk, weaving my way among feet, kids, ponies, camels, blankets, carpets, grandmas, grandpas, hookahs, cool boxes, camel dung, donkey crap and horse shit when suddenly out of the corner of my eye I saw something on the ground that looked like a sparkler. When I got abeam the sparkling fuse, I noticed it was a Roman candle. At that moment it suddenly let out a pop and ignited in a bright flash. It shot off right at me. I ducked, threw my arms over my head and by instinct yelled, "Sheeeeeet!" I saw it rocket near my calves like a Patriot missile just missing my legs and rocketing out to sea in a blinding shower of sparks like Halley's Comet. It exploded in a bright orange flash in a rainbow of colors over the water. From under my arm covering my head, I looked over at where it had been launched and there sat a Saudi man with his little boy holding a smoldering Roman candle stick. The man smiled sheepishly and said, "Sorry."

I quickened my pace, shook my head, and wove my way along the blankets, feet, old men, old women, wives, hookahs, camel dung, horse dung, donkey dung, pot holes, husbands, and gaggles of kids. I get weak whenever I think about what kind of damage that thing could have done to my body. Give me Vietnam any day!

%

As I'd mentioned earlier, because of my background as a HEMS pilot in the States, I seriously believe that if you're going to do it, do it right. It's no good having the *appearance* of an efficient HEMS service if you cannot provide an *effective* one. The day might come when it will be revealed that you are not prepared, a bad system falls apart and tragedy ensues. The people who are paying for the service could die because of your incompetence. What we were doing to train for the job in Saudi could be likened to lifeguards on duty at a public swimming pool not being trained in basic rescue techniques or CPR.

I had vowed in my first tour in Saudi that I would try to address the fact that the training we were doing had no bearing to the job we might be called upon to perform. I saw my chance to effect change on my second tour.

Shortly after I arrived in Jeddah to begin my second tour, Frank Pole left the country for the U.K. to pick up our second helicopter, which had gone through extensive maintenance to ready it for the upcoming cruising season. Once he left the country, with the help of Don Williams – Frank's No. 2 man in charge – I saw my chance. I asked Don if he would be willing to call the hospital at J-Base and ask the general in charge for permission to land at the helipad. Don had always thought it would be a good idea, so he immediately picked up the phone and called the general. The general said he was pleased Don had called and invited him to the hospital the following day to discuss our plan.

Don returned after the meeting the next day and said it had gone very well. He said the hospital staff were in awe of him because he flew HEMS for the king and was based inside the palace grounds.

As it transpired, the general was very receptive to our request and could not have been more accommodating. He said he was looking forward to us flying in and landing on the hospital helipad. He said we could do it any time we wanted! So much for plotting a coup.

The general said he wanted to have a mock drill as soon as we could arrange it, so that his staff would know what to do if the day came when we would have to fly the king to his hospital.

Four days after Don had first called the general, he and I took off from the palace to the helipad at J-Base for the first time ever. The pad was clear of all cars and obstacles and a low chain-link fence had been constructed around it. We were able to see the best approach routing into and out of the helipad and determine nearby obstacles.

Yet the most important benefit of the exercise came when the general let us in on a shocking piece of information. "You know, J-Base is the back-up hospital for the king if you cannot land him at the primary hospital."

We were stunned at his news. All along Frank Pole, Don and I had been led to believe we would take the king to J-Base.

We asked the general, "Where are we supposed to take the king then?"

"King Faud Hospital, of course."

We thanked him for this important piece of information. Don called the King Faud Hospital to arrange for us to practice landing on their helipad day and night. The hospital administrator immediately gave us approval, asking why we hadn't asked to land there in the past. We had no answer for him. What were we going to say, that we were afraid if we did he would think we were plotting a coup?

The day we landed the king's helicopter at the King Faud Hospital helipad it was an exciting time for everyone involved. There was a wonderful happy, almost carnival-like atmosphere, full of excitement. The paramedics were on standby there – nurses, doctors, ambulance crews – everyone I imagine who was able to leave their posts in the hospital came out to watch this special event.

We landed and shut down the engines. When we exited the helicopter we were greeted by the hospital administrator who welcomed us with a huge smile, open arms, a hearty handshake and even a hug. Everyone was patting everyone else on the back, handing out business cards, and inspecting the helicopter's interior. If there had been clowns, cotton candy and helium balloons it would have completed the carnival-like atmosphere we experienced that day.

We practiced landing there at night, too. So now all the pilots: Don Williams, Johnny Grantham, Stuart Gatherer and myself – everyone except Frank, who was ferrying the second helicopter back from England – was current in landing day and night at J-Base and the King Faud Hospital. *Now* we could say we were prepared to supply the royals with the EMS coverage we were being paid to supply them. The four of us felt much better knowing we had landed at the two places we might be called upon to land in an emergency.

When Frank arrived back from the U.K. and learned what we'd done, he was seriously miffed that we had gone behind his back to talk to the general and arrange our landings and takeoffs at J-Base. He was both shocked and glad to learn what the general had told us: that J-Base wasn't the primary hospital where we would take the king if the need arose; rather, that we were to take him to the King Faud Hospital instead.

Even though Frank was angry with us for going behind his back to obtain permission to land on the hospital helipads, it didn't stop him from doing it himself a week later. Now all five pilots were current to do what we were paid to do.

When I returned home after that year's cruising season I received an email from Frank thanking me for pushing for permission to practice landings and takeoffs from J-Base and the King Faud Hospital. He told me that his company had arranged an independent audit of the aviation section to determine if he was doing a good job. Frank told me that one of the first questions the auditors asked him was, "When was the last time you did day and night landings at the helipads where you might need to land? He was able to report that he'd done it within the past two weeks.

The following is a list of HEMS fatal accidents that occurred in the 3 ½ years I had retired after leaving Oman up until the time I took the job in Saudi Arabia.

(Source Air Medical Memorial Website
www.airmedicalmemorial.com)

1998		
Intensive Air	Spencer, IA	August 20, 1998
Valley AirCare	La Gloria, TX	June 5, 1998
Los Angeles City Fire	Los Angeles, CA	March 23, 1998
AirMed	Sandy, UT	January 11, 1998
1999		
Hermann Life Flight	Fresno, TX	July 17, 1999
UK Air Medical Service	Jackson, KY	June 14, 1999
Flight For Life	Indian Springs, NV	April 3, 1999
2000		
Duke Life Flight	Burlington, NC	October 16, 2000
Life Flight III	Sumner, GA	July 24, 2000
Bayflite 3	St. Petersburg , FL	April 25, 2000
LifeStar	Dalhart, TX	March 10, 2000
2001		
CareFlight	Grand Junction, CO	February 28, 2001

CHAPTER 11
Canada

After completing two months of my first tour flying in Saudi Arabia, I flew back to San Diego to attend my son's wedding. I had planned that after the wedding I would fly to Canada for a few days to visit Kaye, whom I had not seen since she left her job at the Royal Hospital in Oman 12 years before. She had left England and was working in Victoria on Vancouver Island.

I was also interested to check out Victoria as a place to possibly stay when not working in Saudi for five months a year. I needed to be out of the U.S. for at least 330 days a year for tax purposes.

Kaye had written me a letter five years earlier, when I was married to Claire and still living in Oman, to tell me that she was considering marrying a man she'd known for 30 years. He was also British; a man she had always carried a torch for. In the letter, she talked about having doubts about marrying him. Apart from the fact he was 20 years her senior, he also had two pre-teen boys from a previous marriage that she would have to look after.

In the letter she expressed great doubts that marrying him could work out so I pointed out that, with all of her doubts and uncertainties, I wouldn't go through with it if I were her.

He was the Anglican chaplain at an internationally recognized boarding school in Victoria. Despite all her reservations, Kaye married him and moved to Canada to be with him. Two years later she joined the school's nursing team.

Kaye and I had kept in touch over the years mainly through Christmas letters as we'd promised we'd do. She had suggested that Claire and I come up for a visit sometime. I told Kaye in an email that I was now divorced but that I would be coming up in June after attending my son's wedding in San Diego. I wrote that I wanted to check out Victoria as a possible place to stay when I wasn't working in Saudi Arabia.

At Wade's wedding reception I saw Shari — my first wife and Wade's mom. She knew Claire and I had recently divorced. Shari was seeing someone at the time but said to me, "If you need a place to stay while you get yourself sorted out you can stay at my place."

I appreciated her kindness, thanked her, and told her I needed to live somewhere out of the country for tax purposes as a way to try to rebuild what I had lost in the divorce with Claire. Shari's thoughtfulness touched me deeply.

After Wade's wedding in San Diego, I flew up to Vancouver, rented a car, then caught the ferry over to Vancouver Island. On the flight from San Diego and on my journey over on the ferry, I kept wondering how I would feel when I saw Kaye again after not seeing her for 12 years. She had always been a good friend, my scuba diving buddy in Oman and someone who I felt always had my best interests at heart. I viewed Kaye like a small shining light in the universe "out there somewhere" who I knew cared for me and would always be a friend.

When we dated in Oman, the timing just wasn't right for us to get together. I was still commitment-phobic back then. I wasn't much better now after experiencing yet another failed marriage. Still, it would be good to see her again and to meet her husband.

Kaye arranged a room for me at Dashwood Manor, a restored Tudor-style house built in the 1890s that had been turned into a bed and breakfast. It is situated on a cliff on the extreme south end of the island overlooking the Juan de Fuca Strait. Kaye had told me that she wanted me to come to dinner on the day I arrived so that I could meet her husband. She also wanted me to meet someone else, a woman by the name of Susan, an unmarried doctor friend of hers. Kaye was playing matchmaker.

As I waited at Dashwood Manor for Kaye to pick me up, I was bristling with anticipation, eager to see her again after so many years. I remember the moment she walked through the front door wearing green silk pants and short-sleeve pale-green silk top. Her hair was cut very short. She'd had it colored almost white-blonde – looking a lot like the singer Annie Lennox. Her skin was pale white – flawless.

We both stood for a long moment in the front doorway of the Dashwood Manor appraising one another, big smiles growing on our faces. Then she threw her arms out toward me, "Oh, Darling, it's so wonderful to see you again," and we embraced.

She looked great. She told me about her doctor friend, Susan, who was her age, 45, and how she was anxious for me to meet her at dinner that night.

Kaye drove us over to her house where I was introduced to her husband. I found him to be a very likeable and chatty guy. There was another couple there visiting from England; plus there was Susan.

Susan was an attractive woman with short hair. She was intelligent and, as I found out through the evening, a good conversationalist. The problem was I couldn't give her my full attention because I was distracted most of the evening. I tried not to be too obvious, but whenever I could, I would glance at Kaye when she wasn't looking in my direction.

There was one point in the evening after dinner when the conversation came around to Kaye's doll-making. When I expressed an interest, Kaye asked, "Would you like to see my studio where I make them?"

"Of course, I'd love to."

Her husband is an excellent story teller and he was busy entertaining Susan and the other guests, so it wasn't rude to leave the table to go down to the studio in the basement to look at Kaye's dolls.

We descended the wooden stairs and she took me over to her small workbench to show me her dolls that were in various stages of completion. As Kaye spoke, I remembered how much

I liked hearing her voice. I had forgotten how much I liked the sound of it, the cadence of her proper English accent. She didn't speak quickly but in a measured, thoughtful way that I found pleasant and soothing to the ear.

I am quite a bit taller than Kaye. She is five-foot two. I am six one. I felt a physical warmth between us as if I were being drawn to her. I wondered if she felt it too. Standing next to her, so close in the confines of the small work area, listening to her explain her doll-making, I couldn't stop myself from gazing down at her ample breasts, wondering what it would be like to make love to her again. It was all I could do to restrain myself from reaching out and gently taking her into my arms and kissing her. But of course I couldn't do that. It was just a wild fantasy. Instead, I listened politely, showing interest.

After several minutes, we walked back upstairs to join the rest of the group in the kitchen. I felt a slight buzz inside me after that, like a slow release of sexual tension. I was glad we went up to the kitchen to join the others when we did.

Kaye seemed very keen for me to hit it off with Susan. She arranged for Susan to drive me back to the Dashwood Manor that night. Before we left, Kaye asked me if I would like to see the sights of Victoria the next day. She said she would act as tour guide so that I could get a feel for the city to see if I might want to stay there during my off time from my job in Saudi Arabia.

"Yes, I'd like that," I said.

"Good, I'll come by Dashwood Manor at ten tomorrow morning to pick you up."

On the drive back to Dashwood Manner, Susan and I made small talk. At Kaye's insistence, I asked Susan if she would like to join me for dinner the next night. She accepted.

When I got back to my room I mulled over the events of the evening. I had forgotten how exciting it was to yearn for another human being. It had been a long time for me. Even though I had only been divorced a matter of months the passion in our marriage had waned many years ago.

It was at that moment that I began to understand what must have occurred between my wife and the guy she fell in love with at the American Embassy when they met in Oman. My attraction to Kaye was something I felt I had no control over. But of course I couldn't give in to the impulse. I was on dangerous ground and I knew it. I needed to watch my step. Besides, Kaye had given no indication that she felt the same attraction for me other than being the good friend that she was. From what I saw that evening she appeared to be happily married. There was no reason to complicate things. Besides, Kaye seemed very eager for me to hit it off with Susan.

When Kaye pulled up outside Dashwood Manor the next morning I was standing in the park across the street talking to a couple I'd met there while returning from an early-morning walk. Kaye approached wearing a green linen dress. Again, she looked stunning.

"Ready?" she asked.

"I just have to change my shoes. Then I'll be ready to go."

She followed me up to my room. As we ascended the stairs I could detect the faint aroma of her perfume. I could feel the little buzz within my body beginning again. I wanted to quickly change my shoes and get on with the tour of the city.

We entered the room and I sat on a chair to change my shoes. Kaye walked over to the window. "What a fabulous view you have from here."

It was, too. The view from the window offered a dramatic panorama of the Juan de Fuca Strait with the 8,000-foot-high, snow-capped Olympic Mountains in Washington State dominating the sky in the distance.

I quickly slipped on my deck shoes, got up from the chair and walked over to join Kaye at the window. We both stood there looking out at the view for a long moment. Then she turned around to look up at me. "Darling, it really is so marvelous to see you again. Thank you so much for coming."

"No, thank you for suggesting I come up for a visit. Your husband seems like a nice guy. It appears everything is working out well for you. I'm pleased."

She looked away toward the window, hesitated then said, "No, not really."

Her admission puzzled me. "But last night … you seemed so content. So happy."

She turned again to look back up at me, "Appearances can be deceiving."

I had to check myself. We were standing very close now. I was aware of nothing else in the room but Kaye at that moment. I had an almost imperceptible feeling of being drawn toward her. I thought I detected the same in her.

There was a slight pause, a moment between us where I could have easily changed the subject, turned and made for the door. But I didn't. Instead, I stood there looking down into that pretty face. It was at that point that I gave in to my natural impulses and leaned down very slowly, giving her time to protest, to halt my impetuous action. Then I leaned down further to make the distance and I kissed her. She reacted by embracing me, softly at first.

Very quickly the repressed passion in both of us was unleashed, taking on a life of its own. We moved over to the large bed and, unwilling to let the other one go, lay down on the bed together as one.

Kaye and I stayed in the room that morning for three hours making tender and passionate love to one another. We were like two starving people released from a desert devoid of love and tenderness, both of us seemingly insatiable, gorging ourselves on a wonderful feast that lay before us after years of deprivation.

After we finished making love we lay on the bed, her head resting on my shoulder and we talked. I told her how I had felt when I first saw her the day before. How I could not stop gazing in her direction over dinner, stealing furtive glances when she wasn't looking. The attraction to her had been immediate from the first time I laid eyes on her standing at the front door of the hotel when she came to pick me up. I expressed my concern that being attracted to her made me very nervous as I didn't want to complicate her life or mine.

"Oh, Darling, I know exactly what you mean. Before you arrived I kept thinking 'I hope I don't find him attractive.' I *really* didn't want to be attracted to you, not at all. I didn't want to be drawn to you. I, too, wondered how I would feel when I saw you again. It sounds like we both felt the same way before seeing one another, doesn't it?"

"Yes. But neither of us needs this complication. I had to fight the urge to kiss you when you took me down to your basement studio last night, but I fought the urge."

She let out a small laugh. "Yes, I felt it too. All last evening, when you were sitting at the dinner table talking, I kept studying your hands and your impossibly long fingers, remembering how you used to caress me with them. I became sad looking at them thinking I would never know your caress again."

I asked her about her marriage. I told her I didn't want to come up to Victoria and complicate matters. If that was going to be the case, I would find somewhere else to live outside the States so that I wouldn't risk wrecking her marriage.

Kaye said that when she returned to England, after leaving Oman, life became very hard. She said she used to buy ball gowns and fancy dresses that would just hang in her closet because there was nowhere to wear them. She thought she would live the same fairy-tale life she'd experienced in Oman, but it wasn't to be. Her reality became working three jobs, driving from the house she had purchased in Folkestone, (near Dover), to London: four hours round-trip, and still not having enough money to live on. She told me she was slowly going bankrupt.

She said the marriage proposal was like being thrown a lifeline. She felt trapped in England, swamped in a sea of debt, going down for the third time. Accepting his proposal, even though she had many doubts, seemed like the only way out for her.

On the morning of her wedding, while sitting in the backseat of a taxi on the way to the hairdresser, she told the taxi driver she was getting married. The unhappiness must have been telling because the taxi driver looked at her in his rear-view mirror and said, "You know, Luv, you don't have to go through with this."

She said, "The other day I looked at myself in the mirror and I didn't recognize the woman looking back at me. It made me terribly sad. I wondered, 'Where did the woman that I once knew go?' What I saw staring back at me was a desperately unhappy, middle-age woman who was a step-mother to two kids she didn't want. I saw a woman longing to be the free-spirited woman she was in Oman. It saddened me to realize that woman had vanished and I may never see her again."

Kaye told me that she was terribly unhappy in the marriage as stepmother to her husband's two pre-teen boys. She felt like he had married her to be his maid. She said that her husband's toxic ex-wife would call the house demanding he take the boys for the weekend or use emotional blackmail on him, saying that if he didn't do this or do that she would pack up the kids and take them back to England to live and he'd never see them again.

Kaye found herself trapped in the middle. Christmas had been so awful the year before that she decided she wasn't going to have another one like it again. She was going to go up-island somewhere to be alone and have Christmas dinner in a fast-food restaurant and stay in a hotel, rather than suffer through another Christmas like the one she'd just had. She and her husband got along well when the kids weren't around. But as soon as they were on the scene, and his ex-wife began to call, the situation became untenable.

She told me that when she arrived in Victoria her first job was cleaning people's houses. She jokingly called it her "Canadian immigrant experience," something she felt she had to do to pay her dues as a new resident to Canada. It was back-breaking work. She then studied to obtain her Canadian nursing license. Once she got it she was asked to be a nurse at the boarding school where her husband worked.

Kaye and I brought one another up to date on what we'd been doing since we last spent time together. After about an hour of talking there was a short lull in our conversation, each of us just enjoying being in the warm company of the other. I rolled her on her back, looked deeply into her eyes for a moment, then leaned down and kissed her again. She responded quickly and we made love for the second time that day.

We finally managed to leave my room so that Kaye could show me around Victoria hoping I would find it attractive and a place I would like to stay when not flying in Saudi Arabia.

Over coffee she asked me what I thought of Susan. I told her I thought she was a very pleasant woman but not for me. Kaye thought it would be a good idea for me to keep my dinner engagement with her that night, which I did.

Susan and I had an enjoyable meal at a restaurant at the Oak Bay Marina. Our conversation was mostly small talk. I had trouble keeping my mind on the conversation because my thoughts kept drifting off to Kaye and what had occurred that morning. Having dinner that evening with Susan was the last time we saw one another. Kaye and I met one more time in my hotel room before I had to leave Victoria to fly back to Jeddah.

I finished the remaining two months of my first tour in Saudi Arabia. It was my intention to rent a small place in Victoria where I would stay when not working in Jeddah. I was adamant nothing should change for Kaye. I didn't want to destroy her marriage. We had talked about it and decided that Kaye would work at the school, stay with her husband, and we would live for any stolen moments we could have together.

I noticed something alarming in this arrangement. I had turned into "the other man," like the man attached to the American Embassy in Oman whom my wife had fallen in love with.

Kaye found a place that I could rent in James Bay that was within walking distance to downtown Victoria and 20 minutes from her house. It was a small heritage house built in the 1880s. It looked to me like a little gingerbread house out of the fairy tale, *Hansel and Gretel.*

As it turned out it was difficult to see one another because of her full-time life with her husband and her job at the school. So, as a way to spend some time together, Kaye and I arranged a three-day weekend on Bowen Island off the coast of Vancouver. I had chosen Bowen Island as a venue for our rendezvous because I figured it would be far enough away from Victoria to keep from being seen by any of the people she knew. Kaye told her husband she was going to stay with a girlfriend in Vancouver.

It was a wonderful three days together. Whenever we left the room at the Vineyard Bed and Breakfast where we were staying, Kaye made it a point to wear a head scarf and sunglasses as a way to keep from being recognized. Unfortunately, her attempt at disguise didn't work.

One evening we left the room to have a meal at a small restaurant near the ferry terminal. We ended up sitting across from a woman who Kaye recognized immediately. In fact, Kaye and her husband had been to her house for dinner. The woman kept eyeing Kaye, most likely trying to figure out what she was doing with me and probably asking herself, 'Why isn't Kaye with her husband?' The irony was this woman wasn't with her husband either. She was sitting with a semi-balding man with glasses who was talking to her in a very animated fashion and gushing like a schoolboy while she sat stoically, nodding her head in reply and glancing over at us. Kaye was pretty certain the woman would not say anything to her husband because she was obviously having an affair herself. It was a perfect stalemate.

The next afternoon we drove to a secluded beach. Kaye and I sat on a massive log, one of many that had washed up on the shore. We looked out on the tranquil, sheltered bay and began to daydream, imagining what it would be like to live together in such a place. We both remember with vivid clarity seeing a small white house that overlooked that beach with two yellow sea kayaks sitting under it. To us the people who owned that house had a perfect situation. We tried to visualize what it would be like to own a house so close to the water like that, offering such a stunning and serene view with our own personal kayaks to take out and paddle any time we wished. It seemed like the perfect fantasy. One we would always remember.

I moved into the house that Kaye had found for me. I had been living there for about a month before her husband figured out what was going on. He was very civilized about it and confronted Kaye one day by saying to her, "We need to talk about infidelity, breach of trust and betrayal."

She told me his statement made her blood turn to ice. They opened a bottle of wine, sat down at the table and talked about what was transpiring. There was no use lying to him, so she told him everything. He listened attentively and after hearing what she had to say he gave her an ultimatum.

He told her, "I think you need to move in with him. See how it goes. The thing is, if you decide to come back to me and the marriage, you will know exactly what you are getting yourself into." His ultimatum to Kaye would be the undoing of their marriage.

Kaye moved in with me in the little house in James Bay. We agreed from the onset that we would be as civil about our arrangement as possible and work hard to keep it quiet. Kaye wanted to be careful not to cause her husband any more pain than he was already going through. Having personally been on the opposite end of a similar situation in Oman, I readily agreed that was the civil way to conduct ourselves. We tried hard to keep our liaisons, and the fact that we were living together, as discreet as possible.

Eventually, however, I grew tired of being unable to even hold Kaye's hand in public or be demonstrative to her in any way because of the threat of prying eyes. So I booked a getaway to Hornby Island in a small cottage on the water.

Once on Hornby and away from anyone who would recognize Kaye, it felt wonderful to feel normal in one another's company. I could put my arm around her or hold her hand and not be overly worried that we'd be seen in public.

The little cottage I'd rented wasn't much, really, but the view from a huge picture window was world-class magnificent. When I brought in our one suitcase from the car, Kaye was standing very still at the window. The view overlooked a few overhanging pine branches and a stunning expanse of water. No other person or structure could be seen. I put down the suitcase, walked over to Kaye standing with her back to me, and wrapped my arms around her waist. She placed both arms over mine.

In nearly a whisper I said into her ear, "Beautiful, huh."

"Stunning. Absolutely stunning."

We were both silent for a long moment taking in the view and this special moment. Then I noticed she was crying. "What's wrong?"

"Not one thing. This couldn't be more perfect."

"What's wrong then, Hon?"

"I'm just thinking how lucky we are to be able to experience this. Then I think about my family when I was growing up in London. Mom and Dad and I were living on the top floor of the house. My grandmother and grandfather lived on the middle floor and my aunt and uncle and three cousins were living in the basement. We had so little. There was only one toilet outside and one inside toilet but no bathroom. We all had to wash from the sink. And now, in comparison, I have so much. And they were such kind people. How I wish I could share this moment with them. I'm living a life now with you they could have never dreamed of. I feel I'm standing on the shoulders of giants. My tears are for them, Darling. My grandmother would have loved this and they really had next to nothing. Life had been so hard."

"So this is a grandma moment then?" I said, not mockingly, but posing a question.

"Yes, Darling, I suppose you can say I'm having a grandma moment. How I wish I could share this with them."

"Well let's drink a toast to your grandma, and to your family members who would probably be thrilled that one of their family members could experience such a moment, such a life." I gave Kaye a peck on the cheek, a squeeze and went over to the cool box and took out a bottle of bubbly.

Two minutes later we were standing at the window again, toasting relatives alive and relatives gone, sharing with them in spirit this splendid moment.

CHAPTER 12
Life in James Bay

Living with Kaye in Victoria soon made me come to realize what a compassionate, kind and caring person she is. I knew she was a kind-hearted person when I knew her in Oman, but I didn't appreciate the depth of her kindness. I guessed it came from being a nurse or perhaps she became a nurse because of this admirable quality. I would later learn it had everything to do with her caring and loving family back home in England. Her compassion was a trait I found endearing.

I witnessed examples of this admirable trait many times, but one incident stands out in my mind. It happened when we were shopping at a local supermarket.

It was raining so I dropped Kaye off outside the market while I parked the car. When I walked inside I saw her standing next to an elderly woman and a man who looked like the store manager. As I approached, I noticed something quite out of character for Kaye. She was chewing out the manager. When I got close enough to hear what she was saying she was speaking to him in a firm tone, but not so loud that she would be overheard by other customers.

"What gives you the right to chastise and embarrass this poor woman in front of everyone, accusing her of eating food in your store? This woman is someone's mother. How would you like it if your mother was spoken to like that? There is another way this could have been handled so as not to cause embarrassment to this poor lady."

"Ma'am, this happens all the time with these old people. It costs the store a lot of money in lost...."

Kaye interrupted, "I don't care about that and neither

should you. You are missing my point. There is a more humane way to handle this. You could take her into your office away from earshot and deal with it there. You don't do it by publicly humiliating her like this. Even if she has been eating food, your handling of this situation is way beyond the pale and you should be ashamed of yourself."

Kaye was trying to speak softly enough to keep the conversation private, but firmly enough to get her point across.

The manager explained, "Ma'am, I am sorry if I have offended her or you in any way, but we do have a problem with this."

"Well I suggest your store adopt some other way to deal with such problems without degrading the person you're dealing with. The elderly people who shop here are mothers and fathers to someone. They could be yours. Don't treat them like someone unworthy of your respect. Be mindful of their feelings."

The manager apologized to the old lady and let her continue to do her shopping. Kaye and I left to do our shopping, too. It took Kaye about 30 minutes to get over her anger with the store manager. She told me, "I kept thinking that could have been my mum and how would I have felt if that had happened to her?"

Even though I was living with a woman I loved and adored, I was still feeling awfully low: I had lost half my net worth in yet another divorce. I was living in Canada during the winter months in a cold and wet climate. I was frustrated by being unable to publicly demonstrate my affection for Kaye, fearing we would be seen by her friends or staff members from the school where she worked, or mutual friends of hers and her husband's, or parents of the kids at school. Keeping our affair and our life together such a closely guarded secret wore heavily on my spirit.

Kaye felt similarly frustrated but to be civil and to be fair to her husband, we had to keep our clandestine affair hidden from public view. I understood her logic, having gone through the gut-wrenching experience I lived through in Oman when my wife met her new man at the American Embassy. It was extremely important to keep our affair discreet. In Oman, my wife and her lover had made no attempt to keep secret how they felt for one another. Their very public display stretched the limit of my sanity.

Kaye worked evenings, often spending the night in the infirmary at school to look after sick kids. She would then return home in the early morning hours, slipping under the covers of my warm bed.

On one such occasion she asked me if I'd ever read the *Paddington Bear* series of books as a child. I told her I hadn't. So the next day she checked out several of the books from the local library. She would read those wonderfully poignant stories to me, with that impeccably soft and proper English accident of hers, like I was some big kid snuggled up in her bed.

I clearly remember one particular rainy morning feeling so emotionally cherished that I marveled at how I, a fully grown man of 55 years old, could be transported back to my boyhood, feeling nurtured and looked after with such tenderness and care, with tears of joy and some tears of sadness and some of pure love streaming down my face, wrapped up in the feeling of being totally in love with this woman. It was a feeling I had not experienced in more than a decade.

Another side of Kaye I hadn't noticed until we moved in together was her tolerant side. I had not realized how conditioned I had become to being criticized in my last relationship until the day I accidentally spilled a full glass of red wine on the white bedspread.

It was evening. We were lying in bed recounting what we'd done that day when I spilled the red wine all over the white bedspread. I immediately jumped up in panic, cowering inside, waiting to be yelled at. I became over-apologetic, waiting for a rocket to be fired in my direction for what I'd done.

Instead, Kaye could see I was flustered and just said,

"Oh-h-h, please don't worry, Darling. That is why they made washing machines."

When I told her how sorry I was she said, "Did you do it on purpose?"

"Of course not."

"Well then, please forget it. It'll come out. If it doesn't, well, it's just a bedspread. Now, pour yourself another glass of wine and get back to bed."

Once in bed she asked me why I had reacted like I had. I told her that I knew it was over between Claire and me when I was sent to the store to pick up some lettuce and nearly broke into a cold sweat because I didn't know whether the lettuce I had chosen was the right one. (I didn't have a cell phone.)

Kaye was incredulous. "What! You, Randy Mains, having flown in combat, having been shot at, awarded the DFC for bravery, were afraid of a woman who weighs no more than 120 pounds?"

"Yep. I'm almost embarrassed to tell you that story, but it was at that exact moment while standing in the grocery store that I knew it was over. And the fact that I could never find a Hallmark greeting card with words that wouldn't make me feel like a hypocrite if I bought it and gave it to her."

"Boy, you *were* in trouble."

"You're telling me. That's why I'm here, divorced again and single."

"And I say her loss is my gain. She doesn't know what she's given up. "

"It takes two. I accept my part of the blame. If it weren't for the criticism I received she and I would still be together. I used to tell her I would get more kudos from people we'd meet at a dinner party than I would from her. I told her about how I felt when I couldn't decide what lettuce to buy. But she said it was never about the lettuce and I fully understood what she meant by that and she was absolutely right. The lettuce incident and my being unable to find a greeting card with words that fully conveyed my true feelings were just indications of problems that ran much deeper. I tried to go to counseling. She did too, but we never went together, which I'm sure was a big mistake. But on the day when we were heading to a joint session I remember that before we went in we talked about whether we thought it would be worth it and we both came to the conclusion that our marriage was dead and over, that there was no use, so we didn't keep the appointment.

"But you know, there was something the therapist told me during my first meeting with her when I went on my own that has stuck with me. Something she said that really made the light bulb come on in my head."

"And what was that?" Kaye asked.

"Well, I talked for over an hour during our first meeting, spilling my guts, telling her my side of the story, what I perceived had gone wrong in our marriage. Then the therapist said something that really resonated with me – something I will never forget and something I had no excuse for. She said, 'And did you know these things about her before you asked her to marry you?' "

"All I could say was, 'yes,' and when I did, all the therapist did was shrug as if to say, 'Well, you went into the relationship with your eyes wide open and you still took the plunge. Why are you surprised?' I tell you, Kaye, that was an illuminating moment for me."

Kaye took a sip of wine, then said, "That's not unlike the letter you sent to me in England before I married my husband, after you read my letter telling you about all the reservations I had about marrying him. You advised me to read my own letter as if it came from a friend of mine, and to contemplate what I would advise them. All the reservations I had? The fears ended up coming true. So, why *did* you marry Claire then?"

"Don't know. It seemed the right thing to do at the time. I guess I could ask you the same question. Why did you marry him knowing the reservations you had about whether the relationship would work?"

"I was drowning back in England, working three jobs, doing four-hour back-and-forth commutes to London from

Folkestone and still unable to get ahead. Marrying him seemed like my only lifeline, my real only option at the time. We'd known one another for more than 30 years back in the U.K. If it weren't for his two boys and the caustic ex-wife of his, I think we could have made it work.

I leaned over and kissed Kaye on the forehead. "We've both gone through quite a lot of pain and personal crap to be where we are today, haven't we?"

"And as painful as it was at the time I would do it all over again if I knew in the end I would be reunited with you."

"I feel the same way, Honey, but holy crap did it hurt getting to where we are now."

She looked at me playfully, "I may have something to cheer you up."

"More wine? Wild, bone-crunching sex?"

"Cheeky bugger!"

She leaned over to the bedside table and produced the Paddington Bear book that she'd started reading to me the previous morning. "This will cheer you up. Now, where were we …?"

I gently settled my head on her shoulder and listened to her sweet, soft voice; and in that perfect English accent of hers she told me how much Paddington liked eating his marmalade sandwiches.

After the dreadful events of 9/11 it became increasingly risky to be an American in Saudi Arabia. By 2003, the compounds where the expatriates lived, like mine, had become fortresses with concrete blocks, arranged to hopefully dissuade any suicide bombers who might try to pass through the gate and blow us up. There were armored personnel carriers posted outside the gates manned 24 hours a day by two soldiers, a driver and one soldier behind a 50-caliber machine gun at the ready.

Frank Pole lived across town in a compound with similar security measures. He arrived at the palace hangar one day and told us that during the night a car had tried to drive through the barricade at his compound's entrance. The guards didn't hesitate to shoot, riddling the car with 50-caliber bullets, instantly killing the driver.

I was on one of my late-night walks when a group of four Saudi youths dressed in traditional Arab dress pulled up alongside me. They waited for me to look at them. When I did, one of the boys aimed his finger at me like a gun and pretended to shoot me.

I thought, OK, it's time for me to say "*ma'a salama*," meaning "goodbye" in Arabic, to my job and the people in Jeddah.

The next morning I told Frank that this would be my last tour working in Saudi.

"Would you stay for more money?"

"It's not about the money, Frank. I feel, for me anyway, that it's time to go do something else. I've decided that on my way home after this hitch I'll route via Abu Dhabi, meet with the chief pilot, and see if I can get a job there."

Frank wished me well and said, "Yeah, I know what you mean. I don't know how long I can last here either."

I knew from my time in Oman that Abu Dhabi, one of the United Arab Emirates, was a very safe country. After my five-month tour in Jeddah, I flew to Abu Dhabi and met with the chief pilot there to inquire about a job with Abu Dhabi Aviation, or ADA, as it's called. The company flew men and equipment to offshore oilfields in the Arabian Gulf and had been doing so for 26 years. On February 15, 2004, I was hired to work an eight-week-on, four-week-off schedule. The company agreed to fly me back and forth to Canada with each rotation.

Back in Canada, it had been a rollercoaster adventure ride for Kaye and for me since we moved in together. She divorced her husband, even though I kept emphasizing to her at the time that I couldn't promise more of a commitment than to be with her one day at a time.

Then Colin Skinner suddenly died and that changed everything.

Colin Skinner had been a much loved and talented drama teacher at the boarding school where Kaye worked as the head nurse. At dinner one evening with Colin and his wife, we learned he had not been feeling well. He was dead three months later at the age of 66.

Colin's death caused me to seriously think about the future. By that time Kaye and I had been living together for more than two years when I was not in the Middle East flying for Abu Dhabi Aviation (ADA). I thought to myself, "I'm not going to live forever so what am I waiting for? I'm living with a woman I love, respect and adore. Kaye makes me feel loved and cherished, she understands me and, probably more importantly, she knows how to handle me. So what am I waiting for?"

I couldn't answer my own question and didn't want to die before I did, so I went to the local jeweler's and bought a ring, got down on one knee (not over pancakes this time) and asked Kaye if she would marry me. She accepted and we were married on December 15, 2003, in our friends' Jean and Jim's house in Victoria with 25 of our closest friends in attendance.

Kaye wore the same beautiful red dress she'd worn on our first date 15 years earlier when we attend the Marine Ball in Oman. I wore a black tuxedo similar to the one I'd worn that night, too. Other than my hair looking a little gray around the temples, the picture of us taken on our wedding day looked very much like the one taken of us on that wonderful night.

After we got married, Kaye discovered the adventuresome young woman within herself that had been dormant when she was stuck in her dreadful marriage. Her rekindled spirit of adventure led her to take a one-year sabbatical from her job at the boarding school to be with me in Abu Dhabi.

⁄⁄⁄

It was Kaye's observation that the accommodation Abu Dhabi Aviation provided its employees only needed a wooden guard tower on each corner of the perimeter and a little barbed wire strung around it and it would look like a prisoner-of-war camp straight out of the movies. Where we lived was commonly referred to by all who lived there as simply, "The camp."

Each accommodation block within the "camp," of which there were 21, housed nine men. The blocks were called Vans and together Kaye and I lived happily for one year in my tiny 11-foot by 12-foot room in Van 17.

After spending an adventure-filled year with me in Abu Dhabi, Kaye returned to her job at the boarding school in Victoria. I changed my work rotation from a two-month-on one-month-off schedule, opting for a more reasonable six-week-on six-week-off schedule. It would mean a reduction in salary but we would have more time together, which was more important to us than the extra money.

Dreams worth dreaming are worth working for. Kaye and I had talked often of that white house we saw with the two kayaks sitting underneath it when we were together sitting on that massive log on that secluded beach on Bowen Island. It made a strong impression on us.

As I write this it takes us one minute to walk from our front door to our sheltered bay, which is perfect for kayaking. Sitting in the back yard against the cedar fence that runs alongside our house are two yellow, 17-foot-long sea kayaks: one for Kaye, and one for me.

Abdul Azziz beginning its journey from Morocco to Malaga, Spain where we were to meet it during the king's visit

Abdul Azziz lying in port, Malaga, Spain. Imagine landing a Bell 214ST on that helideck which can be hydraulically raised three feet. The forward tower can be lowered to accommodate our landing

Prince Sultan's 360' yacht steaming in the Red Sea. The helipad for our Bell 214ST is on the stern

Bell 214ST aboard Prince Sultan's 360' Yacht tied down and chained to the deck.

Standing with Don Williams next to the King's helicopter outside the hangar inside the palace grounds

Kaye and I diving together again in Hawaii after 12 years apart.

On our wedding day – Kaye and I dressed as we were on our first date 15-years prior at the Al Bustan Palace Hotel

The following is a list of HEMS fatal accidents that occurred while I worked in Saudi Arabia for three cruising seasons prior to joining Abu Dhabi Aviation.

(Source Air Medical Memorial Website
www.airmedicalmemorial.com)

	2001	
Enloe FlightCare	Chico, CA	September 22, 2001
	2002	
CareFlight	Doland, SD	September 9, 2002
Mercy Air	Nipton, CA	September 7, 2002
LifeNet	Norfolk, NE	June 21, 2002
Mountain Life Flight	Susanville, CA	March 21, 2002
University Hospital MedEvac 8	Cleveland, OH	January 18, 2002
	2003	
REACH	Redwood Valley, CA	December 23, 2003
IHC Life Flight	Salt Lake City, UT	June 7, 2003
Air Angels	West Chicago, IL	January 28, 2003
IHC Life Flight	Salt Lake City, UT	January 10, 2003
	2004	
EagleMed	Dodge City, KS	February 17, 2004
Hawaii Air Ambulance	Laupahoehoe, HI	January 31, 2004

CHAPTER 13

February 2004

Abu Dhabi Aviation – a Distinct Feeling of Déjà Vu

Accepting the job with Abu Dhabi Aviation was like returning to Vietnam, the place where my aviation career began. I don't mean to imply that Abu Dhabi was as unsafe as a war zone; it certainly wasn't. The comparison to Vietnam came to mind because I could see I would be flying with colorful characters much like the guys I'd flown with in Vietnam.

Abu Dhabi Aviation had a surreal, *Catch-22* feel about it: like the novel by Joseph Heller, the company fostered an insanity, absurdity, and irrationality I hadn't seen in too many places in my career other than the U.S. Army. Working at ADA was as if I'd been transported back to my company in Vietnam in 1968 because I was again being exposed to similar memorable personalities.

I found ADA, and the personalities of the people working there, appealed to my sense of humor. ADA would be a perfect place to serve out my last days in the cockpit before hanging up my headset for good. I could see that working at ADA would make me feel like I had come full circle, like I'd returned to my aviation roots.

Arriving with 36 years of aviation experience under my belt I had this feeling of *déjà vu* for two reasons: The accommodation for the pilots and engineers reminded me of the plywood hootches I'd lived in during my tour of duty in Vietnam where my aviation career began; and because of the wildly quirky and colorful characters who worked there, many of them with eccentric personalities similar to the guys I flew with in Vietnam.

When at ADA I worked alongside personalities like ex-Vietnam pilot, "Too-tall" McCall (because he's short); "Lucky" (because he's not); "Hollywood" (because of his un-Hollywood manner); Robert "Don't call me Bob" Hage (that's how he introduced himself because he dislikes being called Bob); "Bananas" (because it's reported that he was a "little" nuts in Vietnam); "Squeaky Cheeks" (because he has a very odd walk); "Sumo" (because he looks like a sumo wrestler); "Turkey" (because he likes to drink Wild Turkey); "Captain Bipolar" (because you can never predict what mood he'll be in); "Crusher" (because he crushed a man – slightly – with his helicopter while the man was hooking up an under-slung load on a well head); and of course there was "Trackless."

Trackless had been a colonel in the Royal Australian Air Force and had flown fixed-wing in Vietnam. He was a fiery little character so named because he had very short legs, making his ass so close to the ground it dragged behind him wiping out his tracks.

Each man in a Van shared a bathroom with the man across the hall. Every Van had a kitchen with an East Indian cook and a small laundry room used by the East Indian houseboy who washed and ironed your clothes. The Vans were constructed to last only 18 months and had been housing people, sometimes whole families, for nearly 28 years.

Several of the Vans had bars in them that, when I first saw them, looked like the bars in our Vietnam hootches. That's probably no coincidence because many of the pilots who came to work for Abu Dhabi Aviation during its inception back in 1976 were Vietnam vets, so they brought with them their decorating ideas and their wild spirit for adventure.

I'd been told stories by the old timers that in those early days, rules and regulations were pretty lax. Guys flew their aircraft single pilot wearing t-shirts, shorts and flip-flops, many with their hair in a ponytail.

Some of the stories I'd heard made ADA sound like an aviation hippie colony. A few of the pilots wore no shoes at all when they flew. I'd heard one tall tale about a guy who flew nude except for a sock covering his vital bits – an image I would rather not think about.

No Westerner would believe the run-down state of the camp. It looked like a Third-World labor camp, housing employees working there who made a few dollars a day, rather than a place that housed helicopter airline transport pilots and mechanics. In any Western country the camp would have been condemned and torn down to prevent the spread of toxic mold. It was often said that if you could survive living in the camp you could survive living anywhere. I believed it.

The camp was so shocking to the eye that several new pilots arrived after accepting a job with ADA and, when driven to the camp by the company driver, upon seeing it, asked the driver to take them straight back to the airport where they got back on an airplane and flew home.

One of the more famous stories illustrating my point is when a Pakistani taxi driver, who couldn't have earned more than a few dollars driving 16 hours a day, drove his taxi into the camp to drop off one of the pilot's wives. She said the man's jaw visibly dropped when he saw the state of the place and when the pilot's wife tried to pay the driver he wouldn't accept full fare.

When I first arrived to take the job at ADA in February 2004, it quickly became obvious to me that the camp was not the only shocking thing about the company. I could see early on that the management style at ADA was draconian, causing paranoia to run rampant among all its workers.

Admittedly, over time, the mood and the attitude would change for the better, but when I *first* arrived, the mission statement for Abu Dhabi Aviation very well could have been: "No good deed goes unpunished." Or, as Bob Trumble – a former test pilot for Bell Helicopter and line pilot for the company – observed, "We're not happy until you're unhappy." ADA, over the 9 years I was there, was a company that finally came to recognize that its biggest assets were its employees.

This rule by fear and intimidation that I observed when I first arrived came not from the Arabs who own the company, but from the Westerners in management who were advising their Arab bosses. In the 28 years I spent living and working in the Middle East, I learned it usually wasn't the Arabs who would try to screw you. It was the Westerners who had managed to work themselves into a position of trust and authority, with their own agendas, their own interests at heart, who were feathering their own nests, empire building, and not looking after the interests of their fellow expats.

Take our former head of safety, for example. When he took the position, he issued an eight-page memo – a "Matrix of Punishments" – to all the pilots listing all the things they could do to get themselves fired. It reminded me of the old saying, "The whippings will continue until morale improves."

He was hell-bent on finding a pilot who was violating any of the ADA rules and regulations. He became a bit overzealous, however. Using binoculars, he would stand in the Contracts office overlooking the flight line, spying on the pilots, checking to see if they were using their checklists or doing a proper preflight. When an aircraft hovered on the ramp to the terminal or to parking, he'd watch to see if the pilots were following the painted yellow lines drawn on the tarmac to act as guides.

To please the Arab shareholders he would regularly expound to anyone within earshot quite embarrassingly that, "There is no data to support the claim that training in a flight simulator will produce a safer pilot."

Of course, he said that so the shareholders wouldn't have to worry about sacrificing their lucrative 20-to-30-percent yearly dividend to pay for flight simulator training.

The Arab bosses eventually told him to curtail his zeal for continually trying to find fault with the pilots and engineers because his actions were counterproductive to his safety efforts. In short, he was pissing *everyone* off including management and was told to cut it out.

The safety officer was writing a master's thesis on the subject of "Willful Noncompliance;" that is, he was doing a study about the pilots electing *not* to do something because they thought it was a bad idea.

For example, the safety officer would invent ideas to please the shareholders, but many of his notions contradicted good aviation safety practices so the pilots would decline to follow them. We pilots all thought as long as that particular safety officer had a job, his study would be self-perpetuating because the more bad ideas he came up with the more willful noncompliance he would witness which would create more fodder for his reports.

Fortunately for the pilots, that safety officer has left the company, but you still might wonder why a professional helicopter pilot would put up with flying as much as seven hours a day in scorching summer heat in a non-air conditioned helicopter making 45 to 50 takeoffs and landings a day. The simple answer is we did it for the tax-free money and we did it because of the terrific guys we worked with.

The pilots and mechanics at ADA are an international bunch at last count: 160 pilots comprising more than 20 nationalities. To a man, they are all highly experienced, professional and top-notch. When I first arrived they operated safely *in spite* of management not because of it. The pilots looked out for one another – like one does in a combat zone; like we did in Vietnam.

When I first began my training at ADA I had great doubts about whether I would make it. I'd never flown in an offshore oilfield environment before and the way training was handled back then I never really knew how I was doing because I was never told. I felt that every flight was a checkride. The other new pilots I spoke with in training felt exactly the same. The only reason I knew I was doing OK at the end of my tour was because the company gave me a return air ticket to come back.

In the first two months I was with the company, two other very experienced 10,000-hour pilots who were in training with me were let go for what seemed like no apparent reason. Seeing those two guys get chopped made me anxious.

One of the oilfields we used to service was Zakum Field (Zakum as it's called). Zakum is located 50 miles offshore, northwest from Abu Dhabi International Airport. I was told by other pilots who have flown on offshore contracts elsewhere that Zakum is one of the busiest oilfields in the world for radio traffic. I will never forget the first time I flew in Zakum, having to listen to both VHF radios. Like every other pilot who first flies in Zakum, I was completely overwhelmed. The experience was more than daunting – it was mind-numbing.

There could be as many as seven aircraft operating in Zakum at any one time in an area 15 miles wide and 25 miles long, with over 200 wellheads. Keeping track of the other helicopter traffic to avoid a mid-air collision plus navigating to your next destination, talking on two radios, filling out paperwork and accomplishing as many as 20 or more takeoffs and landings before your first coffee break at 9:30 a.m. is enough to swamp and capsize anyone's senses.

To give you an idea what my first experience in the Zakum Field was like I'll describe for you here what the radio traffic sounded like in my headset coming over the two VHF radios.

"Zakum good morning, Alpha Lima, gate in, fifteen-hundred feet for ACPT, fifteen on board.

"Morning, Alpha Lima, wind 330 degrees fifteen knots QNH one-zero-one-zero. Traffic ... Alpha Sierra South Sat to North PC three three. Also, Alpha India lifting Corniche for south Zakum 112. Alpha Victor Central to south eight four.

"Alpha Lima, roger.

"Junana, Junana, Alpha Kilo ten minutes to drop three."

"Roger captain, give a two-minute call, Junana.

"Roger."

"Bravo Mike, two minutes Zap."

"Cleared to land Zap Bravo Mike."

"Alpha Echo holding west PC one one zero for Zakum West."

"Roger Alpha Echo, traffic Bravo Mike leaving west PC 39 for Hilton Main."

"Alpha Echo, copy."

And on and on and on and on like that all day long ....

When I landed back at the airport after my first day in Zakum, Ron Littleton, the head of training at the time, asked me, "Well, Randy, what did you think about your first day flying in Zakum?"

I just shook my head in bewilderment and said, "Great, Ron. If we would have had a fatal accident I wouldn't have been killed in it because I was twenty-five miles behind the aircraft."

It normally takes a new pilot about half a year or more to feel comfortable with the radio traffic in Zakum.

The following are stories and series of anecdotes and observations illustrating what I saw and heard while working at Abu Dhabi Aviation (ADA).

On my first tour as a newly qualified captain at ADA, I flew with a very experienced senior pilot who had been flying for the company for five years. He was a man of few words on the radio. He was as paranoid as many of the other pilots I'd flown with but, as it turned out, he was only paranoid when he was back at base on the Abu Dhabi ramp at the airport.

I had heard from some of the other pilots that Len was a bit standoffish. That he could be a little difficult to get to know. Although Len was probably only 45 years old at the time, he was one of the "old" guys; that is, he'd been with the company when they used to fly offshore single pilot.

The company was making the transition from single pilot ops to two-crew ops. ADMA, the oil company ADA worked for, demanded that Abu Dhabi Aviation fly its oil workers using two qualified captains for safety reasons. Of course I was used to flying in a two-crew environment from my 13 years in Oman and my three seasons in Saudi Arabia so I knew the obvious benefits. I had not been with ADA long but I could see a reluctance by many of the "old" pilots to fly with another pilot. Because of the rampant paranoia at the time, many of the "old" pilots thought the other pilot was there to "tell on him" if he made a mistake.

I had noticed at ADA there was this leftover machismo amongst the "old guys" that they lorded over we "new guys," implying that they were somehow more talented and better pilots because they had shown they could do the job single pilot.

At one point during our flight, Len suddenly remarked over the intercom, "You know we used to do all this single pilot," inferring how much more difficult it had been without the "help" of another pilot.

I wasn't going to let it go and said back over the intercom sarcastically, "Ahhhh, yeah, I see, the good old days, huh? Wasn't that back when you guys worked six-and-a-half days straight, only getting a day off after you'd come off night duty and you had to do all the paperwork yourself and fly the aircraft at the same time, and before the oil company mandated you follow European duty time regs ensuring you get enough rest and it's now mandated you get two full days off? Yeah, I can see how that would be something you'd want to hold on to."

Len thought about what I'd said for a moment, then nodded his head and said, "Yeah, I guess you're right. It is a lot better now."

"Much better!" I added.

Other than that one incident where Len tried to lay his dick on the center console trying to impress, we had spent a very congenial two days together flying in the field. During that first day I learned that Len was a sailor like me and had owned and lived aboard a 40-foot sailboat of his own. As I had owned three sailboats and had lived on two of them we had lots to talk about while flying and, thankfully, our common interest in sailing lightened him up a bit; that is, until we got back to base. It wasn't until we landed back on the ramp at Abu Dhabi Aviation that his demeanor suddenly changed from congenial to surly.

It's customary at the end of a flight to walk around the aircraft to do a post flight inspection to see if there are any puddles of oil or anything wrong visually that could affect the serviceability of the aircraft for the next crew.

On the Bell 412 there is a little indicator in the back of the helicopter in one of the small compartments on the port side called a "doll's eye" that, if you pull too much power you can over-torque the drive train of the aircraft and it trips, turning it white, indicating too much mast torque. The doll's eye is also called the JSI by the pilots – short for Job Situation Indicator. If it trips, the safety manager will find out and you will have a pretty good chance of losing your job. That's how it had been in the past, anyway, before ADA got a new safety manager. Fear of "tripping" the doll's eye caused rampant paranoia with pilots thinking that the doll's eye could trip spuriously; that is, without the pilot actually pulling more than the allowable mast torque, leaving it up to the crew to defend themselves to fight for their jobs.

After returning to the base with Len, I got out and did my post-flight walk-around inspection. I naturally glanced in at the doll's eye to see if it had tripped, knowing full well we had not come close to exceeding the torque limit that day.

Len saw me checking the doll's eye and barked, "Don't you *ever* do that when back at base!" Then he proceeded to walk in the direction of the maintenance line shed to turn in the aircraft's tech log.

I was shocked and a little pissed off at his sudden change in attitude. I began to chase him down but thought, no, I'd ask him what he was talking about when we were on the bus taking us back to the camp.

When I saw him again waiting for the bus to arrive I asked him, "Hey, Len, what was that all about back there on the ramp? Why didn't you want me to check the doll's eye?"

He told me, and this is the best anecdote I have for the paranoia running rampant through Abu Dhabi Aviation at the time, "Well, if the safety manager is looking at you through binoculars from Jack Lunn's office and sees you checking the doll's eye, he's going to *think* that you *think* that you've had an over-torque!"

This convoluted, irrational logic actually made me step backwards. I replied incredulously, "And don't you think that sounds just a *little* bit paranoid? What if it *had* tripped, and you and I hadn't checked it? Then the next crew that comes out to take the aircraft checks it on their preflight and finds that it *has* tripped. Then you and I are going to look like fools for not reporting it. Wouldn't you want to know it if had tripped?"

I could not believe I was having this conversation with such an experienced and competent pilot. I added, "Besides, we're supposed to check it. It's part of our job."

"Well, don't." he said defensively. "Not when you're back here if you know what's good for you."

I told him, "Well, Randy Mains is *not* going to play *that* game. If I'm working for a company where I have to be looking over my shoulder because I'm that paranoid of losing my job, I'm working for the wrong company!"

This incident really puzzled me because it was so foreign to anything I had witnessed in my aviation career up to that point.

That was not to be the last incident I would encounter dealing with the paranoid attitude pervading the company at the time. I am happy to say the attitude has changed for the better, but back then, paranoia was a cancer that was rampant. The mantra could have easily been: "I wouldn't be so paranoid if everyone wasn't trying to get me fired!"

Phil Lee was another larger-than life character who had his own method for dealing with company paranoia. He had been working for ADA longer than any other pilot, for over 30 years. He'd logged in excess of 20,000 hours by the time I flew with him. It was universally agreed by all the pilots that Phil Lee was a smart guy. He had a degree in chemistry. It was also universally agreed that Phil Lee believes everything is a conspiracy. He'd change his point of view during an argument just to keep it going, or in my case, I am certain he did it just to wind me up. For example, he'd argue that there is no health risk in second-hand smoke, a position he would argue till the death, which will most likely be caused by, you guessed it, second-hand smoke.

Phil is an excellent pilot whose view on life is more askance than the norm. For example, he'd tell me he'd seen the other side – you know, life after death. Whenever I'd ask him what he'd seen on the other side, he wouldn't tell me. All he would say was, "You'll find out."

Phil is a big-hearted guy. On one of my first flights out to Zakum, he briefed me as to how I should act to survive not being fired. I was Phil's copilot that day. Once we were leveled off on our cruising altitude heading out to Zakum, and he'd engaged the autopilot, he looked over at me from the captain's seat and said on the intercom, "You have to learn plausible deniability to survive here, you know?"

"What?"

"Plausible deniability."

"How do you mean?"

"Whenever you're called in front of management give them a story that could have an element of deniability that could be plausible."

"You mean tell a lie?"

"No, no no no no, never lie. Tell your story in such a way that they can't quite pin it on you."

"Pin what on you?"

"Whatever you've done."

"Like what?"

"Anything. There are a hundred ways to get fired you know?"

"No I don't."

"A few months back the safety officer came out with a Matrix of Punishments you know?"

"Matrix of Punishments?"

"Yep. It's a matrix he devised that any pilot can refer to so they know what punishment they can expect to receive for any infringement of the SOPs (standard operating procedures). That's why, to survive here, you need to master the art of plausible deniability."

I felt like Yossarian, the main character out of Joseph Heller's book, *Catch-22,* having a conversation with Milo Minderbinder. Because I never really felt I fully understood anything Phil told me, to make sure that I "got it" I always repeated what he'd just told me to determine if I'd understood him correctly. So I repeated back to him what I'd just heard. After I did, Phil said, "Now I didn't say that."

My jaw dropped. Phil was plausibly denying what he'd just told me. I looked over at him. He was nodding his head as if reaffirming in his own mind what he'd just said.

"Got it, Phil. Thanks for that," I decided not to press it, taking his advice for what it was: confusing.

Pilots who survived working for ADA were more likely than not what I call the "gray men." They exist but you hardly know they're there. The gray men at ADA were low-key and barely noticeable to management. They didn't fuss. They were malleable. They came to work, they flew, they went home. In short, they were a hassle to no one. They usually didn't voice an opinion either, because they'd learned early on that they had the power to change nothing. They are the kind of employees where, if they were to quit or leave the company, you could imagine they would still be receiving a paycheck because the finance director or management would never know that they'd left.

Ian MacPhail was one such employee. He'd flown helicopters in Vietnam and had been working at ADA for more than 22 years when I met him. When I asked him how he handled working for the company for so many years he answered with total candor, "I've already fired myself," he explained. "That way I don't fall into the paranoia trap because, the way I see it, each paycheck I receive since I fired myself is a bonus."

I encountered another form of paranoia when I was flying one day with Wayne Handley, nicknamed "Hollywood." In the rich and colorful tapestry of characters at ADA, Hollywood would be its brown shoes.

Hollywood had been with Abu Dhabi Aviation for seven years when this particular incident occurred. He was a very competent pilot who would smoke three cigarettes on a 30-minute break and liked things done "just so" in the cockpit. He had a good sense of humor and came across firm but always with a smile. He was not judgmental but he liked things done his way for the most part. When we flew and he was the captain he included me, his copilot, in the decision-making process, as he did on the flight I had with him when we were flying in marginal VMC weather (visual meteorological conditions) skirting low clouds on our way back from Zakum Field to the airport.

I didn't think anything about the fact that we were flying over a broken cloud layer, then occasionally going into a solid cloud layer, then out again, then back into a solid cloud layer, then making the decision to leave 1,000 feet for 500 feet in an effort to get into the clear using the radar altimeter bugged to 200 feet above the sea in our descent.

We agreed to use 200 feet on the Rad Alt as our decision height if we didn't spot the sea. At that point we agreed that if we didn't see the water we would rethink the situation. That is, until he told me what alibi he was going to use if someone had seen us flying back in something less than visual flying conditions.

I had not given it much thought to what we were doing at all when he suddenly said, "Here's what I'll say."

I looked over at him, "Say about what?"

"About what we're doing."

I looked around, scanning outside the cockpit. "And what are we doing?"

"This."

"What?"

"What we're *doing*."

"And what *are* we doing?"

He explained, "I will just say we're flying in thin broken clouds if anyone should ask. That's legal."

"OK," I answered, a bit puzzled at his statement. I was happy with what we had done under the circumstances and, as I said, I hadn't given it much thought.

He looked over at me, "There are spies out there, you know?"

"Spies! Out where?" I said, looking outside, scanning the sky.

"In the field. There are spies in the oilfield that would like to get me in trouble and report back to Jack if I'm seen to be breaking the rules."

"Oh," I said, thinking this was getting weird.

He continued, "Jack and I have a history, you see."

"A history? A history of what?"

He looked over at me, "Yep."

He didn't tell me what history he had with Jack, our boss. And I didn't ask.

"Well," I said, "We'll just say we descended because we saw some weather ahead and went down to five-hundred feet." I wanted to reassure him I was with him on this.

"Don't lie," he told me, "Never lie."

I wondered if he was talking about coming up with a story that would fall under the category of plausible deniability that Phil Lee had spoken about.

I thought for a moment. Wait a minute: we had just descended out of solid IMC (instrument meteorological conditions) and he was calling it thin broken as if we could see the water below but we couldn't. So he *was* in fact lying, at least to himself anyway, but he didn't see it that way because it was probably a better rationalization of plausible deniability than the excuse I had just come up with, although it is one used all the time by pilots. I didn't say anything more on the subject as I felt we had hit an impasse in the logic. I just took the incident for what it was: confusing and, of course, paranoid.

On more than one occasion in the early days I worked at ADA it seemed to operate in its own alternate reality outside of the aviation standards we practice in the West.

Les Koppe, whose nickname back in Vietnam was "Bananas," was probably one of the most conscientious, meticulous and thorough pilots working for the company at the time. Les had a graph or a chart or a paper to cover every eventuality for nearly every flight he went on. His side of the cockpit was not a cockpit as much as it was his personal office.

It was common knowledge that the preflight he performed on the aircraft he was going to fly was more thorough than any of the other pilots practiced because he opened the aircraft's cowlings so that he could get a *real* good look at all the moving and non-moving parts of the helicopter. He is the only pilot I know who did this.

He told me one day that he'd had a bit of a set-to with management about his practice of opening cowlings. He defended his actions by contending it was his prerogative to open the aircraft cowlings if he is expected to sign for it as aircraft commander. He was told by management – are you ready for this? – that his standards are too high.

One of my favourite characters working at ADA was Duane Kincaid. I remember when I first saw Duane. He was walking from the Gulf Hotel, not far from the camp, on his way to his room. I didn't know at the time he was one of the pilots. I thought he looked like a Hell's Angels motorcycle club gang member. I was to learn just how wrong first impressions can be.

A weight lifter, Duane was built as solid as a tree trunk. He kept his ginger hair neatly shaved, like a military man's. He sported a big, bushy, ginger-color moustache that drooped down either side of his mouth to his lower jaw, which made him look like he ought to own a Harley. Duane spoke with a southern drawl because he hailed from Arkansas (Arrrr-kan-sawwwww).

I walked into the TV room at work one morning where Duane was sitting watching the news and took a seat on the couch across from him. Duane Kincaid is a man of *very* few words. In fact, at that time, I think I may have said "hi" to him once or twice in the hallways in passing and that was it. He wasn't rude. He just kept to himself, listened and spoke only when he thought he had something worthwhile to say. I'd been told he had a very dry wit and that he didn't even know when he'd said something funny. I suspect the opposite is true.

When I entered and sat down he kept watching TV. I thought to be polite I should say "hi" to him, so I said, "Hi, Duane."

He answered in a slow drawl, "Hi, Randy."

I was surprised because I didn't know he knew my name. We continued to watch TV. About two minutes passed when he suddenly spoke, and when he did it nearly made me jump. "I read your book."

"What?"

He looked over at me now. "I read your book." Meaning he had read *Dear Mom I'm Alive – Letters Home from Black Widow 25*, the book I wrote about my year in Vietnam.

"Great," I said. "That's great."

A long pause, then he said, "Liked it."

"What?"

"Liked it."

"Great. Where did you get a copy?"

"Bill Lee." (Our chief pilot).

Another short pause, then Duane said, "Got any more? I'd like a copy."

"Nope, I sold all the ones I brought back with me."

"Oh."

Another slight pause, then he said, "I may only read one book every three years."

"Well that makes me feel good, Duane. I'll bring you a copy in July."

Then he said, "Heard you were writin' a book about this place."

I told him what I had in mind. He just nodded. Like I said, Duane Kincaid is a man of few words.

We did manage to have a very good conversation that day. We talked for about 35 minutes or so. He was really talkative – for Duane, that is. The most words I had ever heard him speak. I found out he learned to fly helicopters in the U.S. Army. He was 42 so he didn't serve in Vietnam. He told me he'd flown helicopter air ambulance (HEMS) for three months back in the States.

"Oh, and how'd you like that? I said, finding common ground.

"Don't like flying at night. Don't like hospitals. Don't like blood. It was all the things I don't like. So I quit."

He mentioned that he flew logging with Columbia Helicopters for three months up in Oregon. "Too much movin' around," he told me. "Dangerous too. I was flying co-pilot. I would hold a piece of paper and we'd pick up two logs. I'd write down '2.' Would've been a co-pilot for three to five years before they'd let me be captain. Boss called me one day. Asked me to drive 2,200 miles from California to Canada to do a job. He told me I had to be there in two days. I figured it was that far to Arkansas where my family is, so I told him I quit and drove to Arkansas instead."

Another recollection I have of Duane is the day four of us, all pilots, were travelling back to the camp in a company car driven by a company driver. Duane Kincaid was sitting in the front seat. Tony Dogandara, one of the new pilots, was sitting in the back seat with me. Tony said he was upset because he'd been told he was going to have to work more than 60 days in his first tour to make up for the training the company was giving him. He said, "This separation is going to really be tough on my girlfriend."

Duane Kincaid turned around in the front seat and said to Tony, "My first tour was 72 days long. When I got home to Arkansas my girlfriend had married another man, the town preacher no less, and she was three-weeks pregnant."

I don't know how many lives I have saved directly or indirectly by piloting my medical helicopter – probably well over a thousand I guess. But the most dramatic lifesaving event in my life presented itself to me quite unexpectedly, causing me to make a split-second decision that could have had terrible consequences if it had gone wrong. You see, in Abu Dhabi, as in many Middle Eastern countries, there are no "Good Samaritan" laws that would protect me should a person I was trying to save died under my charge. A tragic outcome could have meant spending a long time in a Middle Eastern jail – perhaps even for the rest of my life.

The incident occurred at the Gulf Hotel, a 10-minute walk from the Abu Dhabi Aviation housing complex where I was living at the time. After a full day of flying in the oilfields of the Arabian Gulf, it was nearly 4 p.m. when I went to play some doubles tennis with three other pilots.

When I entered the hotel pool area I met up with Steve Charles, a pilot for ADA, a former pilot in the British Royal Navy, and the company's crew resource management (CRM) instructor. Steve was also a tennis buddy of mine.

As we entered the hotel grounds, making our way to the tennis courts, we both heard a commotion taking place by the pool area and noticed a crowd gathering. We quickly walked over to see what was going on.

When we arrived at the edge of the pool we could see through the gathering crowd an East Indian lifeguard pulling the small, lifeless body of a boy out of the water. The lifeguard brought the boy up to the pool's edge, lifted him out and began attending to him. The boy looked like he was about eight or nine years old, of East Indian or Pakistani descent. It was evident to me he wasn't breathing. I could see that he'd vomited and had defecated in his swimming trunks.

I was shocked by what the lifeguard did next. Instead of beginning CPR (cardiopulmonary resuscitation), he grabbed the boy around his waist and, standing up, he held the boy like a rag doll, the boy's feet and head dangling downward. The lifeguard then began to shake the boy up and down as if doing so would somehow revive him. It was obvious to me, and probably to everyone else standing around him, that the hotel lifeguard had no idea what he was doing. I thought, if something isn't done quickly, the boy will surely die. I reacted immediately.

I reached through the crowd and snatched the boy from the lifeguard's arms and placed him on his back on the concrete. The lifeguard stepped back, probably thankful someone had taken charge.

I could see that the boy had vomited and, as suspected, he wasn't breathing. I did as I had learned in San Diego while working as an air ambulance pilot for the Life Flight program more than a quarter-century earlier, when I had taken the EMT (emergency medical technician) class. But I had never done for real what I was about to attempt to do now. I was going to try to resuscitate the unconscious young boy, alone, with my own hands, with no help from a doctor or nurse, with consequences too dire to contemplate if I failed.

I tilted the boy's head to one side and, with my index finger, I scooped the vomit from the boy's mouth trying to clear it. Once satisfied it was cleared, I tilted his head back to open the airway, pinched the boy's nose shut and, leaning down over him, placed my lips over his mouth, and gave him a few quick breaths. I scooped out his mouth for a second time, cleared his airway with my finger again and gave him a few more quick breaths.

It flashed through my mind, only briefly, that if I failed to save the boy's life, I'd be in terrible trouble. The lifeguard would only have to say in his own defense, "Well, this man came out from the crowd and snatched the boy away from me before I could save his life." By inference, I would be accused of preventing the lifeguard from saving the boy – in effect, killing the boy. I would be tried for murder.

But I couldn't stand there and watch as the boy's life slipped away. If I would have allowed the lifeguard to continue, the boy would have died. I couldn't stand by and just watch the boy expire. I *had* to do something.

After administering a few more quick breaths I reached down with my fingertips, feeling for a carotid pulse on the side of the boy's neck. I couldn't feel it. No heartbeat. I laid my ear on the boy's wet chest and listened, straining to hear a thread of a heartbeat. To my great relief, I could hear his heart beating, but only faintly.

I cleared his airway again with my index finger, put my mouth over his, and gave him several more breaths. I remember thinking, "Come on, come on, breathe, breathe breathe." I continued giving him breaths, tilting his small head back, pinching his nose, blowing into his mouth, watching his small chest rise and fall, filling his small lungs with the air expelled from my own lungs.

When I began working to resuscitate the boy, Steve said he'd go call an ambulance, and quickly left for the hotel lobby. Another pilot, Hugh Page, arrived at my side and said, "I'll go try to find an oxygen bottle from reception." He then sped off, leaving me to work on the boy, surrounded by a growing crowd of curious onlookers.

Hugh and Steve knew the grave danger I was in by taking responsibility for the boy in a Muslim country where, by doing so, I would be held responsible for the boy's death if he didn't make it.

Come on, breathe, breathe, breathe ....

I continued giving the boy CPR, breathing for him.

I continued my cadence, my rhythm, leaning down, breathing for the boy like clockwork, doing what I'd been trained to do half a world away, more than two-and-a-half decades previously in San Diego, placing my lips over the young boy's mouth, breathing for him, checking that he still had a pulse, giving him the life-giving air from my lungs, hoping that would bring life into his, my heart racing, my every nerve-ending alive with anticipation, silently praying that he'd come to.

Come on kid, breathe ... breathe ... breathe ....

Then the most extraordinary thing happened. The boy let out a small cough almost like a convulsion, causing his back to arch upward as he coughed. He did it again. This time pool water flowed from his mouth and onto the concrete. After a few coughs and more water coming out of his mouth, to my great relief, and to the relief of the crowd around us, the little boy's eyes blinked open and he began breathing on his own.

I placed him on his side in the recovery position, covered him with a towel, and stayed by his side while waiting for his parents to show up, which they did several minutes later. His mom and dad had been in the changing room and had not been watching their son.

Steve returned to say that when he called the ambulance he was told it would be faster to load the boy into a car and drive him to the hospital rather than to wait the 45 minutes it would take for the ambulance to reach the hotel. When the parents were found they were understandably upset. I told them to take the boy immediately to the hospital emergency room, which they did.

They never thanked me. After learning how they had almost lost their son they were in shock and quickly left to take their boy to the hospital. I didn't mind. Saving the young boy's life was thanks enough.

After the boy was taken away by his parents, the crowd dispersed. Steve, Hugh and I walked over to the tennis court.

On the way over I said, "If the kid would have died I don't want to think about what the police would have done with me."

Steve said, "We had a plan, Randy. If the kid had died we were going to take you to the housing site, collect your passport, money and any belongings you could quickly throw together, drive you to the airport and book you on the first available flight anywhere out of the country before the police could catch up with you."

I played tennis for several hours with the guys. I figured, after such an emotional experience, it was the best thing I could do to work the adrenaline out of my system.

The full gravity of what had taken place that afternoon didn't hit me until I was walking from the hotel back to the camp. It was dark by then and for the first time after the event I was alone with my thoughts.

As I walked, I recalled the ordeal, causing a sudden wave of emotion to wash over me, giving my body and mind permission to let go. I had never saved a life in such a hands-on way before. I had become used to saving lives with the helicopter in my days flying hospital air ambulance and in Oman during the rainy season, but never in a one-on-one situation before.

Alone in the darkness, away from the bustle of the hotel, I became aware of how quiet it had become. I replayed the incident again in my mind. I began to speculate, wondering what impact on people's lives the boy might have when he grew up and became a man. What if I had just saved the life of the man who would become a doctor who would save other people's lives or perhaps a researcher who would discover a cure for cancer, or Alzheimer's, or Parkinson's, or some other terrible disease. Perhaps the boy would turn out to be a great composer, inventor, popular artist or writer. I wondered how many children he might have. How would *his* children's lives impact others, their own children and so on?

Walking alone, halfway to the camp from the hotel where, two hours earlier I had saved the little boy's life, my emotions began to well up within me. I began to cry. It was a sudden, unexpected release that I had no control over. I didn't sob. The tears just came and streamed down my face. I let the tears of relief and the tears of joy flow freely while experiencing the most precious of emotions, the elation and euphoria that comes when you save the life of another human being. I closed my eyes and gave silent thanks that the boy had lived.

Feeling emotionally drained and deeply philosophical at that moment I asked myself a more personal question: "How did I come to reach this point in my life?" How did it occur that I would be in Abu Dhabi half a world away from San Diego, California, at this time of day on this exact date to save a boy's life? How did the serendipitous and fortuitous timing transpire that I would witness the lifeless body of a young boy being dragged from the deep end of a swimming pool and that I would step in and save him from almost certain death?

Thinking back, the journey that caused me to be poolside that day began on December 29, 1984, to be exact. That is the day I left San Diego, California, ending my six-year air medical flying career in the States to return to the Middle East after vowing I would never return.

It all came down to that one decision I made to return to the Middle East 21 years previously when I accepted the job in Oman in December 1984. I am so thankful I made that decision, not the least because it meant I would at that pool, in the right place at the right time on the right day to be in a position to save that young boy's life.

///

As I had been a type rating instructor and type rating flight examiner (TRI/TRE) in Oman as head of training, teaching and examining airline transport pilots there, the training department asked me if I would like to be a TRI/TRE for ADA. I accepted.

It was a requirement by the local aviation authority that before becoming a TRI/TRE I had to attend a three-day ground school course first. In the course with me was a retired Canadian Armed Forces pilot and flight instructor by the name of Dave Skinner. There was also a government GCAA (General Civil Aviation Authority) flight examiner, a local Emirati Arab pilot by the name of Mohammad Khitiri.

After the three of us completed the ground portion of the TRI/TRE course we had to take a 50-question written exam. Skinner, Khitiri and I were left in a classroom alone to complete the test. When we had completed it, Khitiri began asking us what answers we had put down for certain questions. It was obvious to us by his questions that he didn't know his stuff.

After asking us about the test, Khitiri told us that he expected ADA to supply him with an aircraft for his TRI/TRE flight training. He was apparently meeting with some resistance to that request from Mike Burke, the head of training.

Khitiri told us: "I have asked Mike to supply me with an ADA aircraft to do my training in. I can tell you this: if Mike doesn't agree to give me an aircraft to do my training for no charge, I will make life very difficult for Abu Dhabi Aviation."

As Khitiri was the flight-operations inspector for Abu Dhabi Aviation acting on behalf of the government, he had the power to either grant or deny approval for ADA to operate in the UAE. Therefore, his threat to make things difficult for the company if he did not get his way could have had some very nasty repercussions.

Skinner and I thought Khitiri's threat, an obvious abuse of his power, was just bluster; that is, until what he said that day affected me personally.

When I first arrived in the United Arab Emirates (UAE) I quickly learned that there were two standards: one standard for the expats and one for the locals. The ADA trainers I'd spoken with who had dealt with Khitiri said that the man's knowledge and flying skills were marginal at best; and on a professional level he could be extremely difficult to work with.

The standards for the expats were high, comparable to standards in a Western country. The standards for the locals were not as high. It was a fact that irked me because when I was head of training in Oman the Omanis knew they had to achieve and maintain the same standards as the expats. Not so in the UAE.

That double standard would eventually come back to haunt ADA in "the crash that didn't happen" on June 2, 2008. It was termed "the crash that didn't happen" by all the pilots working there because after it happened, it was never really acknowledged by management. Subsequently, no lessons were learned from it and we lost an opportunity to take steps to ensure another crash wouldn't happen.

Everyone knew that the Emirati pilot flying that day was weak on his instrument flying even though he'd retired a full colonel after serving 20 years in the UAE air force, but there was a nod of the head, and a wink of the eye as if to say, "Well, we'll just make sure he is never put into a position where he will *need* to fly on instruments." It would turn out to be a fatal assumption.

As he'd flown in the military he never had to obtain a civilian instrument rating. He was told that he needed to have one to operate ADA's aircraft. He went to a local flying school in Al Ain and in two days he came back with one. It was highly suspected by those in the training department who had witnessed his instrument flying in the Bell 412 that it had to be a paper exercise, that he'd used his influence, his Wasata, to ask one of his buddies there to give him an instrument rating. So on paper anyway he was legal. But, of course, not in reality.

I was told by one of the senior trainers that he wouldn't pass this particular pilot on the instrument portion of his six-monthly checkride because he didn't even know how to follow a VOR radial. Basic stuff. And another expat pilot told me that on a ferry flight to bring an Agusta Bell, AB 139 from Italy to Abu Dhabi, this pilot's basic instrument flying skill had been so weak he would not be comfortable with him flying as captain in instrument conditions.

As often happens when looking at an accident in the rear-view mirror, all the clues were there that this particular pilot was sub-par in portions of his flying skills and in his attitude. He *believed* he was safe to operate an aircraft when indeed he was not. Unfortunately, he had been allowed to operate and live with that belief, and it came back to haunt those in the company who knew something like this *could* happen but were prepared to accept the risk that it wouldn't. In the end it came down to the double standard: one standard for the expats that was higher than the standards required of the locals. It was a fact that always galled me.

There is a well-accepted error chain analysis formulated by Dr. James Reason, known as the Swiss cheese model. On this night all the holes in the slices of cheese lined up that allowed this accident to happen.

The "slices" are weaknesses in the organization, managers, etc., which make up one slice; the team (another slice); the task at hand (another slice); and the individual (another slice). Imagine the slices with holes in them pressed together. If there are weaknesses in the organization, the team, the task and the individual, the holes in each slice of the Swiss cheese may line up opening up an opportunity for an accident to occur.

That Emirati pilot *did* need to know how to recover from an unusual attitude and fly on instruments that night. His lack of skill caused him and five others to lose their lives that night in what was a totally preventable accident … that is, had he been properly trained and suitably tested. But the chain of events leading up to "the crash that didn't happen" was a set of circumstances so bizarre, a Hollywood science-fiction writer could not have dreamt it up. A little history ….

The local pilots had been flying VVIP (very very important people) flights single pilot in the AB 139 only during the day. In doing so, they soon discovered if they allowed the VVIP to sit in the front seat and let them fly a little they would be rewarded with cash, sometimes a lot of it. It was rumored that one local pilot was even given a BMW after such a flight.

Since the expat pilots wouldn't allow anyone other than another pilot to fly in the left seat, the chief pilot drafted a memo for all the local AB 139 pilots telling them that only a qualified pilot could occupy a seat in the cockpit.

About a week or so after the chief pilot drafted that memo the No. 2 man in the country, Sheik Nasser bin Zayed Al Nahyan, the equivalent of the vice president of the U.S., chartered an AB 139 for a sightseeing flight. The chief pilot signed for the aircraft; that is, he was legally responsible, acting as the pilot in command while the local pilot who was known to be weak flying on instruments was his copilot. The sheik was late for the flight so what was supposed to be a day flight ended up being an evening flight.

When the chief pilot arrived at the aircraft the sheik was sitting in the copilot's seat and the local pilot was sitting in the captain's seat. There were three other passengers who had accompanied the sheik who were sitting in the back.

The sheik expressed his desire to sit up front. The chief pilot was immediately faced with a personal and a professional dilemma that could only happen in a country where saying no to a passenger's unusual request could cost you your job.

In his split-second decision, the chief pilot elected to disregard the very memo he'd written only days earlier that said no one but a qualified pilot be allowed to occupy a pilot's seat. He had to be feeling great pressure to accommodate the sheik so he elected to go against his own SOP, and his better judgment by getting in the back with the other three passengers as darkness was falling, knowing full well the local copilot was weak on instrument flying. It was a decision that would cost him his life.

They took off from Abu Dhabi International and were cleared by air traffic control to climb to 1,500 feet on a westerly departure. They were flying over a segment of the departure that took their flight path over water with very little ambient light. That is when the sheik's voice was picked up on the cockpit voice recorder saying, "Let's scare them in the back."

It is assumed the sheik took control and pulled back on the cyclic stick causing the nose to pitch up. Radar tracked them rocketing up to 2,500 feet then descending quickly to 500 feet, then climbing up to 1,000 feet, then disappearing off the radar passing through 500 feet.

"The crash that didn't happen" was so named by all the pilots at ADA because after it happened, in the end, management and the General Civil Aviation Authority (GCAA) acted like it hadn't happened. In effect, any details of the crash were swept under the carpet.

That fact concerned the pilots greatly, especially the expat pilots flying the AB 139 because there were valuable lessons to be learned from that crash – lessons that might prevent a repeat of the accident.

Because the AB 139 had suffered some teething issues due to the fact it was such a new aircraft on the market, the crash caused a lot of sleepless nights for those pilots who continued to fly the aircraft and wondered whether the same thing could happen to them. A collective sigh of relief came from the pilots when they eventually learned, unofficially, that it was pilot error, and not structural failure of any of the major components that caused the crash.

One very good thing came from the tragedy. The leader of Abu Dhabi, the step-brother of the sheik who had lost his life in the crash, decreed shortly afterward that every helicopter pilot in the UAE must go through flight simulator training. This was done as a safety measure to, hopefully, prevent another crash.

At about the same time that the decree came down that flight simulators *must* be implemented as part of every helicopter pilot's flight training, the safety officer at ADA was moved sideways in his job. The information he would regularly put out to the company shareholders – that there was nothing in the literature to support the idea that a flight simulator would produce a safer pilot – didn't hold water any longer. A few months after being moved sideways in the organization, he was gone. Make that two very good things that came out of that tragedy.

I had studied for many weeks preparing for the TRI/TRE checkride with Ron Littleton. The checkride I had with Ron was one of the most difficult I've ever taken. It began at 8:30 a.m. with a two-hour oral exam, with Ron asking me questions. We broke for lunch, then we went to fly for an hour-and-a-half. He debriefed me in his office afterward and it wasn't until the last minutes of that debrief – at 4:30 p.m. – that he finally let me know, with a smile, that I'd done a good job and that I'd passed. The relief I felt came over me like a wave. When he delivered the news after all the effort and worry I'd put in, I could actually feel a huge weight being lifted off my shoulders. Whew!

What would occur after going through that course, the flight training, the tough oral exam and the checkride would be the most flagrant abuse of power and one of the most upsetting professional rug-pullings I have ever experienced in my professional aviation career.

I had been a TRI/TRE for about five days when, as I was taking two new pilots to the flight line to give them an orientation flight, Ron Littleton called me into his office.

"Randy, I'm afraid I have some bad news."

"What is it?"

He read from a letter on his desk. "This came today from Mohammad Khitiri's office. It says here, no TRI/TREs will be accepted from Abu Dhabi Aviation until further notice as of the end of this month."

I checked my watch. "But it's the 30th. Surely it means my paperwork got in before this letter takes effect."

"I thought so too, as I'd submitted your paperwork on the 25th documenting that you'd passed the checkride. I immediately called Khitiri to ask him what your status was. He said what it says here: That no more TRI/TREs will be accepted from ADA. I asked Khitiri, 'Does that mean Randy?' And all he said was that it is out of his hands now, and he hung up."

"Bastard! What an unprecedented, flagrant abuse of his power. You know what this is about, don't you?"

"Yeah, I do, Randy. He's pissed because ADA won't give him an aircraft at no charge to do his training in."

"Yeah, Ron, and I'm caught right in the middle."

He nodded. "Afraid so, my friend. I'll keep calling Khitiri's office to see if I can get him to change his mind on this. Meanwhile, I'm afraid you'll have to go back to flying the line."

I was stunned and, understandably, highly pissed off that Khitiri so blatantly abused his power for his own vindictiveness. I wanted to strangle the little shit for causing me this grief, for indirectly causing me to lose what I had worked so hard to attain; the strain I had put on myself had been colossal. Now, because of Khitiri's maliciousness, my hard work was all for naught.

I'd been working in the Middle East for 23 years up until that point in my career and in that time I couldn't remember ever being personally maltreated by a local. I'd witnessed abuse of power but it had never affected me personally. Up until that point in my career, the locals had always been fair with me.

In Vietnam there were three men who made my life miserable: the commanding officer of the company I was assigned to (Charlie Company), and two captains. In my book, *Dear Mom I'm Alive,* there is a chapter entitled, "Poetic Karma Strikes the Brass," where I describe how karma struck those three men as if balancing a great wrong in the universe. Karma would serve to equal the score with Khitiri with no intervention from me and it would hit him with the force of a steaming freight train. The trouble was, I would have to wait a year-and-a-half for that karmic train to come barreling down the tracks.

Entrance to the old camp. Built to last for only 18-months it had been in existence for 30 years.

One of the Vans at Abu Dhabi Aviation in the old camp

A typical bar in one of the Vans

Eating area in one of the Vans in the old camp

Another bar in one of the Vans in the old camp

Living area in one of the vans in the old camp

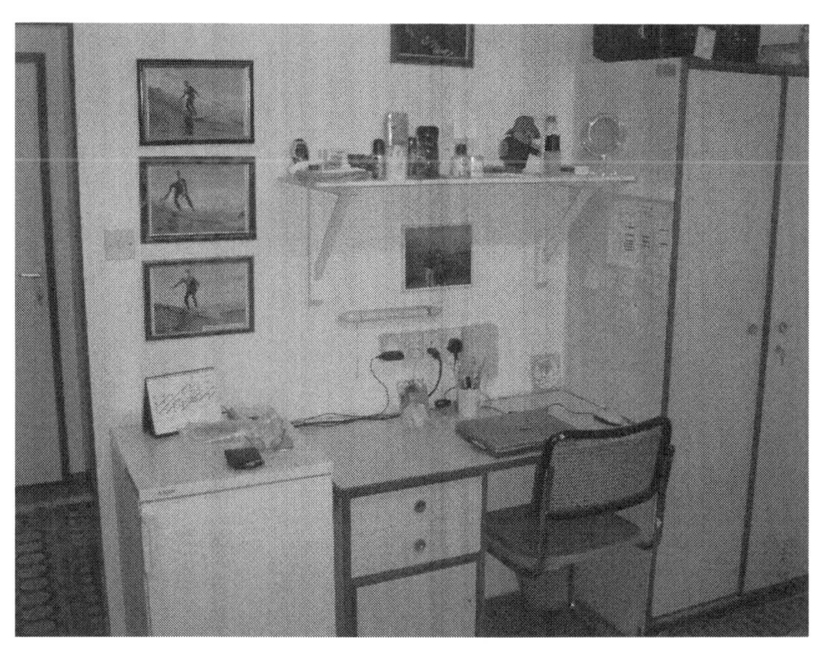

The desk in my 11 foot x 12 foot room in Van 17

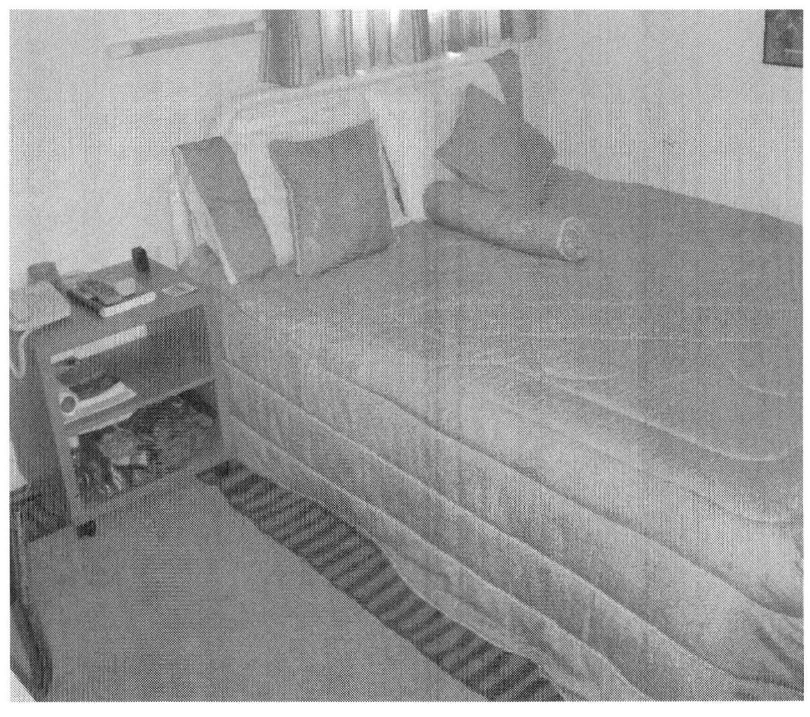

My home away from home Van 17 at the ADA camp

Pilots in my room Van 17 probably with a cumulative 50,000 helicopter flight hours between them. L to R Tom Brown from the U.K., Peter Hill from the U.K., Brian Taylor from New Zealand, Robert Hage originally from Holland living in Canada

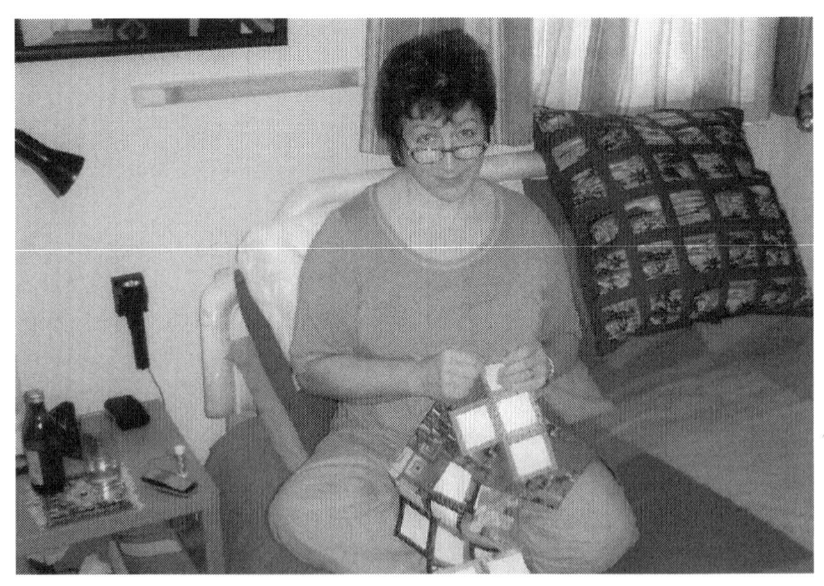

Kaye making a patchwork quilt in our room in Van 17 during her one-year sabbatical from her job at the boarding school where she worked as a nurse

Oil Rig Offshore in the Zakum Oil Field

Winching a generator to a platform in Zakum field

Accommodation Platform Zakum Field could house 300 men

Abu Dhabi Aviation AB 139

In the Bell 412 sim with Dave Skinner practicing for our TRI/TRE check ride

CHAPTER 14

On Becoming an Activist

I had mentioned to Kaye many times that I held the answer for significantly reducing the accident rate occurring in HEMS in the States, but I also told her that I felt I didn't want to get involved.

I was reluctant to enter the fray, thinking that if I did I would be opening Pandora's Box. I'd most likely be drawn in, immersed in a quagmire of politics and petty bickering, exposed to not-so-hidden agendas, and become a personal target for ridicule – perhaps retribution – for offering my "solution" to the problem. What I would propose would be unpopular with those more concerned with the bottom line and profit than investing in operational safety.

I also knew my "fix" would never be adopted in the United States because to reduce the accident rate the way I would propose to do it would require a whole new paradigm. A system that is, in my mind, broken – evidenced by the continued loss of life – would need to be scrapped and replaced.

So I kept quiet, watching from afar, frustrated as I witnessed more and more HEMS crashes occurring in America, knowing I had at least one "cure" to reduce the accident rate. I knew what it took to "do it right" from what I'd seen while living and working abroad, yet I said nothing.

There *were* some operators in the States doing it right in their training and in the way they equipped the aircraft and they did not put pressure on the pilot or flight crews. But on the whole, the majority of operators were putting their flight crews in harm's way. They were sending single pilots into bad weather, virtually unarmed, with no autopilot: pilots who were not instrument proficient. Many of them not even instrument current, yet the industry was still wondering why there were so many accidents.

Most activists will tell you they became an activist quite by accident. Something happened in their lives to spark them into action. Usually they witnessed a grave injustice or an event took place that was so unfair they felt they could no longer keep silent. Once that point was reached they became driven to speak out to the decision-makers, the public, and anyone they thought could make a difference, in the hope that reason and solid, irrefutable evidence could right wrongs that catapulted them into action in the first place.

I know the exact place, time and date when I became an activist. It was as ten o'clock at night on August 31, 2010. That's the moment I learned of yet another fatal HEMS crash in America, this one in Arkansas, killing all three flight crew. There was nothing remarkable about that crash that would make it stand out from the rest. Like many of the others, marginal weather was involved. It was reported that the aircraft emerged from the overcast in pieces because the pilot lost spatial orientation in the cloud cover and lost control. That crash made it six HEMS crashes in eight months with 16 people dead.

Since taking the job with ADA I had watched as the number of HEMS crashes mounted: 68 HEMS crashes had occurred in the seven years that I have been with Abu Dhabi Aviation, killing 47 people. Sixty-eight crashes!

"When will it end?" I asked myself. "When will it ever end?"

That crash in Arkansas was the defining moment for me. It was the catalyst that set me off, launched me into motion. It was the one that *finally* caused me to snap; the crash that caused me to finally say, "Enough is enough!"

The movie producer who had purchased the movie option on my Vietnam book, *Dear Mom I'm Alive*, had emailed me to inform me about the crash. When I read his email something snapped inside me. I stood, launching myself out the door of my Van and into the humid darkness to go on a three-mile walk to think. I needed to ponder what one man could do to bring about change. What could I personally do to stop this senseless loss of life? I "got it." They didn't. I had the answer. I needed to tell them.

As I was walking – thinking – a classic scene from the motion picture *Network* kept replaying over and over in my head. A famous scene from that movie showed the newsman – played by Peter Finch – ranting in front of the TV cameras. He tells the American people, "Go to your windows, throw them open, and put your head out the window and holler, 'I'm as mad as hell and I'm not going to take this anymore!'" In the scene, people can be seen doing just that, hollering out their windows, yelling that they were mad as hell and they weren't going to take it anymore.

That's how I felt after hearing about that HEMS crash in Arkansas. "I'm as mad as hell and I'm not going to take it anymore." I really could not understand why people in America were not taking to the streets in protest over the steady loss of life in the air medical community.

I decided then and there that I needed to do whatever it took to try to get on the stage at one of the yearly air medical transport conferences back in America and deliver *my* message – a message so important that if followed I knew would reduce the accident rate and save lives. I knew my message was valid because what I had to tell the industry in the States is the way I'd seen HEMS operate safely, backed up by the other 160 ADA pilots – those 20 nationalities of pilots from all over the globe whom I worked with – who had told me that the way we do it in America wouldn't be tolerated in their countries because it was so dangerous.

I had the answer. Fly an aircraft with two pilots who are instrument rated and instrument current and instrument proficient (there's a difference) who use night vision goggles (NVGs) at night, do not land to landing areas at night that haven't been checked out during the day, and keep the medical influence on the pilot's decision making (i.e. hospital administrators, program directors, doctors, nurses, paramedics) out of the cockpit. That's one answer to drastically reduce the HEMS accident rate in America. That would be my gift to them: a surefire way to stop the loss of life if the day ever came when they finally decided enough is enough.

I was exposed to true, two-crew operations during my transition into the twenty-place Bell 214ST in the Royal Oman Police Air Wing in 1985. It opened my eyes to a whole new way of flying unlike any I had ever done in my military or my civilian flying career. I was shown a new paradigm, flying with pilot and copilot not unlike the airlines do it.

I had flown pilot and copilot in the military when I flew in Vietnam but in Vietnam the second pilot was there more for insurance in case the other pilot got shot.

The British and Australian pilots I flew with in Oman had been brought up flying regimented two-crew operations using good crew resource management (CRM) which they learned from their military flight training. Nearly every one of them had flown as a captain on the North Sea out of Aberdeen, Scotland, geographically nearly on the Arctic Circle. In doing that job they flew to offshore oil rigs sometimes hundreds of miles offshore where nearly all the flights are on an instrument flight plan. There, they operated in some of the most inhospitable and challenging weather on earth.

Crew resource management (CRM) studies the human factors that can cause aircraft accidents. In the late '60s and up to the late '70s, perfectly serviceable airliners were crashing at an alarming rate, not dissimilar to the terrible accident rate in HEMS today. The shocking number of airline crashes caused the National Transportation Safety Board (NTSB) to ask the National Aeronautics and Space Administration (NASA) to form a task force to study the problem and look into why so many airliners were crashing. What NASA uncovered was alarming. It was determined that nearly 80 percent of all aircraft accidents – dating back to 1940 when records began to be kept – had an element of human error. The task force studied airline accidents from 1968 to 1976 determining that 60 airliners crashed due to an element of human error caused by lack of leadership, communication, situational awareness and decision-making. It was then that CRM, then called Cockpit Resource Management, was born.

Today, CRM is called Crew Resource Management. While CRM is not new to the airlines, it *is* new to HEMS. In 2005 the FAA published an aviation circular AC 00-64 – Air Medical Resource Management – suggesting that HEMS crews undergo yearly air medical resource management (AMRM) training. The FAA's thinking was: if it could turn around a terrible accident rate in the airlines certainly it would work in HEMS.

The circular lays out proposed subjects and suggests areas of study. It lays out how to set up an AMRM program. As is often the case, few, if any, HEMS programs followed the FAA's advice on the subject. The FAA would need to mandate AMRM training forcing HEMS operators to adopt a program.

I was first exposed to CRM when I joined the Royal Oman Police Air Wing in 1985. Since then I've learned or read about most of the errors and pitfalls and many of the reasons we, as human beings, make mistakes. I've learned something else: The "Right Stuff" is a myth.

CRM teaches each crew member to know and understand what effect their actions or inactions have on the safe operation of any flight. Flying in a two-crew environment, the way the British taught me in the Police Air Wing, is a style of flying I hadn't been exposed to before. It took me about six months to break the old habits that I'd acquired when I flew single pilot, where I would want to take on every task myself. I had to break those habits and learn how to delegate some of the tasks to the other pilot. I had to learn how to be an integral part of the crew and become comfortable with that new role. I have to say, initially, it wasn't easy.

However, once I was comfortable with it, I found flying as part of a properly trained two-pilot crew to be much easier and a much safer way to operate an aircraft. When I finally adopted this "new" way of flying with another pilot who had also undergone crew resource management (CRM) training, I didn't want to fly any other way.

The two-crew concept is much different than one would expect because when you think of proper two-pilot operations you would be wrong in thinking it is two pilots who are used to flying an aircraft single pilot who just so happen to be flying in the same aircraft. The concept is much more than that.

In a proper two-crew cockpit the pilots operate as a well-orchestrated team that when brought together creates a synergy greater than the sum of its parts. They are two pilots who know what their roles are at any point in the flight from pre-start, start and after-start checklists, climb checks, cruise checks and pre-landing checks. They are taught to memorize the immediate actions they must perform in any emergency and what role they play in dealing with that emergency before referencing the emergency checklist. Pilots know what is expected of them using good crew resource management in normal operations and in an emergency.

When I arrived at the Police Air Wing, I had ingrained habits to break if I was going to successfully fit into a two-crew concept the way they were used to doing it. I had come from an environment where I flew single pilot IFR (instrument flight rules), using an autopilot as my "second pilot." Being alone, I had to take on every bit of the responsibility and the operation of the flight myself. I wasn't used to having a second pilot to share the workload. With a second pilot I, as captain, could concentrate on the sole task of flying the aircraft, concentrate on keeping it upright, not flying into anything, while staying situationally aware. I found that flying with another similarly trained pilot to share the workload was a much safer way to operate an aircraft than the way I'd been doing it back home.

In learning to become part of a two-crew operation I had an epiphany, a real "light-bulb," moment as they say. I could see that if a similar way of flying were mandated in the States and adopted for flying a helicopter air ambulance, there would undoubtedly be fewer accidents.

Examining the main cause of why HEMS helicopters crash, one obvious solution is easy to see: because the majority of HEMS accidents are controlled flight into terrain (CFIT) – where a pilot inadvertently flies into a cloud or fog; or on a dark, moonless night where there is no visible horizon and loses spatial orientation and crashes – it makes sense that at the very minimum it should be mandatory that every HEMS aircraft be equipped with an autopilot, like I had available in my aircraft when I flew single-pilot IFR in San Diego.

An autopilot is like having a second pilot in the cockpit to reduce the workload on a single pilot, and can be programed to fly the aircraft if you inadvertently fly into a cloud or lose spatial orientation for any reason. Having an autopilot is the only option if it isn't possible to supply a second pilot. Because the FAA knows, understands and has identified the problems as to why most HEMS helicopters crash, I cannot understand why equipping every air medical helicopter with an autopilot hasn't been mandated.

I often fantasized about what it would be like to fly on a HEMS program in America if it operated like they do it in Oman with the Police Air Wing using two pilots with an autopilot or like we did it when I flew HEMS for the king using two pilots or when flying medevac missions with the benefit of two pilots at Abu Dhabi Aviation. The advantages far outweigh the disadvantages.

The dynamics of having two pilots in the cockpit instead of just one balances the HEMS team. In many programs in America, like the ones I flew with in Houston and San Diego, the pilot is often seen as the "employee" supplied to the hospital by an outside vendor, whose job it is to keep the customer "happy." In the pilot's role the cockpit gradient sometimes referred to as the "trans-cockpit authority gradient" – that is the gradient of who is in charge in the aircraft and to what degree – may in fact be giving power to the customer (medical personnel), thus making the pilot a subordinate. This could create undue pressure that could possibly compel him to make a decision that could cause him to exceed his ability, thus causing an accident.

An example would be the pilot pushing bad weather when

he should have turned around much earlier in the flight but felt pressured to continue for some reason. The cockpit gradient between the medical staff and two pilots, on the other hand, would be balanced more on the side of the pilots – where it belongs to operate safely.

Flying with two pilots reduces the workload. Because much of the workload in the cockpit is shared, it allows each pilot to operate at a more relaxed capacity so there is less stress, thus less chance of loss of situational awareness, which is one of the primary reasons HEMS helicopters crash.

Another safety issue gained by flying two-crew is that the captain is free to fly the aircraft and not become distracted with other tasks as could happen if he were flying alone and had to fly and deal with the running of the whole flight himself. One pilot can concentrate on just flying while the other pilot takes on more responsibility with other tasks, like radio calls, programing the flight management system, monitoring the instruments, etc., thus freeing up the flying pilot to just concentrate on flying.

Having two pilots doubles the experience level brought into the cockpit. Imagine, for example, two pilots flying together who have each logged 4,000 hours in their respective careers. You have a combined 8,000 hours of flight time in the cockpit, meaning 8,000 hours of experience and 8,000 hours of problem-solving. With that experience level, more options are available to consider in any given situation whether it is in flight planning or in an emergency.

Options can be discussed between the two pilots weighing the pros and cons of any crucial decision that needs to be made, backed up with hours of experience, which would most likely result in the most considered decision being made.

Error avoidance, error trapping and mitigating error – all factors in good CRM – are much better dealt with by two pilots than by just one. Two sets of eyes and ears and two brains experienced in aviation are more likely to catch errors early on, before they become links in an error chain.

Two pilots could mean heightened vigilance. With two

pilots there is constant monitoring of what is occurring in the flight, again something pilots are taught in their CRM training. This increased vigilance helps avoid a dangerous situation before it progresses and turns into a link or links in an error chain.

Another benefit of the two-crew concept is that a more-experienced pilot can pass along his years of experience to a less-experienced copilot. Flying with a more seasoned captain allows the less-experienced pilot to learn, thus ensuring that when that experienced captain moves on, or retires, there will be someone competent to fill their shoes.

I found flying in a two-crew environment using good CRM to be much safer than flying on my own. Once I finally "got it" and later on began teaching the concept myself, I wouldn't want to fly any other way.

The downside about having two pilots in air medical programs in the States is the cost to provide it. The salary of a second pilot, additional training to keep them proficient plus the purchasing and operating costs of larger helicopters are considerations most operators cannot afford if they want to remain competitive. That fact causes the operators and medical personnel to accept a certain level of risk by not operating to the safest standard possible.

In the current climate in the HEMS industry in America, to offer a hospital a two-pilot, twin-engine machine would go against the current status quo of using single-engine aircraft flown by a single pilot. It would be too expensive for a vendor to compete against other companies vying for a HEMS contract who can (legally) offer a much cheaper option: a single-engine machine flown single pilot.

Flying a HEMS helicopter single-pilot may not be the safest option but it isn't illegal and that's a large part of the problem. It comes down to what a hospital is prepared to pay and how much it values its staff. The decision makers have to decide how much safety they want to invest in. They have to decide what is an acceptable level of risk. Empirical evidence shows me that hospital administrators are willing to accept a pretty high level of risk because HEMS helicopters keep crashing. The industry could use tough government regulation where it becomes mandatory for HEMS programs to operate with a pilot and a copilot (or that all HEMS helicopters must be fitted with an autopilot to help the pilot out if he gets himself in trouble), or the tally of lives in HEMS crashes will continue to rise.

Something I've noticed over the years that perhaps no one has thought about: Why is it that every HEMS helicopter has two medical team members? Would they ever consider flying with only one? If the answer is no – and it must be otherwise they'd be doing it – then couldn't the same argument for the use of two medical team members be used to support the argument for two pilots? After all, if the medical team makes a mistake, a critical error in judgment, it's the patient who suffers. If a single pilot makes a fatal error in judgment everyone in that aircraft suffers.

While on that three-mile walk with all these thoughts going through my mind I kept asking myself, "How am I going to get my message out there to the people it can help. What can I do personally, to try to bring about change?"

I returned back to my room in Van 17 a changed man. I was now a man on a mission to make myself heard and, hopefully, get on that stage to address those people who can make a difference. I composed an email and sent it to the producers of the Oprah Winfrey show asking for 10 minutes to get the message out to millions. (Why not aim high?) I am still, unfortunately, awaiting a reply.

I took down a copy of *The Golden Hour* from my bookshelf to take offshore with me. I wanted to re-read it, having not read what I'd written for more than two decades. After such a long break I saw the story in a new light. Two things struck me: First, how relevant it was to what was still happening. The second thing that stuck me was that it was a page-turner.

I called Kaye to tell her what had transpired. I needed her to do something for me. "Honey, get a copy of *The Golden Hour* from the bookshelf and please read it. I need you to tell me what you think, OK?"

She agreed. I called her three hours later. "Have you started reading it yet?"

"Yes, Honey, but I'm upset."

"Upset. Why?"

"Because I started reading it after you called. I began fixing dinner and I am desperate to get back to it. It's really good!"

I wrote *The Golden Hour* to highlight the practices and attitudes that if they were allowed to continue, would certainly cause more deaths. I wrote the book mainly to highlight the long duty hours and grueling 48-hour shifts the pilots were made to work, causing them to become dog-tired and less sharp in the cockpit, making them less safe. I wrote it as a way to expose an ineffectual FAA, NTSB and Congress. I also wrote it to expose the practices and attitudes that were putting pressure on the pilots to make bad decisions.

But after re-reading it I realized that when I wrote the book, I didn't have the definitive answer to the problem – an answer I would not discover until I left America and was exposed to a different paradigm – a different way to do things, a much safer way to fly. But I now had the answer to make flying in a HEMS helicopter a whole lot safer and I needed to get it out there.

I sat down and rewrote *The Golden Hour.* By this time my second book, *Dear Mom I'm Alive – Letters Home from Blackwidow 25,* had been optioned to be made into a movie. From that experience I learned what Hollywood was looking for in a story, so I wrote in a love interest for my protagonist, Billy Lee Ream, from Mineral Wells, Texas.

I also made him win in the end, something he hadn't managed to do in the first version of the book. In fact, in the first book, by fighting to change the HEMS system, he becomes blackballed in the very industry he helped to create, making his situation more disheartening. I wanted to enrage readers into action when I wrote the first version of the book. In fact, back in 1985, I didn't make the hero win because back then I didn't know *how* to make him win; but by 2010, armed with the answer, I re-wrote the ending.

I knew from personal experience how long it took to find a publisher for *Dear Mom I'm Alive.* After I signed a book contract with Avon Books in New York, I waited more than a year before the book finally saw the light of day. From writing the book, to finding a publisher, to having the first copy in my hands took 2½ years. I couldn't wait that long. In that length of time 20 or more people could lose their lives. So I paid to have the new edition of *The Golden Hour* self-published through a book printing firm in Victoria, Canada. I had copies of the *new* book in my hands in a month. Then I set about the task of writing *Journey to the Golden Hour – My Path to the Most Dangerous Job in America: Flying a Medical Helicopter.*

Journey to the Golden Hour was practically already written. After my best friend and former Army buddy, Joe Sulak, had been killed in a helicopter crash in 2008, due to a control malfunction while flying tours in Kauai, I was asked by his family to deliver his eulogy. Kaye and I went to Folsom, California, where Joe had once lived when he worked on the UC Davis Life Flight Program and where the memorial was to be held in his honor.

The gathering took place in a park near to where he used to live. As Joe was originally from Big Spring, Texas, it was a Texas-style barbecue with 60 of his close friends and family members in attendance, many of whom he had worked with when he was a HEMS pilot there.

His two grown kids, Andrew and Carrie, had laid tablecloths on several of the picnic tables and placed some of Joe's memorabilia on those tables. I had noticed a blue, dog-eared spiral notebook sitting at one end of one of the tables. I walked over and opened it up, curious as to what it was. Inside were notes Joe had written, the beginning of his autobiography he wanted to write for his new granddaughter so that she could know what kind of man he was. He never got to finish it because he died in that helicopter crash, having written only five pages and a few notes of stories he wanted to recount.

As I stood there reading his notes I felt like Joe was giving me a gentle nudge from the grave as if to say, "Come on Randy, if you're going to write your autobiography do it now. Don't wait like I did because it might be too late for you too."

So I responded to Joe's gentle nudge. I wrote my autobiography, *One Helicopter Pilot's Story*, not for public consumption but only to give to my family. Taking relevant sections from that book I wrote *Journey to the Golden Hour* in about four months.

The motivation I had to write *Journey to the Golden Hour* was to have another "go" at the HEMS industry in America by recounting my personal story, detailing the journey I took leaving the United States Army in February 1971, 13 months after leaving Vietnam, and how I would eventually become a HEMS pilot. Writing *Journey to the Golden Hour* was my chance to finally tell my non-fictional account of how it was in the early days of helicopter EMS, how dangerous it was and how I got there.

There is one chapter in that book entitled "Twenty-six Years On" that is an exposé on the industry, exposing it for what it is by describing how and why it turned so deadly. That one chapter holds the essence of why I wrote *Journey to the Golden Hour* in the first place.

Now I had two books to get out there to try to bring about change. *The Golden Hour,* with the new ending that offered a solution to the problem; and *Journey to the Golden Hour,* my non-fictional account telling it like it is in the hope it would shock people into action. With both books completed it was time to start trying to get the message out to those who are in dire need to hear it.

I knew I would not be able to manage it alone. Like the turtle you see sitting on a fencepost you just know he didn't manage to get up there by himself. I would need lots of support and help from other like-minded people if I were going to get my message out there. I'd know soon enough if I would have that support. With both books written and ready to go it was time to start making some enquiries.

The first thing I did was to go online to see if there were any other like-minded people in America who were as fed up with watching the carnage in the industry as I was. I wasn't surprised to learn that there were quite a few.

One Ezine (electronic magazine) article on HEMS immediately caught my eye. It had been written by a former HEMS pilot by the name of Byron Edgington, a former Vietnam helicopter pilot who had flown HEMS for 20 years and had since retired.

His excellent article, "How to Fix the Helicopter EMS Accident Rate," mentioned many of the "fixes" to the industry that I wanted to see implemented. Byron was the first person I contacted to see if we could form an alliance.

I sent him an email to say I'd read his article and that I believed wholeheartedly in everything he'd written. I asked him if he would like to read a copy of *The Golden Hour.* He said that he would so I sent him a copy. I also sent him a copy of *Journey to the Golden Hour.*

He wrote back to say that he thoroughly enjoyed reading both books and to say that things hadn't changed much since I wrote *The Golden Hour* all those years ago. He said he saw many of the same characters, hospital administrators, programs directors, etc., in the programs where he had worked. He said the attitudes I wrote about, for the most part, are alive and well in the industry. I suspected as much, but Byron confirmed it. He would not be the only person to do so.

Several months later, Byron emailed me with a proposal that would be the ignition – the spark – that would launch me on my mission to become heard and deliver my lifesaving message. He said he'd been approached by a Mr. Fred Jones, President of the Helicopter Association of Canada (or HAC, as it's referred to by its members), asking him if he would be the keynote speaker at their annual meeting to be held in Vancouver at the end of March 2011. Byron told Fred that he had prior commitments but he put my name forward with my contact details.

Fred Jones called me the following day.

I asked Fred over the phone, "How many people will I be talking to?"

"About five-hundred."

"Five hundred?" I said, trying to sound as if I were casually making a note of it. What I was really thinking which was "Holy shit!"

"Would you be willing to do it?" he asked.

"On what date would I be speaking?"

"The conference will start March twenty-fifth and end on the twenty-seventh. You'd be speaking on the twenty-sixth."

I did a quick mental calculation. "Yep, that'll work. I'll be home on rotation from my job at Abu Dhabi Aviation. What would you want me to talk about?"

"Safety, of course. That's a given. But how about a speech on working through these tough economic times?"

"Great. Yep, sure I can do that," I said.

Fred continued, "Alison DeGroot, the associate publisher at *Helicopters* magazine, will be contacting you to sort out the details. *Helicopters* magazine will be sponsoring you. You should hear from her shortly."

"Great, Fred. Thanks for the opportunity. I won't let you down."

"Well, Byron told me you've been around the traffic pattern a few times. Your CV is impressive. I'm looking forward to meeting you in person."

"Same here, Fred."

"By the way, Randy, you ever speak in front of a large audience before?"

I hadn't but I didn't want to let on and possibly blow this opportunity with him. Thinking I could handle it I said, "Well, I used to speak to hospital groups and first responders when I was chief pilot of the Life Flight program in San Diego. I see no problem, Fred." I needed to put his mind at ease.

"Good, great, terrific to hear. Well, as I said, Alison will contact you shortly to firm up the details. Looking forward to meeting you, Randy."

"Same here, Fred. Bye," I said and hung up the phone.

I took a moment to go over what had been said.

Five-hundred people.

Hmmmmm ....
Five-hundred people.
Hmmmmm ... Five-hundred people.
No problem.

%

Alison DeGroot, managed to contact me after I returned to Abu Dhabi to do another six-week tour. We'd made arrangements for me to call her, which I did on my cell phone while on an oil accommodation platform in the Persian Gulf. We spoke for an hour.

I knew one of the reasons she wanted to speak to me was to find out whether I could string a coherent sentence together before she committed to sponsoring me to speak at the Helicopter Association of Canada convention. During that phone conversation I felt I was being given a job interview from halfway around the world. All went well, though, and a deal was struck.

I didn't want to think about what that conversation would cost on my cell phone bill. It wasn't important. What *was* important was to get on that stage.

Transportation and accommodation at the Gateway Hotel in Vancouver was to be provided for Kaye and for me. My speaking fee would be the equivalent of $11,000 – not in cash, but in half-page ads in *Helicopters* magazine advertising my books for three months.

The magazine would also stock and sell my books in its Annex Bookshop. Fred Jones said he wanted to purchase 50 books that I would sign and hand out to the first 50 members who came to the HAC booth on the convention floor. I could then continue selling books after the first 50 were handed out.

I had never spoken to a group so large and I knew that helicopter pilots can be a pretty tough audience because they are all extremely individualistic and opinionated.

Someone once said that trying to organize helicopter pilots is like trying to herd cats. That's one of the reasons there isn't a large helicopter union in the States, whereas the airline pilots have had a union for years. If there were an industry-wide union for helicopter pilots it would give them a strong collective voice to force safety changes in the HEMS industry in America, and they wouldn't be putting themselves and their passengers at such risk.

I wrote my keynote address when I wasn't flying on my six-week tour in Abu Dhabi, putting the speech on 3" x 5" note cards as bullet points. Then I practiced it over and over, timing my delivery to fit the 50-minute time slot I'd been allotted. Luckily the Toastmasters training that I'd had when I retired for that short time in San Diego was beginning to pay off.

///

I wrote to several other people I had found online who were championing the cause to try to increase safety in the HEMS system: CNN anchor, blogger and aviation journalist, Christine Negroni, is a strong advocate for HEMS safety; Lisa Tofil, a lawyer working impossibly long hours in Washington to draft a bill looking after patients' rights on helicopter flights; Tom Judge, Executive Director of Life Flight of Maine and former head of the Association of Air Medical Services; Kent Johnson, the past president of the National EMS Pilots Association (NEMSPA); Ron Fergie, also a past president of the National EMS Pilots Association, and Rex Alexander, then president of NEMSPA.

I contacted them, then sent each of them copies of *The Golden Hour* and *Journey to the Golden Hour* and was told – like Byron Edgington had told me after reading them – that many of the attitudes and practices were "still out there." Kent Johnson arranged for the two books to be advertised on the home page of the National EMS Pilots Association website.

Another fellow by the name of Ron Whitney was a HEMS pilot and the editor of a publication called *Rotorcraft Pro Magazine*. I sent Ron a copy of each book and after he read them he contacted me asking if I would like to sell copies of my books at the upcoming HELI-EXPO (the largest helicopter convention in the world) sponsored by the Helicopter Association International. It was going to be held in Orlando, Florida, March 5-8, 2011. It was going to take place 18 days before I was scheduled to give my keynote address in Canada. I gladly accepted his offer, jumping at this first opportunity to get my books and my new message out there.

I arranged to have an assortment of 90 books shipped to the hotel that I'd booked in Orlando. Copies of *Dear Mom I'm Alive, The Golden Hour* and *Journey to the Golden Hour* would be waiting for me when I checked in. As the dates for HELI-EXPO dovetailed with the beginning of my leave from Abu Dhabi, I planned on stopping in Orlando on my way home at the end of my six-week tour.

After a 27-hour journey from the Middle East I rented a car and booked into the hotel in Orlando where I arranged to stay near the convention center. I called Ron Whitney to say I'd arrived in town.

"Good to hear you made it back from the Middle East, Randy. Say listen, I've arranged through the National EMS Pilots Association for you to sell your books at their booth. Because your message is geared toward HEMS safety I spoke with Rex Alexander, the current NEMSPA president, and he ran it by the board and they approved that you can sell books from their booth."

"Terrific, Ron, I look forward to meeting him.'

"I've arranged a pass for you to get into the convention hall with no out-of-pocket expense to you. Rex and the team are anxious to meet you face-to-face. If you can meet up with them around eleven tomorrow they'll be expecting you. Good luck!"

I was pretty jet lagged – make that *real* jet lagged – but I was on a high thinking about this great opportunity to finally be given a venue to get the updated *The Golden Hour* and *Journey to the Golden Hour* into the public's hands.

I worked from the NEMSPA booth for three days, speaking to people who would pass by, while selling and signing my books. I managed to sell every one of them.

Working the booth were Ron Fergie, who had been the past president of NEMSPA, and the current President of NEMPSA, Rex Alexander.

I had long conversations with Ron and Rex in an effort to bring myself up to speed as to what was going on in the industry. I had this drive, this passion deep in my gut to deliver my lifesaving message but I had not been actively involved with the industry since leaving San Diego for Oman 25 years prior. I needed to re-educate myself to try to understand the politics going on in the industry. Sure, I had witnessed from afar – from Oman, Saudi Arabia, Canada and Abu Dhabi – that helicopters kept crashing and people kept dying and it appeared to me it was the same scenario over and over again. I needed to know *why* it had been allowed to continue.

Ron Fergie told me that while he was reading *The Golden Hour* he realized that a lot of the same attitudes that were prevalent 25 years ago are still out there in some programs. He said the industry hadn't changed much in that regard since I flew HEMS back in the '80s despite those prevailing attitudes. He told me, "The industry's made many positive changes over the years but it still has a long way to go."

I had suspected as much but I was still disheartened to hear it from someone so knowledgeable of the industry. What he said was confirmed by Rex Alexander. As members of the National EMS Pilots Association they were still fighting a battle to make the industry safe. They told me they appreciated my efforts to bring about change. I thanked them for giving me the opportunity, hoping to keep up the momentum.

CHAPTER 15
The First Step to Delivering a Crucial Message

The Pan Pacific Hotel, with its distinctive five sails, is situated on the Vancouver waterfront next to the convention center where I would be speaking. The room that Kaye and I were given was magnificent, offering a stunning view of the mountains, the harbor, Stanley Park and the city skyline.

As Kaye was standing at the window looking out at the spectacular view I came up behind her, placed my arms around her waist and kissed her lightly on the cheek. "Thinking about your grandma and your family members when you were growing up again?"

"Afraid so, Mr. Mains. They'd love this." She turned to face me and said with mock sternness, "I would like to know who gave you permission to turn my life upside down so?"

"I didn't know I needed permission."

"Well you do. So please check with me next time," she paused for a moment then said, "You nervous about tomorrow?"

"Nope."

"Not even a little bit?"

"Honestly no. Not even a little bit. I feel it's such an important message I need to deliver and this is such an important first step for me – where I hope to eventually get on that stage in the States at one of the air-medical conferences to address the people who really need it. I really can't wait to speak tomorrow."

"In front of five-hundred people?"

"The more the better. Luckily, I've landed right in the

middle of friendly territory so this'll be a good warm-up for hopefully better things to come."

Kaye understood what I meant about landing in "friendly territory." She knew that one of my arguments for making HEMS safe in America was to do it as they do it in Canada. In Canada, HEMS programs fly two-crew, pilot and copilot, who are instrument rated and current. Many of the crews use, or are planning to use, night vision goggles (NVGs). The pilots are not allowed to land at unprepared landing sites that haven't been checked out during the day and, mainly because of the nature of their healthcare system, there is no influence whatsoever over decisions made in the cockpit from medical personnel, medical directors or hospital administrators. Because there is no pressure on the flight crews to pick up patients to bring in revenue – like there is in the States where healthcare is a business – there is no pressure that can filter down to the Canadian pilots that could cause them to make unsafe decisions.

Kaye said, "I think I'm more anxious about tomorrow than you are, Mr. Mains, and you're the one who has to get up in front of all those people."

"Yes, I do believe you are more anxious about it than I am."

She knew that for the past four days I'd been practicing my 50-minute keynote speech three or four times a day in my small study addressing a make-believe audience of 500. I hadn't wanted Kaye to hear it. I wanted her to hear it for the first time when I delivered it. Unsure of what I was going to say or how I was going to say it, I think that's why she was more nervous than I was.

We both knew what a big deal this was. Succeeding in Canada could launch my speaking career on HEMS safety. If I bombed, well, it could very well be the end. We both knew so much was riding on my success, not only for me, but for those in need of my lifesaving message.

The room where I was to deliver my keynote address was long and narrow. One wall running the length of the room was floor to ceiling glass windows overlooking the water and the mountains.

Five hundred people, mostly men – helicopter pilots, helicopter company owners, journalists, aircraft and engine manufacturers, and engineers – sat 12 to a table eating lunch. At our table; Alison DeGroot, associate publisher at *Helicopters* magazine, the woman who had done the phone interview with me when I was offshore in Abu Dhabi, was sitting next to Kaye who was to my right.

The small stage and podium sat some distance back from the first row of tables, which I found distracted a bit from the intimacy between the speaker and the audience. There was a disquieting echo in the room, too. Not the best acoustical setup, but it would work.

Two video-camera teams were ready to film the keynote speech that was about to be announced. I thought, "Well, here goes. The moment I've been waiting for has finally arrived. It's show time!"

Matt Nichols, editor of *Helicopters* magazine, took the podium. The 500 attendees who had by now finished lunch fell silent. Matt introduced himself and proceeded to read my bio. As he did, Kaye reached across, squeezing my leg as a way to offer her support. I placed my hand on top of hers and gave it a gentle squeeze.

I could feel the cameras tracking me as I switched on my lapel microphone and took the podium, thanked Matt, and then I began to deliver the speech that I had spent so many hours preparing for.

Glancing down at Kaye sitting at a front table with Alison DeGroot and several others, she smiled, nodded and unconsciously held her clasped hands under her chin as if she were praying. I was fine. A little nervous at first gazing out at all those expectant faces, but I was fine.

The 50 minutes passed by quickly. I told a few humorous anecdotes that, thankfully, brought a few laughs. After about five minutes I knew I'd be OK because I sensed I had them on my side.

Kaye told me later that when I recounted my 10-minute war story, taken from my book *Dear Mom I'm Alive*, about a mission I'd flown in Vietnam that had turned into a living nightmare, she said the room was so silent she felt that everyone was holding their breath.

The story I recalled was how at 22 years old I'd dropped off a four-man recon team into a hover hole surrounded by 100-foot high jungle and how, after I'd departed, they became pinned down by the enemy so I'd gone back in after them. My feeling at the time was that I had put them in there so it was my job to get them out.

Trying to ascend to clear the 100-foot trees after picking the team up, we were being shot at by the enemy from below; I was running out of power, which made it impossible for the helicopter to make it the last 25 feet to clear the trees around us. With two gunships firing rockets on either side of our ship – "Whoomp, whomph, whomph" – my gunner and crew chief firing their M-60s at the enemy below, the four recon team members I'd picked up firing down at the enemy, as well as the two F-4 Phantom Jets dropping their sortie of napalm on either side of me to help keep the enemy's heads down – "Whooommmphhhh, whoooommmmmphhhh!" – when it looked like that was how I was going to die, hovering there, unable to climb, sitting like a tin duck in a shooting gallery, I kicked in right pedal to deliver horsepower to the main rotor, causing us to spin but allowing us to clear the trees to fly away to safety. I told the audience that for that mission I'd been awarded the Distinguished Flying Cross.

I recounted how it transpired that I was speaking to them today. I told them how, on August 31 of 2010, seven months previously, I had heard of yet another HEMS crash – the one in Arkansas that killed three crew members – and how I'd thrust myself out the door of Van 17 in Abu Dhabi, enraged, asking myself what one man could do to bring about change. What could I *personally* do to bring about change?

I told them how the scene from the movie *Network* kept replaying in my mind where Peter Finch's character rants on national TV and tells Americans to, "Go to your windows, throw them open, put your head out the window and holler, 'I'm as mad as hell and I'm not going to take this anymore!' "

I told the audience how I had come back to my room after that walk and emailed Oprah Winfrey. They laughed when I told them I was still waiting for her to get back to me. I told them about rewriting *The Golden Hour* to make the protagonist win, with the new ending I wrote that throws it right back on how they do it in Canada: i.e., the right way, the way we should be doing it in America.

I spoke about my mission to bring about change in a broken HEMS system in the States. I mentioned how, on that night, I became an activist for change. I told them about writing *Journey to the Golden Hour* as yet another way to drive home the message to the American public that they needed to change a deadly system that was broken and how the answer is supplied in that book.

The 50 minutes passed by quickly. When I had finished I thanked them and to my great surprise everyone in the room rose and gave me a standing ovation.

I signed and gave away my books that Fred Jones had purchased to give away as gifts to the first 50 members visiting the Helicopter Association of Canada (HAC) booth. I sold about 50 more after that.

Many of the attendees stopped by the booth where I was doing book signings to shake my hand and to tell me how much they had enjoyed my speech.

Kaye and I must have spoken to what seemed like all 500 members while she collected the money and I chatted to the person I was signing a book for.

There was one man who came by the booth on several

occasions. His name was Jack Todaro, business and marketing manager for Oregon Aero, a company that designs and manufactures aircraft seats for military and civilian aircraft. They also fabricate aircraft interiors and are well known for seat cushions specially designed to relieve the stress in a pilot's back, which can suffer a lot of abuse when flying.

When Jack told us his age, Kaye and I were both taken aback. He said he was over 70 but to outward appearances he had the manner and carriage of a man decades younger.

We couldn't have known then how significantly Jack would figure in our lives.

Another individual stands out in my mind. He was a pilot serving with the Canadian Armed Forces on leave from flying Blackhawks in Afghanistan. He came up to have a book signed, to shake my hand and to deliver a message.

"I just wanted you to know that right pedal trick still works. I've used it in Afghanistan several times. And I want to thank you for your service so many years ago in Vietnam."

"And thank you for yours. And thanks for taking the time to stop by."

///

Kaye told me later that day, when we were standing on the waterfront outside the convention center, that she'd been really nervous for me as I took the stage, but from the first words I spoke I didn't look or sound nervous at all, which put her at ease. "You looked like Clint bloody Eastwood up there." She told me, using British slang.

"Yeah, it felt real good. Really good, in fact. Wonder what's next in our future?"

The answer to that question would shock us both.

Crew members of the HEMS helicopter that crashed in bad weather in Arkansas August 31st 2010.

Pilot Ken Roberson, Flight Nurse Kenneth Meyer, Flight Paramedic Gayla Gregory

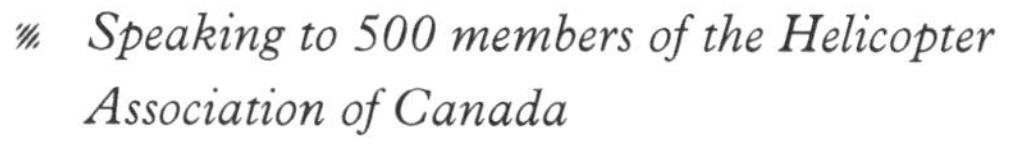

Speaking to 500 members of the Helicopter Association of Canada

Recounting the Vietnam story where I am almost shot down to 500 people at the Helicopter Association of Canada convention.

CHAPTER 16
The Abu Dhabi Continuum

Mohammad Khitiri, the flight ops inspector who had revoked my TRI/TRE certification because ADA's head of training, Mike Burke, had not agreed to supply him with a free helicopter to do his flight training, suffered five heart attacks. It was reported that he died twice on the table, meaning his heart stopped and the medical team managed to get it started again.

I heard the news from Mike Burke. It still angered me to think back on how Khitiri had made my life so miserable by his abuse of power, revoking my TRI/TRE certification after I'd put myself through so much stress to ensure I would pass it. Khitiri's karmic train had finally pulled into the station. Overkill to be sure, but his medical condition signaled the end of his aviation career.

With Khitiri out of the picture, Mike Burke and the No. 2 in training, Pat Smith, saw this as an excellent opportunity to re-request that I be made a TRI/TRE. The approval came back within days. Apparently my paperwork was still on Khitiri's desk, which streamlined the process.

When Mike and Pat told me the news that I had been reinstated, I was jubilant. I went to the bottle shop and bought two bottles of Moët & Chandon and gave each man a bottle as my way to show my gratitude.

In mid-August 2010, seven months before giving my speech in Vancouver for the HAC, while home on my six-week leave, I received a frantic phone call from Mike asking me if I could fly back to Abu Dhabi early to train to become a flight simulator instructor and flight simulator examiner, SFI/SFE. Mike hit me with the news that Dennis Troup, my good friend and ADA's head of training in the Bell 412EP flight simulator, had been diagnosed with leukemia and had to begin chemotherapy immediately.

Making the situation more pressing, 50 new pilots needed to be trained for the new Saudi HEMS contract that ADA had landed. Hearing the news about Dennis came as a blow but I leapt at the opportunity.

ADA had been training pilots for about two years in the flight simulator, often referred to as "the sim," after "the crash that didn't happen." It had always been a dream of mine to finish out my flying career by "giving back" and teaching in the sim. I had, of course, been an instructor and flight examiner in a "real" aircraft and I knew the value of the flight simulator training because you can do so much more in the sim than you can in a real aircraft.

The Level-D flight simulator in Dubai is a $14-million, full-motion state-of-the-art training device that rents out for $2,000 an hour. It is fully certified by aviation agencies from several countries: e.g., the FAA in the States, the CAA in England and Transport Canada. After a pilot is trained in the sim all they have to do is have one flight in a real aircraft and to be shown the walk-around preflight inspection.

In the sim, an instructor can give more than 180 emergencies and that doesn't include variations in the weather conditions. He can make it a sunny day or take the ceiling and visibility all the way down to zero-zero in fog where you can't see more than a few feet down the runway. An operator can give moderate to severe turbulence, lightning, simulated rain, wet runway – the works. When a pilot lands the sim on the runway you can even hear and feel the metal skids sliding along metal against tarmac.

Things can be done in the flight simulator that can be quite frightening, like simulating the loss of a tail rotor where it departs the aircraft or making the tail rotor stop turning altogether: both emergencies cause the aircraft to spin to the right uncontrollably.

The sim can simulate the loss of engine or transmission pressure, high temperature, gearbox failures, hydraulic failures, driveshaft failures, electrical failures, engine fires, baggage fire – all with the associated bumping, grinding and vibrations you'd hear and feel in the actual aircraft if it were happening.

The flight simulator experience creates its own reality. That's because when you go flying in a *real* aircraft you are not expecting problems to occur. When a pilot has a session in the flight simulator that pilot *knows* there's going to be a problem – probably a lot of problems. This fact often makes pilots quite nervous because a session in the sim can find weaknesses in a pilot's ability that could easily be missed when giving a checkride in a real aircraft.

Many of the emergencies an operator can give a pilot would be impossible to simulate in a real aircraft because it would be too dangerous or impossible to do without killing everyone on board. So in the sim, pilots have to demonstrate skill and judgment when dealing with emergencies they would never be able to practice in a real aircraft. That is why even the most competent pilot becomes a *little* nervous when training or doing a checkride in the sim.

Some events in the sim can be quite frightening to pilots. Even though they know they are sitting in a building in Dubai they soon become wrapped up in the moment and, to them, the flight becomes real.

Probably the scariest thing I see in the sim is when a pilot "loses it" in the clouds while flying on instruments. He loses spatial orientation and loses control of the aircraft. It doesn't happen often but it does happen, usually if he is made to hand-fly the aircraft as he would during a failure of the autopilot. If a pilot loses control it serves to humble him and – unfortunately – the experience can destroy a bit of his confidence because before it happened he thought he was invincible. It's an attitude, unfortunately, that many HEMS pilots have before actually "losing it" for real in the clouds before crashing.

If a pilot inadvertently flies into the clouds and has to suddenly transition from visual flight onto the instruments, it takes a proficient pilot about 40 seconds to one minute before he has the situation fully under control. A pilot who is *not* instrument rated, *not* current and not *proficient*, will most likely crash if hand-flying the machine. I have seen quite a few pilots "die" in the sim, that is, get a red screen – which occurs when they crash along with the accompanying sound – which is something that can be quite frightening.

That is why a HEMS pilot back in the States must have an instrument rating but more importantly, it's imperative he must be current and *proficient* to fly by sole reference to the instruments. What that means is that a pilot must keep practicing – and practice often – to ensure he doesn't lose his instrument flying skills. Any pilot will tell you that flying on instruments is a skill that degrades very quickly if not routinely practiced.

The FAA has documented that – of those pilots who have lost control of an aircraft and died while inadvertently flying into instrument conditions – 25 percent of those pilots held an instrument rating. The Aircraft Owners and Pilots Association reported a much higher percentage saying, "That 43 percent of the pilots who inadvertently ran into IMC and had accidents were instrument rated." Once a pilot flies into inadvertent instrument meteorological conditions (IIMC) – that is, the pilot accidentally flies into a cloud – he now has to join the instrument system. That's when it becomes dangerous.

When a pilot is flying visually, flying according to visual flight rules (VFR), he is in effect "off road." If he enters a cloud or loses the horizon, like on a black night with no moon and has to reference the flight instruments to keep the aircraft upright, he now must get the aircraft on a published instrument route that has protected airspace well clear of all obstacles. He must join the instrument flight rules (IFR) system set up for flying on instruments.

Think of the IFR system as established highways in the sky called "airways." The pilot can follow these airways using his radio navigation instruments to get him to somewhere where he can do an instrument approach down to a minimum descent altitude or decision altitude where, hopefully, he will break out of the clouds, see the ground and land safely.

Whenever I see a pilot enter a cloud who has weak instrument flying skills while hand flying the machine, it can be a sobering, often frightening experience for that pilot.

I have often thought it would be a good idea to allow the medical crews back home to go into the sim so they can experience firsthand what it is like to fly in clouds or on a dark night with no visible horizon by sole reference to the flight instruments. Put them in the pilot's seat to let them get a good taste for what the pilot sees feels and experiences. It would give them a healthy respect for weather and may even cause them to request that a helicopter be turned around sooner on a real HEMS mission.

I have a simple method for determining if a pilot passes or fails his checkride: I ask myself, "Would I put my precious wife Kaye in the back of the helicopter, confident that the pilot will bring her back home to me safely?"

The full-motion flight simulator is the best training tool I have ever used. I flew a full-motion flight simulator for the first time in Fort Worth, Texas, back in 1982 when I met David Sutcliffe when he and I flew in the Bell 222 sim together. I had to obtain my helicopter instrument rating in it. I was told by Bell Helicopter at the time that I was the first American to receive my civilian helicopter instrument rating based on a flight simulator. The checkride I had to pass to get it was the checkride from hell. After it was over a picture was taken for the Bell newsletter touting the achievement. In that picture I looked like I'd done 15 rounds in the ring with a heavyweight prizefighter. The pressure and the effort totally wrung me out.

Acquiring the HEMS contract in Saudi Arabia came just in time for Abu Dhabi Aviation. The company had recently lost the lucrative oil contact in Zakum Field that, for 30 years, had been a cash cow. The Saudi contract would serve to fill up the coffers that had been steadily decreasing.

The chief pilot, Bill Lee, approached me one day with a question. Bill was my vintage. We'd both flown helicopters in Vietnam about the same time and had often flown together while at ADA.

Anytime Bill had a question for me it always made me nervous. That's because he usually asked me to perform some herculean task. The last time he had a question for me he asked me how long I had on a particular hitch before going on leave and I told him, "I have two weeks, Bill."

"Great, then would you mind writing an SOP that a new pilot can look at that will tell him *everything* he needs to know about all the operations we do offshore?"

"Bill, are you kidding me? Do you know how much information that is?"

"No, but you will."

He handed me Sumo's notes that he had kept in a blue spiral notebook similar to the notebook my friend Joe Sulak had used to begin writing his autobiography. I took the notebook from Bill and paged through it. His notes seemed thorough enough.

Bill told me, "I'll take you off the flying program for a week. You can have the office in contracts. Use the computer in there."

It *was* summer and hot, real hot out there. And humid too. We had no air conditioning in the aircraft. Let's see. Sit in a cool office for a week or fly offshore doing 45 to 50 takeoffs and landings six or seven hours a day in 110° F and 85-percent humidity. Even though it was a mammoth task, I agreed to do it.

I had a 60-page SOP done in five days.

Now he was going to ask me *another* question.

It started with the usual inquiry, "How long do you have on this hitch"

"I go on leave in six days, Bill"

"You've heard about the Saudi EMS contract right?"

"Yep."

"Well it begins in seven days. With your HEMS background I thought you would be the perfect man to write the SOP for it."

"Bill, did you hear me? I go on leave in six days." I held my two hands with six fingers showing. "Count 'em, six days."

"You can use the contracts office again. The first day you and Herbert Brantle can get your heads together. The second day you can have Philip Marshall. The last three days you can have Wayne Handley to help you finish it up."

Admittedly three very experienced HEMS guys. Herbert and Philip had been HEMS pilots for 15 years in Germany flying two-crew using night vision goggles in a Bell 412. They certainly knew how to do it safely and the right way. Wayne, a Canadian, was also used to doing it right, having flown the Bell 222 IFR in Canada. It certainly was a good team.

I said, "Bill, can I write the SOP any way I want to, that is, to make it as safe as it *should* be?"

"Yep, here," he handed me two folders. "Here is the SOP that the last contract used. And here's CHC's SOP."

I knew that Canadian Holding Company, or CHC, operates helicopters in more than 30 countries, operating to a world-class safety standard.

"But Bill, how can you expect us to write an SOP when we haven't been on the contract. Of course I've been in Jeddah before but that was flying HEMS for the king. This is totally different."

"Just do the best you can, Randy. I'm sure you'll do OK."

"And I can write it any way I want? As safe as I want?"

"Be my guest."

"OK, I'll do it."

In five days Herbert, Phillip, Wayne and I hammered out an SOP for the Saudi contract just the way we'd want to fly it. Of course it would be two pilots who were instrument rated and current. I mandated use of NVGs because I knew how dark it can be in Saudi and how many towers, wires and obstacles there are. We wrote that no landings would be allowed at night to landing sites unless a full recce had been done during the day. There would be no problems keeping the medical influence out of the cockpit because the Saudis had unlimited funding, so there was no pressure to bring in patients as revenue to pay for the service. I handed the completed SOP to Bill at the end of office hours on the fifth day.

Six months later I asked several of the pilots working on the contract if they had seen the SOP. They told me they hadn't. They said no one had seen it.

Great!

Most helicopter companies I've worked for *react;* they don't plan. In this case, Abu Dhabi Aviation was no different. They secured a lucrative HEMS contract in Saudi, then it appeared as if management just woke up one day and said "Hey, wait a minute. We need fifty pilots."

Let the fire drill begin! The thing is it wasn't *my* fire drill. But it would become mine.

Bud Jarvis, Philippe Berling and I were the main sim instructors who would train the majority of the new pilots hired for the Saudi HEMS contract. There would always be two instructors in country while we rotated through our respective work-and-leave cycles.

Abu Dhabi Aviation needed copilots for the Saudi operation and, to their great credit, they decided to bring in some new blood to the organization by hiring pilots who had recently acquired their airline transport license. Many of them had never flown a turbine-engine helicopter let alone a medium-twin engine helicopter like the Bell 412EP. It was a gamble for the company because of the expense to train them, and because it was a pretty big step for these guys, many of them coming from a Robinson R-22 background.

To our great delight they did just fine. In fact, ironically, the few pilots who didn't make it through the training were the older, supposedly more experienced pilots.

The new pilots who had only flown single-pilot had to learn how to operate in a two-crew environment; a major step for them. For example, when the copilot read from the checklist and came to the part where it said, Captain's Brief, the guys who'd only flown single-pilot were at a loss as to what to say. Understandably, most of them were not clear about their roles when flying as captain or copilot. So I came up with a training device so simple I was actually shocked at how effectively it taught them two-crew ops. This high-tech training device is called a "couch."

Philippe Berling would fly his two new pilots on the evening sessions and I would fly my two guys on the morning sessions. When Philippe and I had time between sessions to talk we both remarked how the new pilots didn't know what to do in their respective roles. So I came up with a plan.

When we were not in the sim I brought Philippe's two guys and my two guys to my hotel room where we stayed during training. On the wall in my room, I put a poster of the Bell 412EP cockpit that I'd taken from the Flight Safety Training Manual. Swinging around the couch to face the wall, I had one of the new pilots sit next to me on my left, while I sat in the captain's seat to his right. I had the other three pilots sit behind us to observe.

The copilot would read the pre-start, start and after-start checklist and I would show him what the captain should be doing and what he should be saying. Then I gave him the captain's brief before takeoff. I told him to envision from the point of hovering, to accelerating, to climbing, to leveling off and what he would say. It would sound something like this.

"OK, we'll be doing an IFR Alpha 31 departure to Zakum Field. I want you to call out airspeed alive, TDP (takeoff decision point) at 45 knots, Vy (best rate of climb speed) at 70 knots.

"If an emergency occurs *below* 500 feet no switches will

be switched until mutually confirmed *except* for an engine fire in which case I want you to pull the illuminated T-handle for that engine and fire the fire bottle.

"If we have an emergency *above* 500 feet I will do the initial actions and I will call for follow-up actions as per the checklist.

"I want you to call 1,000, 500 and 100 feet from assigned altitudes.

"Please advise me plus or minus 10 knots from my assigned airspeed, plus or minus 10 degrees from my assigned heading, plus or minus 100 feet on my assigned altitude. It you see anything you don't like or have a question about anything please bring it up and we'll discuss it.

"Any questions?"

Then we would do an imaginary flight to include takeoff and climb out. During the climb I would announce that we had an engine fire, talking them through the emergency. I had the new pilots rotate into the left seat as the imagined flight progressed. As they made the mock radio calls I would also act as air traffic control, giving instructions and answering back. We'd do a whole flight that way, requesting radar vectors for an ILS (instrument landing system) approach for runway 31 back at Abu Dhabi while on single-engine.

We would practice doing all the checks, imagining that nothing could be seen of the runway environment at the decision height at 200 feet. Then we'd imagine doing a single-engine go-around using the go-around button on the collective pitch lever and climb for another approach doing radio calls, checks, everything just like the flight in the sim, except we'd be doing it while sitting on the couch in my hotel room.

The results Philippe and I saw after that session were astonishing. It was like the four new pilots had been struck by lightning. They "got it." I was amazed. So was Philippe. After that initial session in the room with the couch and the picture on the wall of the cockpit layout of the Bell 412EP, we included it in our training with all the new pilots.

I found it funny that we could get so much accomplished

using a $400 couch. I wondered how many couches you could buy with $14 million, the price of the flight simulator. Probably a lot.

///

The Air Medical Transport Conference for the next year, 2011, was going to take place in St. Louis, Missouri. It was my first opportunity to try to get on the stage at one of these annual aeromedical conferences to deliver what I knew to be a lifesaving message. I was told I had the support of the guys with the National EMS Pilots Association whom I'd met in Orlando at the HAI HELI-EXPO, where I'd sold 90 copies of my books. All I had to do was to send in an application to be considered for a keynote speaking position, which I did. I couldn't help but wonder what chance I'd have as I'd been out of HEMS flying in the States for so long. One thing's for certain, like winning the lottery, you'll never have a chance to win unless you buy a ticket.

In my application I was asked to supply a video tape or a CD of keynote speeches I'd done in the past plus any recommendations from those who'd heard me speak. I sent in the taped speech of the keynote address I'd given in Vancouver at the Helicopter Association of Canada convention, plus a glowing recommendation of my speaking ability written by Alison DeGroot, the associate publisher of *Helicopters* magazine.

I sent in all the requested information and waited. If ever there were a moment to find a four-leaf clover, polish my lucky horseshoe, stroke a rabbit's foot, this was it. I knew I was an unknown commodity in the HEMS community, having been out of HEMS flying in the States for 27 years. But I felt it all came down to this one moment. If I could just get on that stage and deliver my message I would be satisfied that I had at least tried. What the audience members decided to do with the knowledge I would give them would be up to them.

I also had an idea how to graphically show the audience members how many people the industry had lost since I wrote

The Golden Hour. At the time, 358 people had lost their lives in aeromedical helicopter crashes, leaving nearly 600 crash survivors. I couldn't remember wanting anything more than I wanted this.

I received acknowledgment via email by Ms. Natasha Ross, CMP Director of Education and Events at the Association of Air Medical Services (AAMS) that my application to speak had been received.

There was nothing else I could do but just sit, hope and wait.

CHAPTER 17

September 18, 2011 • St. Louis, Missouri

Air Medical Transport Conference

Standing on stage in front of 700 air-medical professionals I could see Kaye sitting in the front row. I imagined she was holding her breath while I got started, knowing what an important moment this was for both of us.

The glare of the spotlights, the huge video screens on either side of me projecting my image to the audience, and a sea of expectant faces listening very intently ....

The organizers of the Air Medical Transport Conference had paid to fly me from Abu Dhabi to St. Louis to deliver my safety message – a message that had been locked inside me since I began flying with the British pilots in Oman back in 1985.

My voice echoed off the walls and ceiling of the cavernous room, enveloping the early-morning audience. I secretly wondered whether I was overstepping my bounds. Would I go too far with my message? Would I create dissention or anger in the ranks, or turn them all against me when they finally heard what I had to say?

From all that I had seen, lived and experienced since leaving America more than 27 years ago, I felt I was delivering a message so important and so timely that, if adopted and embraced by those in the industry, it would most assuredly stem the tragic flow of blood, suffering, pain and death that I'd witnessed for over three decades.

I'd worked so hard to get up on this stage. Of course I couldn't have done it alone. That fact, in itself, was heartening because it signaled to me that people were ready to listen. Perhaps people had finally had enough and, dare I say it, were ready to make a change.

So there I was, addressing the decision-makers, pilots, flight nurses, doctors, hospital nurses, respiratory therapists, communications specialists, dispatchers, emergency medical technicians, paramedics, program directors, and coordinators, to try to convince them there is a better way to do it without sacrificing lives. For I had witnessed it outside America and I was there to bring them the "good news," eager to share with them what I had witnessed while away, hoping they would understand and fully embrace my message. It was a wonderfully sweet moment. It was also a very scary moment. How would they react? I'd know soon enough.

I worried my message would be unpopular because implementing my cure would cost the helicopter operators lots of money – money that would need to be shaved from their bottom lines. My "cure" would mean battling one of the greatest of human motivators of all, what I would later call the 500-pound bacterium in the emergency room that everyone knows is there but no one dares acknowledge: it's money, and that desire to make money over flight safety is killing people. Throughout history that appetite has more often than not trumped the right moral decision, even if it meant sacrificing lives to do it. What is going on in the HEMS industry is a classic example of that way of thinking.

I began my 50-minute speech at eight in the morning. I spent the first half-hour drawing my audience in with anecdotes and humor to establish my credibility before I drove home my message.

As my enthusiasm and conviction overtook my initial bout of nerves, I left the podium and stepped away from my prepared notes. I was on a roll, as if on autopilot, because my message was flowing freely now, not from how I'd rehearsed it or from my notes, but emanating straight from my heart. I could tell by the overall reaction of the audience they sensed my passion and my sincerity.

I had their full attention. They seemed to be on board with what I'd said so far but would they join me by committing to fix a broken system? I doubted it because money was involved, but that couldn't deter me. I had to deliver my "solution" anyway.

Perhaps they'd become so fed up with the system that they were finally ready for any solution to stem the bloodshed, no matter how much it might cost to implement or how much it might upset the status quo. The status quo wasn't working. The status quo was, and always has been, deadly. The status quo was killing people. Were they really ready for change? Only time would tell.

My hope was that those in the industry had finally become so weary of watching their colleagues die year after year, as I had, that after three decades of slaughter, they would be ready to act.

I was coming to the part in my speech where I would ask them: "How much is a human life worth?" To me it was an irrefutable argument. A question with only one logical, acceptable and moral answer: No one can put a price on a human life.

But, unknowingly, they had. How much would it cost to install an autopilot in each HEMS aircraft: $120,000 or so? The head of the FAA, Randy Babbitt wrote in a letter to the NTSB in September, 2009 saying that in the absence of a second pilot, use of an autopilot might enhance a pilot's ability to cope with high workload, such as in inadvertent flight into IMC (IIMC) something that occurs all too frequently in HEMS.

Babbitt strengthened his argument by offering statistics, saying that a review of the NTSB Aviation Accident Database revealed that during the eight-year period from 2000 to 2008, 123 HEMS accidents occurred, killing 104 people and seriously injuring 42 more. He said: "Pilot actions or omissions, in some capacity, were attributed as the probable cause in 60 of the 123 accidents and that most of these 60 accidents might have been prevented had a second pilot and/or an autopilot been present."

I wondered whether the audience was aware of a presentation NTSB board member Robert L. Sumwalt delivered just five months previously where he appealed to the hospital decision-makers to consider using aircraft that had an autopilot installed if a second pilot wasn't available.

After I read what those two high-ranking government officials had to say about the problem, the question that popped into my head was this: If Randy Babbitt, then head of the FAA, and Robert Sumwalt, a board member of the NTSB, were both saying essentially the same thing as their answer to '"fix" the problem in HEMS in America, and they were supposedly in the best possible position to get the ball rolling to do just that, then why hadn't a law been passed or a regulation been enacted following their recommendations?

So, in fact, it *is* easy to figure out the cost of a human life. It's the price of an autopilot. The math goes like this: Three people die in a crash, which is typical in these HEMS crashes, and that makes a human life worth $40,000, the price of an autopilot divided by three people. The cost of a human life would be more, of course, if the industry added a second pilot, which would require a helicopter big enough to carry the added weight. Take the added cost for an operator to do it safely and divide that cost by the number of lives lost. It's simple math. Simple but deadly math.

I explained to the audience how I came to be standing in front of them having travelled for more than 28 hours door-to-door to arrive the previous evening from my job in the Middle East.

I mentioned what the other airline transport pilots I flew with in Abu Dhabi thought of our HEMS system. I told them that they said HEMS in their country wouldn't be allowed to operate in the same way in their countries because the way we do it in America is far too dangerous.

I mentioned how I inadvertently became a pioneer, one of six ex-Vietnam helicopter pilots operating three Alouette III helicopters, desperately trying to prove that the helicopter could save lives in peacetime as we had seen it used so effectively in Korea and Vietnam. But I admitted that, in the process, we unknowingly and unwittingly made the helicopter air ambulance industry dangerous because we pushed the weather and tolerated working those grueling 72-hour shifts and how we and our helicopter bosses pandered to the "customers" by allowing hospital administrators and some medical crews to take over the decisions that we pilots normally made in the cockpit.

To lighten the mood a bit I asked, "Do any of the pilots in the audience still use the trick I used to use to fool the medical team to make them think that we were flying faster?" I told them, "When I flew HEMS in San Diego if we were flying a really sick patient into the hospital our medical director, Dr. Baxt, would often say to me, 'If you can make this thing fly any faster it could make the difference.'

"I was flying an Alouette III. Have any of you seen an Alouette III? It's an exercise in induced drag. I was flying as fast as it would fly already. But to fool Dr. Baxt and the flight nurse on board into thinking we were flying faster, I would descend to 500 feet above the city, which would give the *illusion* that we were speeding toward the hospital. Then I would open the air vent and lean forward, putting my face into the 110-knot slipstream, causing my hair to blow straight back. Flying lower, while leaning forward, with my hair blowing back in the breeze always caused Dr. Baxt to remark after landing, 'Thanks Randy, The added speed made all the difference.' I never told him my secret."

I explained to the audience how, through the help of other concerned members of the HEMS community, I managed to get myself on that stage in St. Louis. I mentioned how 13 months earlier, while working on one of my tours in the Middle East, I'd heard about yet another helicopter EMS crash, the one in Arkansas that killed three people in bad weather, which was the most common scenario in the majority of HEMS crashes over the years. I told the audience how I'd "snapped" when I'd heard the news and how, at that very moment, that very instant in time, I became driven to get on stage to deliver my lifesaving message in what I termed, *"My gift to you."*

I was at the point where I was going to take that final leap of faith, to deliver the message that had been burning deep within my gut for 27 years. Imagine possessing a cure for a virulent disease for that length of time and after 27 years you are finally being given the opportunity to deliver it to those in desperate need of it.

Everything was ready. The special envelopes I had prepared weeks earlier had been passed out to random members of the audience when they filed in. The people in the audience now held those envelopes in their hands but had no idea what was inside them.

Inside each envelope I had placed the name of a person, pilot, doctor, flight nurse, paramedic, whose life had been tragically cut short in an air medical helicopter crash since I wrote *The Golden Hour:* 358 names.

It had been odd printing out those names on my printer, then carefully cutting each one out then placing each name individually into a white business envelope. It had taken me nearly half a day to do it and it felt eerie to me, like I was placing each person in their final resting place.

It was like giving them an opportunity to speak out for one last time in a desperate effort to warn others of the dangers of the job. By inference they would be saying, "Please, don't let what happened to me happen to you. I, too, thought that these crashes happened to others and would *never* happen to me. Not true. Take heed. Please be careful. Look out, be vigilant, and listen to what this man has to say because what he says could save *your* life."

As I carefully placed each name into an envelope, folding each flap over and sealing it, I knew they were not simply names on a white strip of paper. They had been living flesh and blood, breathing, loving, laughing, caring mothers, fathers, sisters, brothers, husbands and wives who no longer walked with us on this earth.

I'd heard many of the stories over the years of the family members of these HEMS crew members who were deeply concerned because of the dangerous job they knew their loved ones had embarked on. When they voiced their concern they were always told, "But I'm doing what I love doing. Please don't worry." But the concerned family members would often say "Please be careful, honey," in their final sendoff whenever their loved ones left for work.

There were orphaned kids left behind, too. The tragedy of that thought made it much more frustrating to me because I knew if there were a collective consciousness in the industry to stop the carnage, it could be stopped overnight.

There was one name I specifically remember cutting out and placing in an envelope. Sandy Sigman, an Australian flight nurse I'd flown with in Houston. Sandy had been the flight nurse on the very first scene call I flew to during my initial flight training to become a Life Flight pilot. I remembered feeling awkward and out of place as I stood on the highway, observing as she and the doctor began working on the motor-vehicle accident victim. While on her knees, working on the male patient, she must have sensed my discomfort, knowing I had no idea what I should be doing. She looked up at me and gave me a smile that seemed to tell me, "It's OK. Just watch and observe. You'll do just fine."

Sandy lost her life on July 9, 1994, in Granite, Colorado, while trying to rescue an injured hiker at 12,500 feet. The helicopter's rotor blades stuck the steep mountainside, causing it to bounce over the rescue crew, then tumble 1,000 feet down the mountain.

I had no idea how the envelope stunt would be received, but it was too late. I was determined to go through with it. I was *hoping* the audience would be shocked.

I continued my speech by asking them, "Have any of you heard the allegory of Plato's cave?" I took a moment to survey the faces in the audience, and then continued.

"Imagine a community living in a cave. Inside that cave, all of Maslow's hierarchy of human needs are met. The cave in my case represents America. Those living in the cave have their biological and physical needs met: air, food, drink, shelter, warmth, sex, sleep, etc. Their safety needs are met: protection from the elements, security, order, law, communal limits, stability, etc. A sense of belonging and the need for love and companionship is met. I think you get the picture.

"Now imagine you're living as one of many in that cave. Every 12 hours you notice a shaft of light appear on the far wall of the cave as it filters down from a hole at the top of the cave, slowly making its way from one end to the other until it climbs the cave wall on the opposite side until darkness falls. Then as you gaze up through the opening of the cave, you notice twinkling specks of light set against a dark backdrop, stars in the night sky, but you have no idea what they are.

"Twelve hours later the shaft of light appears again as it creeps down the wall and the cycle continues like that day after day. You begin to wonder what's outside the cave. You ponder this question for a while until you finally ask your close friends and they reply, 'Why would you care what's outside the cave? We've got everything we need right here.'

"You look up to the opening of the cave and pause for a moment to consider what they've said and say, 'Yes, but there might be something better up there.'

"They laugh. 'But how could it be better than what we have right here in the cave?'

"One night, you escape from the cave by climbing up the walls and out of the hole and soon you discover a whole new and exciting world out there. You witness a new paradigm, a new way of doing things that is different from anything you've done in the past. A lot of what you see and do is much better than the way things are done back in the cave.

"You're excited to share this new found knowledge so you return to the cave to tell everyone what you have learned. To your great surprise and disappointment you're ridiculed by the masses. Scorned. Scoffed at for even suggesting change. In many cases the community back in the cave is loath to alter the status quo because of self-interest, apathy or even the most powerful of human emotions, the quest for greater wealth.

"That pretty much sums up my story. I was lucky to leave the cave in December 1984, when I accepted a job in the Sultanate of Oman to set up a country-wide HEMS program there. I witnessed a new paradigm in the world of aviation, so different from the way I had been taught when I lived in the cave. I soon realized that if the same practices, procedures and attitudes were adopted and followed back in America, back in the cave, the slaughter in American helicopter EMS would stop.

"I learned a new way of flying while in Oman. The pilots I flew with there were former British armed forces pilots who had flown challenging instrument flying on the North Sea. They were used to flying two-crew operations practicing good crew resource management (CRM). The lessons were later reinforced when I flew as a HEMS pilot with British and Scottish pilots in Saudi Arabia, operating from the king of Saudi Arabia's 500-foot yacht. My resolve was further cemented while flying for Abu Dhabi Aviation with those 20 nationalities of airline transport pilots.

"If I could bring to the U.S. what I had learned overseas, flying in a medical helicopter might not have to be the most dangerous job in America."

The time had finally come for me to deliver my message ....

CHAPTER 18
Time to Deliver

I moved to my right, stepping away from the podium, pausing for a moment to collect my thoughts. Then I looked up at a sea of expectant faces. Everyone appeared to be listening attentively.

"I'm going to give you the gift to solve all these terrible accidents in your industry, and it's from watching how they did it in Oman, in Saudi Arabia and in Abu Dhabi. I fly with 20 nationalities of pilots right now, and do you know how most of them do it in their countries? They fly two-crew using night vision goggles. The two pilots are instrument rated and current. They don't land at night to unprepared landing sites that hadn't been checked out during the day. And the medical influence is kept out of the cockpit.

"That's my gift to you. Now, what you decide to do with that gift is of course up to you. But I guarantee that you will reduce your accident rate by a minimum 80 percent if you do it that way. I know I am fighting against the tide here because there are economics to think about here, too. But my question to you is this: 'How much is a human life worth?'

"I feel like Peter Finch. Most of you are probably too young to remember this but there was a movie in 1976 called *Network*. And there is a scene where the actor Peter Finch goes on a famous rant. He's a TV news anchor and he tells the TV audience, 'First of all, you have to get mad. You have to say, "I'm a human being, my life has value." So I want you to get up now, get up and go to the window, open it and stick your head out and yell at the top of your lungs, "I'm as mad as hell and I'm not going to take this anymore." '

"That's what kept going through my mind when I went on

that walk after hearing about the HEMS crash in Arkansas that killed those three people. I kept asking myself: 'What can one man do? More importantly, what can *I* do? And I'm mad as hell and I'm not going to see one more life lost in a medical helicopter because it's preventable.' "

I walked back behind the podium and asked for the house lights to be brought up. The spotlights were so bright I couldn't tell whether the house lights had been brought up. After a few moments I said, "I can't tell if they're on. Are they on?" Then I laughed, "You don't want to fly with me if I can't tell the lights are on." My comment brought a laugh from the audience. Then I continued.

"Now, as you all filed in this morning some white envelopes were passed out. I would like those of you holding envelopes to please stand up."

I paused as half the room's 700 people rose from their seats. Once they were standing, I continued. "Inside each envelope there is a name of a person who died in a medical helicopter since I wrote *The Golden Hour.* Look around. This is how many colleagues we've lost since I wrote that book."

I could see people surveying the room of those standing; some wearing flight suits, others in business attire. Then they began to open their envelopes to read the slips of paper inside with the names I'd printed out.

Something I wasn't expecting was the sound of 358 envelopes being torn open at once. The ripping sound filled the conference hall, adding to the tension in the room.

I continued. "If you don't want to see any more people die, please remember the gift I am giving you today: How to do it right."

I took a few moments for my words to sink in as the envelopes were being opened. Then I spread my arms out to encompass the whole room and said, "But look around. Look how many people are standing. Look how many people we've lost."

I watched as people reluctantly look around the room at all the people standing. Then I said forcefully, "Please join me, like

Peter Finch, and say 'I'm mad as hell, and I'm not going to take it anymore.' Thank you very much."

The audience erupted in applause. Of course half the people were standing already but the remainder rose to their feet, applauding. A standing ovation. It was at that precise moment I knew my message had been well received.

%

After I'd given the speech and stepped down off the stage, Dr. Kevin Hutton, the CEO of MedEvac International, hopped on stage and said something to the audience that made my heart swell. He said, "That was one of the most moving keynote speakers we've ever had. The message is clear. We can't take it anymore,"

Afterward, people came up to me as I stood at the foot of the stage, many of them very emotional. Most I could see were mustering as much sincerity as they possibly could. Some even had tears in their eyes. Each person shook my hand and thanked me, "For saying what's needed to be said for more than 20 years."

%

I received an email a few weeks after the conference from Dr. Kevin Hutton to say he'd read the copy of *Journey to the Golden Hour* that I'd signed and given to him in St. Louis. He wrote to say that he was going to make the book required reading for his staff at his HEMS billing firm, *The Golden Hour,* in San Diego, California. I could see I had a strong ally in trying to spread the "good news."

Kevin placed an order for a copy of *Journey to the Golden Hour* to give to Rick Sherlock, the new CEO of the Association of Air Medical Services (AAMS), to give him an idea of the history of HEMS in America. It would also be a quick primer for Rick to get a handle on the state of the industry at that time. In short, it would give him an idea of what he was getting himself into.

More positive things were happening in my life as a result of my obvious commitment to increase safety in the HEMS industry. The HELI-EXPO for 2012 was going to be held in Dallas and I hoped to sell my books on the convention floor like I did the year before. Unfortunately, a change in policy meant this wouldn't be possible.

Then something totally unexpected happened. About one month later Lyn Burkes, the owner of *Rotorcraft Pro Magazine*, said he might be able to help me out. He asked if I would be willing to supply his magazine with four long articles a year that he would run quarterly. He suggested they be excerpts taken from my three books. I leapt at the opportunity.

The first article I supplied him was a scene taken from *Dear Mom I'm Alive – Letters Home from Blackwidow 25*. I sent him the story about rescuing the four recon team members whom I had inserted into the 100-foot hover hole in the jungle, then rescued when they became pinned down by the enemy. He ran that article soon after I submitted it and he came back to say the article had received an incredibly positive buzz both from his readership and from the magazine's advertisers and sponsors.

About a month later he called to ask, "Randy, what would you think about having your own monthly column in *Rotorcraft Pro Magazine*? I was thinking about calling it "My Two Cents Worth" and you could write about anything pertaining to aviation. I was thinking, to help you out, we could put together a half-page color ad advertising your three books. Is that something you'd be interested in doing?"

I couldn't say "yes" fast enough.

"Great, then it's settled. I was thinking around 800 words per article or thereabouts."

"Terrific, Lyn. When do you want your first article?"

"How about the first of July. That's enough lead time for it to appear in the August issue."

An unexpected spinoff from having my articles appear each month in *Rotorcraft Pro* is that Lyn also owns the website *Justhelicopters.com*, the largest helicopter website in the world. He often runs my articles from the previous month on the home page of his website, giving me double exposure.

But I wanted to make a greater impact. How could I *personally* try to bring about change? I wanted to do more than what I was doing but what? The answer came to me when I read a new regulation passed by the FAA that would affect all the HEMS operators and programs.

The FAA had mandated crew resource management (CRM), or air medical resource management (AMRM), a derivative taken from the principles of CRM, for all Part 135 air taxi operators, which included all HEMS programs.

Of course I'd been exposed to CRM back in 1985 when the Police Air Wing sent me to do my Bell 214ST course at Flight Safety in Fort Worth. I'd evaluated CRM in the cockpit when flying for the Police in Oman. I was a CRM assessor at Abu Dhabi Aviation in the sim and had attended yearly CRM courses while with Abu Dhabi Aviation. I figured I had the background to effectively teach it. Because CRM was so new to the HEMS community in America I saw this as an excellent opportunity to pass along what I'd learned as my way to make a personal difference.

I'd been asked to deliver a safety speech at the Mayo Clinic in Rochester, Minnesota, and while there, I met an accident investigator from the FAA by the name of Matt Rigsby. I asked Matt who the FAA would consider to be qualified to give these CRM/AMRM courses and was there a place where one could go to become certified? He couldn't tell me at the time but he said he'd get back to me.

I decided to do some checking of my own. I was in Abu Dhabi at the time and went online to do a search. At that time I could not find a CRM train-the-trainer course anywhere in America. Perhaps there was one out there but what kept coming up in my search was Global Air Training based in Cheshire, England.

I then asked our two CRM instructors at ADA if they could recommend a world-class CRM train-the-trainer course. They both said, hands down, Global Air Training in Cheshire, England, because they had been teaching CRM train-the-trainer courses and CRM to flight crews for 16 years.

I then made arrangements to attend their train-the-trainer course that was to take place on my next leave. My total personal out-of-pocket expense would be nearly $6,000.

Also attending that one-week course was a recently retired British Airways 747 captain, a Royal Air Force Nimrod captain, an Airbus 330 Captain from Romania, a military F-16 pilot from Belgium, two helicopter pilots from Belgium, a helicopter pilot from Holland and a Chinook crew chief serving in Afghanistan with the British forces. There were also three senior flight attendants: two from Romania and an Australian working for the Royal Flight of Bahrain.

Our day began at 8:30 a.m. with lectures and facilitation finishing at 5 p.m. Each night we had a minimum of three hours of homework. We each had to do three presentations/facilitations in front of the class, one 10 minutes long, one 25 minutes and on the last day we had to facilitate an air crash investigation taken from more than 140 final accident reports in the school's archive. The last facilitation lasted 45 minutes and it was videotaped. Everyone in the course agreed it was one of the most difficult but one of the most worthwhile courses any of us had ever taken.

Now, fully trained, I needed to keep up the momentum ....

Seventy days after I delivered the keynote speech in St. Louis, a chartered Bell 206 Jet Ranger flying a Mayo Clinic heart-transplant team in Eastern Florida crashed in foggy weather in the early-morning hours, killing cardiac surgeon Dr. Ernest Bonilla, transplant specialist David Hines, and the charter pilot E. Hoke Smith.

Unfortunately any change I suggested would come too late for those three men who lost their lives on December 26, 2011. Sadly, it would not be the last fatal HEMS accident following my speech. The carnage would continue unabated as if everything I had said that morning had been spoken to an empty room.

On Stage St. Louis, Missouri

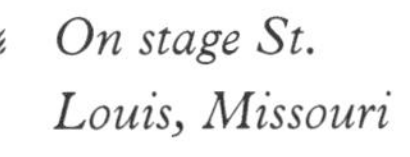

On stage St. Louis, Missouri

In St. Louis giving the speech of my life – delivering a lifesaving message to an audience of 700 medical professionals

Mid Speech St. Louis

Making a point about HEMS flight safety in St. Louis

E. Hoke Smith

Seventy days after I delivered my safety speech in St. Louis, these three men died in Florida while on a heart-transplant run in a Bell 206 helicopter chartered by the Mayo Clinic.

CHAPTER 19
Onward and Upward

For the first time in nearly nine years of working at ADA I came back off home leave thinking, "I don't want to be here any longer." That revelation hit me as I was filling in the simulator sign-in book to begin my first simulator session of that tour.

It was as simple as that. A little micro-switch in my head just "tripped" and that was it. It was time to follow advice I had followed throughout my 45-year career – advice I had passed along to other pilots and mechanics I'd met over the years. If you are not having fun doing what you're doing try to figure out what you have to do to change it, or move on. I knew it was time to move on.

I kept that thought in my head, revisiting it throughout the rest of that tour. On the second-to-last day of my six-week stint I called Kaye to tell her I was going to resign. She didn't protest or ask me why I had come to that decision, she just said, "Darling, you will never know what door will be open to you until this door closes."

She had no idea how prophetic her words would be.

I met with Mike Burke, head of training, to give him notice that after my next tour I would be leaving. He understood and wished me well.

Mike had been a strong influence in the HEMS industry in the early days when we were both heavily involved with it. HEMS was as much ingrained in his marrow as it was in mine, mainly because we both believed so strongly in the concept.

During my time at ADA I would often sit with him in his office and we would have long chats about the state of the HEMS industry back home as we saw it, the seemingly never-ending loss of life and the appalling safety record, and how it was just as dangerous to fly in a medical helicopter then as it was when we did it.

As previously mentioned, Mike had helped found the National EMS Pilots Association back in 1985 to try to bring back the voice from the cockpit that had been hijacked by the medical people. Also in that year, he allowed himself to be interviewed by Peter Van Sant, a popular investigative journalist working for the well-known news program *60 Minutes*. To prevent him from being identified as a troublemaker in the industry, Mike gave the interview with his face blacked out and his voice altered, describing the problems in the HEMS industry, and warned Van Sant and the viewers that if the attitudes and the same practices were allowed to continue more people would die. The piece won Van Sant an Emmy but wasn't enough to bring about change in an industry turning deadly.

In 1986, Mike, was asked to testify before Congress where he issued the same dire warning that he reported to Peter Van Sant on *60 Minutes*. In the end, nothing was changed and Congress missed a window of opportunity to stem the bloodshed by enacting stricter regulations on the industry.

Mike's efforts, along with the support of Al Gore, who was then serving on the Senate Subcommittee for Aviation Safety, managed to bring about strict duty-time policies as a way to address the grueling shift-hours the pilots were forced to work.

During our frequent chats I would often tell Mike what I was doing to try to bring about change. I told him about that August 31 walk that night in Abu Dhabi after I'd learned of the HEMS crash in Arkansas. I told him about speaking in Vancouver at the Helicopter Association of Canada conference. How I became driven to get on stage at an air medical transport conference in the States. What I'd managed to achieve in St. Louis including the envelope "stunt" and my speaking engagement at the Mayo Clinic following the helicopter crash where the Mayo Clinic lost two medical colleagues. I told him about the CRM train-the-trainer course I'd recently taken in the U.K.

"So what do you see yourself doing after you leave ADA then?"

"I think it's time to give back, Mike. Now that the FAA has mandated that all air taxi operators must have CRM training, I see myself giving CRM and AMRM courses to HEMS pilots, medical crewmembers and any staff member in a flight program who has an influence on the safe outcome of a flight."

"Sounds great, Randy. Got any leads on how you're going to do that?"

"Nope, not yet. All I've got is the desire and the passion. I'm hoping the rest will come. When I told Kaye on the phone that I was going to tender my resignation today, she said, 'You'll never know what door will be open until this door closes.' "

"You've got a jewel there, my friend."

"No one knows it better than I do, Mike."

Then Mike said, "HEMS in the States is such a mess. Even worse than it was when you and I tried to prove the concept."

"I know, Mike. What happened?"

"I call it predatory capitalism. It used to be if someone had a good idea and followed it up with hard work they could expect to be rewarded. Nowadays, everyone seems to be out to screw everyone else. It used to be 'shame on you' if you screwed your neighbor. Now it's 'shame on you' if you allow yourself to get screwed."

"I know what you mean. Did you know that operators are charging up to $16,000 a flight in a tiny Jet Ranger for a short 15-minute flight? And while doing research for an article I wrote for *Rotorcraft Pro* called, "A Surefire Fix for one of the Most Dangerous Jobs in America", I read in the 2009 winter edition of the *American Journal of Clinical Medicine* that many of the patients being flown aren't critical. I was shocked to read that in a meta-analysis of 22 papers reviewing more than 37,000 trauma patients transported by helicopter, approximately 60 percent of those patients were felt to have had only minor injuries, and 24 percent were discharged within twenty-four hours."

Mike nodded in agreement. "The pure concept that you and I were trying to prove back at Hermann Hospital is gone, buddy. Now it's like a feeding frenzy out there, the equivalent to ambulance chasing."

"That same article said that a Washington, D.C., study of nearly 4,000 pediatric trauma patients transported by HEMS found that nearly 85 percent of those kids were over-triaged and didn't require helicopter transport."

"It appears helicopters are being sent on just about everything."

"You're right, Mike. I received an email the other day from a senior member of the board of the National EMS Pilots Association. He said some programs monitor scanners and launch before being called so they're over the scene before the call is dispatched. They're after those patient dollars. He told me he recently landed on a helipad and four other helicopters were circling overhead. Apparently, helicopter shopping is still going on out there too."

I was making reference to the practice where a flight dispatcher will call a pilot, telling him of a flight. If the pilot refuses the flight because he doesn't feel comfortable with the weather, the dispatcher will call another flight program and ask that pilot if he will take the flight, not telling him that another pilot has already turned it down. There have been several documented cases where this practice has occurred and the pilot who accepted the mission was involved in a fatal accident due to bad weather.

Mike said, "I'm afraid the only answer is strict legislation like Part 121 of the federal regs that regulate the airlines. That's the only way to fix a broken system. Right now operators are allowed to fly single-pilot single-engine machines, without an autopilot, under visual flight rules so what motive is there for them to operate any other way if they aren't breaking the law? There's one operator out there who operates on the cheap. In fact, it's part of that operator's business model and everyone in the industry knows who that operator is. They've had at least 12 crashes since they've been in business. Who can blame that operator, though, if there's nothing in the federal regulations to stop them from operating that way?"

"I agree, Mike. Until the feds make the regs and enforce them I'm afraid we'll continue to see helicopters plowing into the ground as has happened for the past 30-plus years."

"Sad fact, my friend, sad fact. But it's a noble crusade you're embarking on, buddy. I know I can't talk you out of your decision to leave the company so I won't try. You'll be missed, you know, by me and all the guys. All I can do is wish you the very best of luck. When would you like your last day of work to be?"

"I'd like to come back on my next tour and work eight weeks instead of the usual six, to top up the kitty a bit. So I'm thinking January 16."

"That would suit me. That gives me 12 weeks to find a replacement. What do you and Kaye have planned for this leave?"

"Well, looks like I didn't manage to piss everyone off too much last year at the air medical conference in St. Louis because they've invited me back to be a keynote speaker at their conference in Seattle this year to talk about CRM."

"That's terrific. Keep them on their toes. Anything else planned?"

"Yep, Lyn Burks, the owner of the magazine I write for, has invited me to speak at the conference he puts on in Vegas every year for up-and-coming pilots who want to hear how they can succeed in the business. He calls it HELISUCCESS. This'll be the fourth year he's put it on. He's asked me to be one of 10 speakers he's bringing in who have been in the business for more years than we all care to remember. My topic will be 'Survival Tips 101 – Nuggetts to Live By.' "

"Sounds like a worthwhile enterprise and a great opportunity for the up and comers. Tell the new pilots when you see them that ADA will need more pilots in the near future for the new oilfields that'll be opening up offshore."

"Will do, Mike."

"Keep me informed and have a great leave. Sounds like you'll be busy."

Mike could never have imagined just how busy we'd be ....

The front of my new villa #57 – the new camp Abu Dhabi Aviation

Pool Area at the new camp Abu Dhabi Aviation

Entry into the new clubhouse and gym at Abu Dhabi Aviation

Living area in the new accommodation Abu Dhabi Aviation

CHAPTER 20
An Unexpected Door Opens From Nowhere

With only one more eight-week tour to work in the Middle East I thought I would send out inquiries to two men I thought might be able to help me fight for flight safety in the HEMS industry. Those two men were Dr. Kevin Hutton, the CEO of MedEvac International, and Rick Sherlock, the retired two-star general who had recently become the CEO of AAMS, the organization that promotes safety for HEMS flight programs across America.

When I emailed Kevin and Rick to tell them that I'd put in my notice at ADA and would soon be free to offer support at the end of January, they both sent me what I interpreted to be very positive responses. I had the impression that perhaps they had an idea how they could use me in some capacity as another voice for safety. Kaye and I were both very hopeful that with their contacts, perhaps their organizations could sponsor me to go to HEMS programs across America to teach CRM/AMRM courses. We'd know more in a week when we saw them at the air medical transport conference in Seattle.

Kaye and I took the car ferry from Canada to Washington State, electing to drive rather than fly to Seattle to attend the air medical transport conference. We checked into the hotel opposite the Washington State Convention Center where I would be delivering my keynote address in two days' time. We were excited and very anxious to meet up with Kevin and Rick, thinking they might be able to use me to facilitate CRM/AMRM courses to HEMS programs across America.

Kaye and I thought it would be a good idea to attend the pre-conference wine "meet-and-greet" hoping to run into either Kevin or Rick. While walking over to where the meet-and-greet was going to be held, we ran into Kevin. Kaye and I became excited to see him, eager to talk with him about my future.

We exchanged greetings, then he said, "What do you plan on doing after you leave Abu Dhabi?"

It was a perfect lead in. "Well, Kevin, my dream is to go to HEMS programs and teach and facilitate AMRM and, if I may be so bold, my dream involves you and your organization."

"We all need to have dreams. What is it?"

I told him I was hoping that his company, The Golden Hour, or perhaps MedEvac International could sponsor me to give AMRM courses.

He thought about it for a moment then said, "I'm afraid I can't help you there."

My heart sank. I know Kaye's did too.

"I *can* give you some contacts, though. You can find these folks here at the convention and perhaps they can help you."

He brought out his wallet and gave us the names of people to contact who might be able to help me. We thanked him and he went on his way. It was a very kind gesture to be sure, but certainly not what we'd hoped for.

"Well, Hon, there's always Rick Sherlock. When we bump into him we'll see what he can offer me. He sounded pretty positive in the email he sent to me."

"So did Kevin."

"Yeah, well, fingers crossed. Come on. Let's go to the meet-and-greet and see who's there."

///

It was as if our lives were scripted because as we walked into the room where the meet-and-greet was taking place we immediately ran into Tom Judge, the program director for Life Flight Maine and Lisa Tofil, a hard-working lawyer championing patients' rights in Washington, D.C., for patients picked up by medical helicopters.

I was thrilled to finally meet Tom and Lisa face-to-face. We'd corresponded once or twice because I knew they were both proponents for HEMS safety. Tom was one of the first people I had contacted when I went online looking for like-minded individuals who were fed up, like I was, with the unacceptable accident rate.

Kaye and I had been speaking with Tom and Lisa for about five minutes when I spotted Rick Sherlock talking to another attendee across the room. I recognized Rick from his picture on the AAMS website. At that moment the two men shook hands and Rick began walking in my direction.

I'd never met Rick, but Kevin had purchased my book for him to read, and Rick and I had exchanged some very positive emails about HEMS safety. I was excited and anxious to finally meet the man who might hold my future in his hands. I'd tell him about my proposal when the time was appropriate.

"He approached with a warm smile and an extended hand. "Well, Randy Mains. We meet at last."

"And I've been so looking forward to meeting you too, Sir." I thought as a retired general he'd like that. I introduced him to Kaye.

I continued, "We ran into Kevin Hutton as we were coming in just now. I was anxious to ask him if his organization could use me as a CRM/AMRM instructor and facilitator. Unfortunately, he said he couldn't create a niche for me but he did manage to give us about five leads, people to contact, etc., who might be able to help me out."

"Well I'm sure you can find a role you can fill with the experience you have to bring to the table."

I was disappointed that he didn't immediately say that the AAMS organization could use me. I continued. "It's my desire to teach AMRM now that it's been mandated by the FAA that all HEMS have the training."

"Yes, there certainly is a need."

This isn't how I thought this would go at all. I know that Kaye, standing next to me, would be feeling the same way.

Rick and I shared polite conversation for about five minutes. Then he excused himself, saying he had another commitment. But before leaving the room he said, "I hope the leads Kevin gave you pan out. If there's anything I can do, please let me know."

I was thinking about hollering out, "Offer me a job!" Instead I said, "Thanks, Rick, I'll be sure to let you know how it goes."

"We'll catch up later Randy. There's lots of time." With that, he left.

Kaye and I just stood there looking at one another. In less than a half-hour at the conference the two most hopeful leads had evaporated. We still had three days to follow up on the leads Kevin had given us. It seemed like someone had torn up the script we'd mapped out and thrown it out the window.

"Hadn't Kevin or Rick read the script?" Kaye said, shaking her head.

"Well *that* was uneventful." I said, unable to hide the disappointment in my voice.

"Oh, it was eventful, all right. Just unproductive."

We both began to laugh at how quickly our balloon had burst. Then Kaye said, "We can follow up on Kevin's leads when the conference begins tomorrow. Hopefully something will come from that."

"We can only hope, Hon. A bit discouraging, though.

"We've still got three days, Darling."

"Yeah, three days."

To say that we were both downhearted and our spirits more than a little deflated at that moment would be the mother of all understatements. We felt like we'd gone back to square one. I was thinking I had one more tour to go in Abu Dhabi with no prospects for the future to teach CRM or AMRM to medical crews. To do it with clout I'd need a sponsor. We had three days to find one. Three days.

"Come on, Hon. Let me buy you dinner."

"And how about a stiff whisky?"

"That, my beautiful lady, goes without saying. You buy the first, I'll buy the second."

"Who'll buy the third?"

With that, we slowly made our way back to our hotel.

On the convention floor the following day, Kaye and I tried to make contact with the leads Kevin had provided. We heard the same line at just about every booth we visited, "Oh, well, he's just gone into a meeting. You can probably catch him later." Or checking their wristwatch they'd say, "She'll be here around 4 p.m. You might be able to run into her then. She's got a very busy agenda over the next couple of days though. Keep trying. That's about all we can tell you."

We kept striking out.

Kaye and I had been bouncing around the displays and booths for about three hours, feeling like pinballs in a machine getting knocked around but getting absolutely nowhere: ding, ding ding, ding, ding ding, kwaaammmmm!

Finally, after traipsing around the convention floor for hours, Kaye said, "Darling, my feet are killing me. Can we find a place to sit for a moment so I can give them a rest?"

"Good idea. There are two chairs over there. Let's grab them before someone else does."

Kaye had a shoe off and was rubbing the bottom of her left foot when I said, "You know this isn't going at all like I thought it would,"

"I know, Darling, but this is only the first day, hopefully something will …."

Kaye's face seemed to suddenly brighten as she obviously saw something or somebody over my left shoulder that caused her to perk up. Before she could speak from behind me I heard ….

"Hey, you two, imagine seeing you here?"

I recognized that voice. I turned to look behind me. It was Jack Todoro, the manager for business development and marketing at Oregon Aero. We'd met at the HAC in Vancouver about a year-and-a-half earlier.

Kaye and I recognized him immediately. "Jack, how you doing?"

"Great. I didn't think I'd see you guys here."

"Yeah, well, I'm delivering the keynote address tomorrow. Right after the survivors' network gives their keynote. Hey, it's good to see you."

"Same here. Resting, huh? Worn out already? You still have three days of this, you know." He was making reference to Kaye rubbing her sore foot.

We told Jack about how our day had gone so far. How I had done the five-day CRM course in England because I couldn't find one in the States. That I was there because I'd been invited to give a keynote speech on CRM. I told him that I had put in my notice with Abu Dhabi Aviation and that it was my dream to teach and facilitate CRM/AMRM courses to air medical programs across the States.

Kaye and I both related how Rick Sherlock and Kevin Hutton had sounded upbeat and positive in their emails, giving me hope that they might use my services after I told them I would be quitting ADA. And we admitted how it looked like nothing would come of it and how we were feeling pretty low.

I said, "Kevin gave us some good leads but no one is available so far to talk to us. Everyone seems to be in a meeting."

"I've got some contacts. Maybe I can help you out. Do you have a business plan?"

His question caught me off guard. "Jack I wouldn't know what a business plan looked like if it came up and bit me."

"You *need* a business plan. Then you can proceed. Busy? Got a few minutes?"

Kaye and I could tell Jack was becoming revved up. He seemed to come alive, not that he didn't seem like he was alive earlier, but he appeared to us to be a man on a mission, a man who appreciated a challenge and ours was one that had suddenly fallen in his lap.

The three of us I walked over to an empty part of the building near floor-to-ceiling windows and sat down on a padded bench seat. Jack pulled out a yellow legal pad and started to ask me questions while writing down my answers. In 90 minutes he'd sketched out a business plan.

"You've done this before, haven't you Jack?" Kaye said.

He chuckled and nodded, "Yeah, a few times."

I shook my head, "I'd say more than a few times, Jack."

Kaye and I felt we'd finally met someone who truly understood my mission and my passion to try to make a personal difference and was willing to use his experience and years of expertise to ensure I got a good start to accomplish that mission.

He told us, "I've got some contacts I'll search out and enquire for you. How long you home on this leave before you have to head back to the Middle East for your last tour?"

"Well, after the conference we go home. Then I'm speaking at HELISUCCESS in Las Vegas on the fourth of November. We plan to stay a few nights in Vegas after that, then fly home. I fly back to Abu Dhabi around the eleventh of next month, why?"

"I'd like to bring you and Kaye to Oregon to meet the CEO and owner of the company, Mike Dennis, and perhaps you can give a little talk to the employees at Oregon Aero. Let me work on this, see if I can put it together and I'll get back to you. I've gotta go make some phone calls, meet a few folks ...." He stood to go. "I'll get back to you." He checked his watch. "You want to meet up, say, around six for dinner? I should know more by then."

I looked at Kaye, who must have looked as perplexed as I felt, and nodded "yes" and said, "Yeah, great Jack, OK, six will be fine."

"Great. How about meeting up in the restaurant across the street in the hotel? I'll have more for you then."

With that he was off, like a man on a mission to find a home for me to deliver my message. Kaye and I just stood staring at one another while letting the dust settle.

Then I said, "Did that really happen?

"This is incredible," She said. "I can't wait to see what happens next."

"Well hold on to your hat sweetheart and I'll hold on to mine because I think we're in for one heck of a ride."

CHAPTER 21
Lights, Camera, Action!

Jack Todaro, Kaye and I sat in the front row of the convention hall listening to the six HEMS crash survivors recount their personal stories. I was thinking, "Man, this is going to be a tough act to follow."

Not that I wanted to top their presentation but where, honestly, do you go after six people tell their harrowing stories about cheating death in a HEMS helicopter crash?

Then I thought, this isn't unlike my last situation where I had to speak at the Mayo Clinic when the previous day's speaker was, of all people, the Dalai Lama!

I'd told the lady host at the front desk of our hotel, where Kaye and I were staying, that I was speaking at the Mayo Clinic that day and that I was following the Dalai Lama.

She said, "Unless you can bring a cure for cancer to your speech you can pretty much count on being number two."

I knew the crash survivors would be delivering an emotional presentation. Each had a harrowing tale to tell of surviving a HEMS crash. I had already gone through about three reams of tissue paper, dabbing my eyes thinking I should have brought a roll of kitchen towels.

The Survivors Network for Air & Surface Medical Transport is an organization representing more than 600 survivors. The organization was formed by Krista Haugen, a former flight nurse who survived a helicopter crash from a rooftop helipad in Olympia, Washington, in 2005. The experience made her aware that the resources needed after surviving such an accident were not readily available.

Reaching out, she met with other crash survivors: flight

nurse Megan Hamilton, flight nurse Teresa Pearson and flight nurse Jonathan Godfrey. The four of them shared their post-crash experiences with one another.

Seeing a need, they founded the Survivors' Network so they could share what they had learned with others in the industry, and to bring the survivors' perspectives to the conversation on risk mitigation, preparedness for incidents/accidents, effective responses to incidents/accidents, and long-term recovery from incidents/accidents.

The Survivors have become staunch allies, fully behind my CRM/AMRM message because each and every one of them – and there were over 600 across the nation – knew better than anyone the mental and physical trauma caused by each and every HEMS accident. Their message that morning was powerful, emotional and raw. Every story the audience heard had everyone's rapt attention.

With each heart-rending story I listened to, the more frustrated and angry I became. Those six individuals wouldn't be up on that stage had the Federal Aviation Administration, National Transportation Safety Board, and the helicopter operators done their job to make sure it was as safe as it could be for every passenger who flew on their helicopters.

By getting into that aircraft, each crew member, passenger and patient says to the pilot in effect, "I trust you implicitly and without question. I trust that you will guard my life."

For the six on stage plus the other 600 crash survivors and the nearly 400 people who have lost their lives over the years, the system did not honor that trust. Congress, the FAA and the NTSB had not ensured they were being transported in a safe system. Because of the way our system is set up in the States, medical crew members are allowed to be placed in harm's way. A good lawyer could probably argue that allowing a broken system to continue to operate borders on being a criminal offence. Why aren't people asking: "What exactly is the role of the FAA, the NTSB and ultimately Congress, if it isn't to look after the safety of those who entrust their lives within the very system they regulate?"

The survivors and those who've lost their lives have also been let down by the companies who supply the helicopters and crews because they did not do everything in their power to supply the best equipment nor practice the highest safety standards, as the airlines do, to ensure flight crews and patients would not be hurt, injured or lose their lives. There *are* some operators out there who have the conscience and the moral commitment to honor that sacred trust. There are operators who value life over maximizing profit.

Since writing my column in *Rotorcraft Pro* and writing longer articles on HEMS safety and two books on the history and the problems with HEMS in the States, pilots have emailed to tell me that they receive no pressure whatsoever to accept a flight. They are never questioned when they turn down a flight for weather if they think they might put the flight crew and patients at risk. It's promising to hear those pilots tell me they feel the programs they fly on are safe.

But I also receive correspondence from pilots who tell me they still feel pressured to fly. They feel the pressure from their bosses who supply the helicopter services. They feel pressure from hospital administrators and program directors. They even occasionally feel pressure to perform from the medical crews.

I often hear from pilots who say the pilots themselves are their own worst enemies. The goal and mission-oriented nature of most pilots' personalities often gets them into situations that are irretrievable.

The stats have been in for more than 30 years. There is no need to try to figure out how to make it safe for the people who fly on these medical helicopters because the answer is already out there. As I said in St. Louis, "Look north over the border to Canada, or across the Atlantic to Germany, Italy or Switzerland. Look at Australia. Emulate how they do it."

Medical crews – and sometimes the patients they carry who have no say whatsoever in whether they fly in a HEMS helicopter – are dying or becoming injured or becoming crash survivors.

The last lifeline being thrown to the industry is a change in attitude that can come from crew resource management (CRM) and air medical resource management (AMRM). I'm hoping to convince the audience that CRM can work. The absolute key of CRM/AMRM is communication and knowing the proven pitfalls – the human factors – that can significantly contribute to an aircraft accident and knowing what everyone's personal role is in ensuring the safe outcome of each and every flight. For CRM to work, everyone from top management on down must buy into the concept if the industry expects to see a significant reduction in the appalling accident rate.

The airlines proved it could be done. They were in the same dire straits back in 1979 that the HEMS industry faces now. A similar turnaround can happen in HEMS in America. We can reach a point where a patient's sacred trust that they'll arrive safely will be fulfilled, and we won't have to attend any more conferences where we listen to survivors' harrowing tales.

I checked my watch. Rick Sherlock had run a bit long with his introduction prior to turning over the stage to the six crash survivors, so I could see I was going to be pinched for time, possibly losing as much as 10 to 15 minutes from what was supposed to be a 40-minute speech.

As in the speeches I'd given in the past, I had practiced this speech many times in my small study. I really needed every one of the 40 minutes to finish it.

The survivors' stories had me in tears. Tears of sympathy, tears of anguish, tears of compassion, tears of anger and frustration that nothing had been done over the years to prevent these folks from having to experience this. I'd anticipated being emotional. I can cry watching a dog food commercial on TV. Luckily, Kaye had come prepared with a large supply of facial tissues.

The last survivor, Mike Eccard – who'd been thrown clear of the aircraft during his crash – was finishing up his story. I discreetly tried to blow my nose and wipe the tears from my eyes in preparation for my turn on stage.

This was a much larger room than the conference hall in St. Louis. The hall in St. Louis was huge. This one was mega-huge. There were the two familiar 20-foot by 20-foot video screens to the left and right of the stage, projecting the speaker's image so that those sitting too far back from the stage could see.

The survivors received a standing ovation, as they should have. They filed off the stage, Rick Sherlock took the podium, ran through a short bio as way of introduction and I was "on."

When I speak I like to give the audience a description they can easily visualize like the envelope opening in St. Louis. I came up with one I thought would be a good analogy and maybe shock them to the reality of fatalities the industry had experienced over the years. I began....

"Imagine you are in the waiting lounge at the airport. You look out and see three Boeing 777s sitting on the ramp side by side. They are painted white and each aircraft has a big red cross painted on the tail.

"You notice people with various colored flying suits filing up the aircraft stairs. Some of the passengers are wearing medical scrubs, while others are being carried aboard on stretchers by ambulance attendants. If you'd taken the time to count each person boarding the plane you would have counted approximately 331 people boarding each airplane.

"Now imagine for a moment you boarded one of those planes. As you file past the cockpit you notice there is only one pilot. What you couldn't have known is that the plane doesn't have an operable autopilot and that the pilot has had some instrument training but is not current to fly on instruments; that is, he's out of practice. In fact, because of the rules he must follow, he has to avoid flying into any bad weather at all costs, which is weather less than what he can legally fly in.

"You return to the departure lounge and look back at the three aircraft sitting on the ramp. You notice all three planes start their engines, then taxi out to the runway and take off, disappearing over the western horizon.

"Several hours pass and you hear on the news that all three

aircraft have crashed, killing 364 of the 964 people on board. Would you be outraged? Would you wonder how the regulating powers could allow such a thing to happen? Would you wonder why there was only one pilot and not two? Would you wonder why that one pilot did not have an autopilot to help him? Well that is *exactly* what has been going on in many of the air medical programs over the years and yes, we've had that many people involved in HEMS accidents: 964."

I then go on to say that every HEMS helicopter should have, at the very least, an autopilot to assist the pilot in case he gets into a jam or needs relief from manually flying to tend to other tasks. An autopilot could save the day if the pilot inadvertently finds himself in the clouds, experiences spatial disorientation (a leading cause of these accidents as noted by the FAA) or gets into a situation where he cannot see the horizon, like on an inky-black moonless night.

Not having an autopilot is like being sent off into modern battle with a bow and arrow. Next time you are at an airport ask any airline pilot if he would consider flying without the benefit of an autopilot and he will look at you as if you had lost your mind because there isn't an airline pilot out there who would *ever* consider flying an aircraft without one.

I told the audience how I was asked to write an article for a U.K. publication, *Waypoint AirMed and Rescue* magazine, and how that article also appeared in *Rotorcraft Pro.* The title of that article: "*A Surefire Fix for one of the Most Dangerous Jobs in America.*" I said that if they wanted to stop the terrible loss of life that has been plaguing the industry the answer was in that article.

I talked about crew resource management (CRM) and air medical resource management (AMRM) and how the HEMS industry can learn from the airlines because they managed to turn around their high accident rate beginning in 1979 – a rate that, at the time, was as unacceptable as the HEMS accident rate was in 2012.

By adopting the principles of CRM through good leadership, error avoidance, error trapping and mitigating an error when it occurred – plus knowing what the human pitfalls were that could cause an accident – the airlines kept improving their safety record, experiencing fewer and fewer accidents, until they managed to have one of the safest years on record in 2012, with 2011 being the safest year before that.

Knowing the value of CRM on air safety, as has been demonstrated over the years by the airlines, the FAA finally mandated that as of March 22, 2012, all Part 135 air taxi operators, which include all air medical programs, must have CRM/AMRM training. The FAA hopes CRM/AMRM can turn around the accident rate in HEMS by making it mandatory for all air taxi operators.

With the collective acceptance from top management, all the way down to the person who refuels the aircraft, if everyone in the team knows how his or her actions or inactions affect the safe outcome of a flight, the accident rate *can* be reduced. There is no reason to reinvent the helicopter. The answer is out there. We can stop these terrible crashes as the airlines proved so resoundingly, but it is up to everyone in the organization to be informed and ever-vigilant. However, without full commitment to the concept, it is doomed to failure.

So what is the simplest definition of AMRM? In its purest definition it is what I call in my CRM/AMRM course the CRM/AMRM mantra. It's easy to remember and it goes like this:

CRM/AMRM is a team member's awareness of what effect his or her action or inaction has on the safe and successful outcome of a flight.

And who would be considered a team member? Not just the pilot and crew. *A team member is* anyone *who has a bearing on the decision-making of the flight crew.*

My time on that Seattle stage flew by quickly. I wanted the audience to buy into two important messages: One, that every HEMS helicopter operating in American airspace should have an autopilot available to the pilot if a second pilot is not available. Two, that CRM/AMRM can save lives and is the last line of defense for avoiding an accident.

Future accident statistics will indicate whether my message was embraced or not.

///

The remaining time that Kaye and I spent at the conference is a blur, mainly because we were attached to the coattails of a master businessman, Jack Todaro, which, because of his high-energy and drive, made us feel like we're riding on a shooting star.

Jack *had* made arrangements for us to visit Oregon Aero. He told us, "I talked to the people back there and they're up for it. We were thinking around the tenth of the month. Does that work for you? We'll get you both out there; arrange your accommodation, expenses, etc. You can meet the CEO and founder, Mike Dennis, and the board members. Perhaps you could give a little presentation to him on CRM; then talk to the employees. I was thinking you could tell them about how you've become an activist for change in the HEMS industry. It's up to you. What do you think?"

"We'd be delighted."

"Good, I'll finalize the details and get back to you."

///

The curtain wasn't ready to be drawn just yet on our Seattle adventure. The script had yet to be fully played out. The finale occurred when we ran into Dr. Dan Hankins and his wife, Joan.

Dan Hankins is a past president and CEO of AAMS and an emergency medicine staff physician at Mayo Clinic Emergency Medicine. Joan works as a flight nurse there. What a team!

Dan had figured significantly in helping me get my safety message into the HEMS community, as he had been one of the people who had approved my request to be a keynote speaker at the air medical conference in St. Louis. Dan also had a hand in inviting me to speak at the Mayo Clinic at their annual *Safety Stand down Day*.

When Kaye and I saw Dan and Joan approaching us he said, "What do you two have planned for dinner tonight?"

"We haven't made plans."

"How about joining us and a few others, then? Dr. Greg Powell, the founder of the Shock Trauma Air Rescue Society (STARS) program in Calgary, and his wife Linda will be there. Dr. Andrew Berry, the head of neonatal HEMS in New South Wales in Australia will be there. He's involved with NETS. (Newborn Emergency Transport Service). They'll be lots of interesting people for you to meet."

Kaye and I glanced at one another, then I said, "We'd love to, Dan. Where and what time?"

Later that evening an unlikely invitation would come our way that neither Kaye nor I could have ever imagined happening even if *we* had written the script.

We met a group of about 12 doctors and program directors, many from other countries, in a private dining room off the main dining room of the restaurant. We enjoyed a truly memorable evening with lots of laughter, good wine and lively conversation.

I was able to speak to Greg Powell, who founded the first HEMS program in Canada in the 1970s. His program figured in a very positive way in my book, *The Golden Hour.*

Another definite highlight to that evening occurred when we were just about to leave the restaurant. Dr. Andrew Berry walked over, knelt down by the back between our two chairs and said – quietly so that only we could hear – "I'd like to invite both of you to come to Australia in August. I was wondering, Randy, if you would be willing to speak to members of several of our HEMS crews there and perhaps be a keynote speaker at our HEMS conference in Melbourne next August?"

"We'd love to come, Andrew, but why? I think you guys do it right down there. We here in the States could learn from the way you do things."

"I think your message would be very well received. I heard your keynote address in St. Louis last year and your safety speech today on CRM. I like your passion for safety and your message is definitely something we can all learn from. What do you say? Is coming to Australia and speaking to our crews down there something that would interest you?"

We could not say "yes" fast enough.

Forty-eight days after I stood on that stage in Seattle, at approximately 8:30 p.m., Central Time, December 10, 2012, Rockford Memorial Hospital's REACT helicopter crashed in a field south of Rochelle, Ill., in Lee County. There were no survivors. The crew members on the aircraft were Pilot Andy Oleson; Flight Nurse Jim Dillow, R.N.; and Flight Nurse Karen Hollis, R.N.

The last radio transmission from Andy Olesen to his hospital dispatcher was that he was turning around due to weather. It was reported by witnesses that there was sleet in the area. One witness said he saw the helicopter emerge from the overcast and crashed straight down. It is suspected the pilot lost spatial orientation.

Andy was one of the most experienced HEMS pilots in the industry. He had served as a helicopter pilot in the US Army for 23 years and had flown as a HEMS pilot for 19 years. The crash happened on a Monday. Andy was set to retire that Friday, just 10 days before Christmas. The aircraft – a BK 117, did not have an autopilot, meaning Andy was hand-flying the aircraft in that awful weather when it crashed.

On stage Seattle speaking about crew resource management

Article I'd Written my answer to 'fix' the HEMS system in America

Kaye and Jack Todaro sitting in the front row Seattle

The crash survivors who each told their heartrending stories during the Air Medical Transport Conference in Seattle. I followed them to give my CRM/AMRM keynote address. Front row L to R: Teresa Pearson, Megan Hamilton, the Author, Mike Eccard, Krista Haugen. Back L to R: Mike Moyer, Jonathan Godfrey, Danny Kelly

Six weeks after giving my keynote speech in Seattle, on December 10, 2012, Rockford Memorial Hospital's REACT helicopter crashed in a field south of Rochelle, Ill., in Lee County. There were no survivors. The crew members on the aircraft were Pilot Andy Oleson; Flight Nurse Jim Dillow, R.N.; and Flight Nurse Karen Hollis, R.N.

CHAPTER 22
Oregon Aero

Kaye and I arrived in Scappoose, Oregon, home of Oregon Aero, on November 10. Scappoose is a small town with a very small airstrip situated 20 miles north of Portland.

We were anxious to see Jack Todaro again, and were also eager to meet with the company's owner, president and CEO, Mike Dennis.

Like most people in the aviation industry I'd heard about Oregon Aero. I knew that the company did headset conversions to make them more efficient and more comfortable, eliminating what aviators call, "hot spots" that can occur on the human skull like a centralized pain that feels like heat. In fact, I had ordered oversized headset cushions from Oregon Aero after they were recommended to me by another pilot when I flew offshore with ADA. He had told me that they were more comfortable and blocked the noise much better than the jell-filled ones that come with the standard David Clark headset worn by most pilots. They worked as advertised, too. I knew Oregon Aero also did helmet conversions and designed seats for aircraft.

When Kaye and I arrived in our hotel room in Scappoose, arranged by Oregon Aero, there was a bouquet of flowers and a bottle of champagne to welcome us.

Kaye took the welcome card from the bouquet of flowers and after reading it said, "Lovely. Jack's obviously read the script. I'm so anxious to see what's in store for tomorrow. What do you think? Do you think Oregon Aero will want to sponsor you to give CRM/AMRM talks to medical crews?"

"It would be my dream. But sponsoring me would be such a departure from what the company actually does."

"Darling, I can't stand it. I can't wait to see what transpires."

I gave Kaye a big hug. "Exciting, huh?"

"Darling, you have no idea …."

///

The next morning we met Jack in the parking lot at Oregon Aero so he could arrange clearance for us to enter the building. He told us, "We're scheduled to meet Mike Dennis after we get you both signed in. You have your presentation ready?"

I pulled out my flash drive. "Right here."

I'd worked on it for about a week and was extremely happy with the result. I felt like I was interviewing for a job – a job that hadn't even been created yet.

Jack said, "Great. We'll just get you to sign the non-disclosure form, give you your passes and we'll be ready."

I was dressed in blue blazer, dress slacks, shirt and tie. Kaye was smartly dressed as well. When we entered the small conference room there were three people in the room already. The man farthest from me stood up. Casually dressed, he extended his hand and said, "Glad to meet you, Randy. Mike Dennis. Please, have a seat."

He introduced himself to Kaye and introduced us to the others. The man sitting to Mike's left, Tony Erickson, was the chief operating officer, and the woman sitting to my left was Gail Mellegard, the business development manager.

We made small talk as is usually customary in such situations. They asked about our drive up (in the rain). We thanked them for the kind gesture of champagne and the flowers in the room when we arrived.

It was hard to tell how old Mike was. I suppose 50, maybe

55. I'm lousy with guessing ages. He had a gentle, relaxed demeanor about him. He would sit, listening, his hands clasped behind his head in an open and relaxed posture, open for communication. When he spoke he took time to think and had a quiet, measured voice. He had what I would call a country-boy charm about him but when he spoke I could tell his mind was sharp – his brain firing on all 12 cylinders. Like Jack's.

Mike soon got to the point on why we were there. "Jack tells me you're trying to make a difference out there in helicopter EMS."

"Yes, sir, I am."

"Jack says you're pretty passionate about the subject."

"Very."

"And that maybe you can make a change in the accident rate with CRM."

"Yes sir. You familiar with CRM?"

"Yes, I'm a pilot. I know the benefits and try to practice it whenever I can."

Mike asked me to tell him about my background, so I did. I could feel my internal engine revving up as I began to describe the subject I'm so passionate about. I sensed those in the room could pick up on my enthusiasm.

I gave him a quick overview of my career up until that night in Abu Dhabi on August 31, 2010. I told him about becoming enraged at hearing of another HEMS crash, asking myself: "What could I do to bring about change?" because, in my mind, I held the key, the answer from what I'd seen "outside the cave" while living and working abroad.

I told Mike and the group how I'd emailed Oprah Winfrey (still waiting for an answer). How I'd rewritten *The Golden Hour,* which supplied an answer. Then contacted like-minded individuals in the industry to gain their support; sent out books; spoke at the HAC in Vancouver, and met Jack for the first time. I told him about writing *Journey to the Golden Hour* as another way to further my message.

I told him about the world-class CRM train-the-trainer

course I paid for and attended in England and about being offered my own monthly column in *Rotorcraft Pro Magazine.* I talked about being invited to speak in St. Louis (and the envelope opening), speaking at the Mayo Clinic on their *Safety Stand Down Day*, HELISUCCESS in Las Vegas, and speaking in Seattle on the subject of CRM a few days before coming to Oregon Aero. And now, Kaye and I were there in his boardroom.

That's when Jack said, "You have your presentation ready?"

"Sure do. Right here." I produced my flash drive and had Jack plug it into the Apple laptop sitting on the conference table. Big mistake. I didn't know at the time the video clips in my PowerPoint presentation wouldn't play on the Apple laptop.

I was fully wound up now – brimming with enthusiasm for the topic. The small group listened attentively as I began my presentation, at first describing the history of CRM, how United Airlines 173 from Denver to Portland had run out of fuel in December 1978 because the three crew members had lost situational awareness. They'd become too focused on a landing gear light that hadn't come on, which made them think they had an unsafe gear situation.

After that crash, the NTSB finally said "enough" and instructed NASA at the Ames Research Center to find out why perfectly serviceable airliners were crashing.

I had been speaking for about 10 or 15 minutes, clicking through the PowerPoint slides when I came to my first video clip and it wouldn't play. That moment was like hitting a solid barrier with a freight train. "Bang!" Stopped dead in my tracks, losing all momentum as Jack and I tried to fiddle with the computer, trying to make it work.

Mike had seen enough and said, "You're on a noble cause here but I'm afraid it won't work."

I know Kaye must have felt as crestfallen as I did when Mike uttered those words, like he'd put both feet on the brakes and stood on them.

I asked, "Why?"

"Unless you can show the operators out there how your course will save them money they won't buy into it."

I knew exactly what he was saying and he was right. In St. Louis I had said that I didn't think the operators would add a second pilot who was instrument-rated and current, or an autopilot to help out a pilot flying on his own, because I knew the operators would say, "Yes, but it's too expensive," to which I would argue "But how much is a human life worth?"

Mike continued, "Unless you can show them how much it costs to have an accident I'm afraid your idea of trying to save lives through your CRM course won't fly."

Neither Kaye nor I had to worry about Mike sugarcoating his response to my dream. The sickening thing is that he was dead right. I had too much of a Pollyanna attitude about this whole thing. I was *expecting* operators to do what was *morally* right. But if they hadn't done the morally right thing by supplying the safest combination of two pilots and twin-engine helicopters in the first place, how could I expect them to buy into paying someone like me to come to them to deliver my CRM/AMRM course?

My real fear was that the operators would get their own personnel to toe the company line and do the CRM training themselves; or worse, have their employees sit in front of a computer and do the CRM course that way. Computer-based CRM courses will not change attitudes. If they could, the airlines would be doing it. An effective CRM/AMRM course must be facilitated so the attendees come up with the answers themselves.

Mike's observation and comment, while 100-percent true and totally irrefutable, served to totally deflate me. I now felt like a ship becalmed, dead in the water, quickly taking on water, floundering. In my mind – and I know in Kaye's mind as well – the meeting was over. The very reason we'd been brought in to meet Mike Dennis today didn't manage to bring him on board. The trip had been for naught.

Mike said if I could find statistics from the insurance companies as to how much an accident actually costs an operator and if there could be some kind of break given on a company's insurance premium for having CRM courses taught to their people, then maybe I could get them on board.

It all came down to money again. My mind flashed back to the six crash survivors on that stage in Seattle recounting their harrowing stories. When will it end? When will it ever end? Another good idea blasted out of the water and it boils down to dollars and cents again.

Before we accepted the invitation to come to Oregon Aero, Jack had asked me if I would like to address the company's 70 or so employees – to talk to them for an hour about my story, how I became an activist for change. I said I would be glad to.

Jack checked his watch then said, "I think the employees are ready for you now, Randy. If you'll follow me."

I stood and thanked Tony Erickson and Mike Dennis and Gail Mellegard for their time. Then Kaye and I followed Jack through the building to where the employees were waiting.

The employees at Oregon Aero were a very attentive audience. For 50 minutes I recounted my story. It was a derivative of the story I'd told in St. Louis, at the Helicopter Association of Canada conference and the Mayo Clinic, including the Vietnam rescue story of the four recon team members. A woman told me afterward that while listening to my recollection of the Vietnam story, she was hardly breathing and began to cry.

After I'd spoken to the employees I answered a few questions, then Mike came up to me and said he would like to give Kaye and me a tour of the facility.

"The company was founded back in 1989 because of a headache." Mike began with a little grin on his face, knowing we'd take the bait.

"Headache?" I said.

"Yep, the headache belonged to my wife, Jude. She'd get a headache every time she flew with me."

He told us how he set out to tackle Jude's headache problem. After a great deal of research, thinking and experimentation, he created what has become a very popular item in the

Oregon Aero catalogue, the SoftTop® Headset Cushion made from leather and sheepskin wool. The SoftTop® Headset Cushion worked, too, because Jude's headaches disappeared. Thinking there may be others with a similar problem Mike and Jude began selling the Headset Cushions at local fly-ins.

Customer feedback was very positive. He continued to improve the design, adding custom designs for various headset models. Dozens of headset cushions were piled high on the kitchen table as they were sewn by hand; bolts of leather and other materials filling his garage.

From that unlikely beginning grew a company that today has become a leader in engineering and manufacturing in advanced seating systems for military and civilian aviation, and other industries where comfortable seating enhances job performance.

Mike told us that the main focus of the company still targets the same issues addressed back in 1989 with the SoftTop® Headset Cushion – the core philosophy being geared to making the interface between the human body and manufactured hardware pain-free, safer and quieter.

He said that Oregon Aero designs and manufactures maximum-comfort seating systems for military and civilian aircraft, land vehicles and experimental aircraft. The company also does interior conversions, manufactures portable seat cushions, does flight-helmet and headset upgrades to make them quieter, more comfortable and individually tailored to suit the individual who wears it.

His tour was enthralling and I soon forgot that my idea and my dream of being a CRM instructor for his company had been unceremoniously trumped by Mike's business acumen and logical thinking. Kaye and I soon realized we were in the presence of a brilliant, inventive mind.

"I've got dozens of patents and even more in the works waiting for approval."

Listening to how he approached a problem from every angle and managed to come up with a solution had us spellbound. I told Kaye later, after what would amount to a three-hour tour, "Thinking as hard and as much as Mike does, I would need one of his headsets for the permanent headache I would have."

Mike's kindness would overwhelm us. He showed us a mat he had designed that was a sponge-like material but had the texture of human skin. He told us, "I am trying to market these mats to hospitals to prevent bed sores. We have them on trial at three hospitals and they work. They're proven. But even with our data to show they work we can't get other hospitals to buy them."

"Why not?" Kaye said.

"Cuz the hospitals get money from Medicare for treating a treatable problem."

"That's sick," I said.

"That's our healthcare system," Mike answered with a shrug.

The bed mat was something Kaye was very interested in. She told Mike, "My dad in England has Parkinson's and has a hospital-style bed at home. If he isn't careful he can get pressure sores. He has a mat on the bed already but he doesn't like it much."

"Well, we'll send him one. How about foot droop? Does he suffer from that, too?"

"He wears these little bootie things but they aren't great."

With that, Mike went to a box and pulled out some specially fabricated booties that looked a bit like ski boots made of the same material as the mat. "We'll send him some of these, too."

"Oh, Mike, you are way too kind. My dad would so much appreciate it. Can we pay you for them?"

"No, Kaye. It's alright. Just let me know your dad's home address and we'll ship them to him."

You don't experience kindness like that very often. "Mike that is so kind," I said. "You have no idea what your gesture will mean to Kaye's dad and to her mom, who is his full time care-giver."

"My pleasure. Glad to do it."

Mike was very free with his time and showed us Oregon Aero's product line and some other new projects he was working on. What a mind. We said our goodbyes to Mike, thanked him for the tour, for paying our expenses to bring us from Canada to meet with him and his board, and for sending the mat and the booties to Kaye's dad in the U.K. He said it wasn't a problem and he was glad to do it. He said he needed to leave us to go pack because he and his wife were leaving on vacation in the morning.

I gave Mike copies of my books, *Dear Mom I'm Alive* and *Journey to the Golden Hour.* I signed them for him and told him he would have something to read during his vacation.

Jack then took us to meet a woman by the name of Jeannie Krieger. He said, "Jeannie has been compiling information for me about CRM."

Jack showed me a very large notebook with dividers that Jeannie had been putting together for him. I took it, thumbed through it, then said, "Looks like a lot of good information here. Good job, Jeannie."

"Thank you."

"Yep, she's been busy."

"Looks like it, Jack."

Then Jack said something that struck us as odd considering how my presentation had gone this morning. "I have allocated Jeannie to be working with you to put this thing together. Are you and Kaye free to meet for a few hours tomorrow?"

Wondering why he would want to meet with us and thinking the idea of my being sponsored by Oregon Aero was a dead issue after Mike's reaction in the boardroom I said, "Yes, we're free. We'd planned to stay for the full three days."

"OK, how about we meet here about ten tomorrow morning?"

"Great. Ten it is."

Jack escorted us to our parked car and said goodbye. As I was about to turn the key to start the engine, Mike walked over. To show respect, I opened my door and got out of the car. So did Kaye.

Mike said, “Just wanted to say that quite a few of the employees have come up to me and told me how much they enjoyed your talk. You made a real impression in there and I just wanted to thank you again.”

“It’s been our pleasure Mike. And we want to thank you for your extreme generosity. You have no idea how much the mat and booties will mean to Kaye’s dad.”

“Glad to do it.”

Kaye chimed in, “You can expect a hand-written thank you letter from my mom when it arrives, Mike. Thank you so much.”

“Like I said, glad to do it. Well, gotta get to the house and finish packing. Jude will be waiting on me.”

///

Our drive to the hotel was not a happy one. Kaye and I were feeling pretty low. Jack still seemed upbeat as if what Mike had said in the boardroom had no bearing on his “big picture.” He acted as if I still had a chance. But we told ourselves that if Mike didn’t buy into it, and he’s the owner, the CEO, and the boss, how could I still have a chance? The mixed signals were confusing.

As we pulled into the hotel parking lot, Kaye said, “Well, Darling, when we get back to the room we’ll pop the cork on that bottle of champagne they gave us. We’ll meet with Jack tomorrow and maybe we can find out exactly where you stand.”

“That sounds like an excellent idea. You can’t say we didn’t try. At least we did that.”

///

When we met with Jack at 10 the next morning he seemed as positive, energetic and upbeat as ever.

I had to ask, "Kaye and I were a little confused when we left yesterday afternoon about just where I stand. Mike seemed so negative on the idea. He brought up some very good points on why my effort to teach CRM/AMRM to medical crews wouldn't work."

"We're going to press on. Are you with me?"

"Of course … but …."

He brushed off my obvious skepticism, brought out his yellow legal pad and asked, "How much were you hoping to make this year if you do this?"

I think I shocked him with my answer, "What's important to me, Jack, is to get this message out there. If I come away breaking even then that's good enough for me."

Jack looked at me, shaking his head. "You're obviously not a businessman."

"Jack, I'll leave that up to you. My job is to try to make a difference. If I make a buck, fine, but it's not my motivation for doing this."

With that Jack set to the task of formulating the skeleton of a plan. I still wasn't convinced, nor was Kaye, considering Mike's reaction. But we felt we had nothing to lose by keeping on the coattails of Jack, who didn't seem to be put off at all by the negative reaction of his boss.

"Jack, you've obviously done this before."

"I've owned six businesses. Built them up to multi-million-dollar enterprises." He shrugged and said, "What can I say. I like a challenge."

"Well you've certainly got one in me."

"You'd be surprised. Piece of cake."

Kaye and I told Jack about the extremely kind gesture Mike made by offering to send a hospital mat and a pair of hospital booties to Kaye's dad in England. When we told Jack this he said, "You know how much those mats are sold for?"

"Nope."

"Three thousand eight-hundred dollars."

"What?"

"My God, I had no idea." Kaye said, obviously shocked. So was I.

"Mike's a kind and generous man."

I said, "That he is, Jack."

Kaye said, "He has no idea what that will mean to my family."

Jack just smiled and said, "Oh, I think he does."

///

Jack saw us off in the Oregon Aero parking lot, wishing us a safe drive back to Canada the next morning. The way we left our arrangement with Oregon Aero was still confusing to both of us. Mike, the boss, had looked at the venture as being a non-starter unless of course I could somehow convince the vendors that they wouldn't lose money by employing me to give CRM classes to their flight crews. How could I convince them of that?

Jack, on the other hand, was pressing on as if Mike hadn't been in the conference room that morning.

I told Kaye, "I'm still confused."

"Yeah, me too. I find it weird after seeing Mike's reaction that Jack would press on with his business plan and want to meet with you this morning, ask you how much money you'd like to make the first year, and tell you that Jeannie Krieger will be working with you to promote you and your effort. I guess all we can do is wait for Jack to contact you to tell you where we go from here."

"Looking back to when I resigned from ADA, with no plan other than a passion to teach CRM, thinking at the time that Rick Sherlock or Kevin Hutton offered us the greatest hope of sponsoring me, then that not panning out, then Jack coming on the scene from virtually nowhere … I can't believe he still seems so positive about the prospects." I shook my head. "I really don't get it and to be honest I don't know where the heck I stand."

"Darling, we just have to wait and see. You go back to Abu

Dhabi to work your last shift in a few days' time. Perhaps things will become clearer when you're gone and Jack's had time to work on it."

"Yep, OK, we'll see. All I can do is wait, I guess."

%

Kaye and I had an early dinner at a funky little restaurant called The Village Inn, within walking distance from the hotel, and returned to our room to pack. We'd need to get up around 4 a.m. to be on the road by 5 a.m. to ensure we wouldn't miss the ferry from Port Angeles to Vancouver Island.

Kaye and I were ready for bed now and before turning out the light I decided to check my email on the laptop one last time.

"Hey, Hon, there's one here from Jack."

Kaye came to look over my shoulder as I clicked on it. It read:

> *Dear Randy.*
> *Just had a word with the board. Your new title will be:*
> *CHIEF CRM/AMRM SAFETY INSTRUCTOR*
> *OREGON AERO.*
> *More to come.*
> *Welcome to the Oregon Aero family!*
> *Regards, Jack.*

Kaye spoke first, "Oh, Darling! What wonderful news. I am so proud of you!" she said, hugging me tightly.

I shook my head, feeling elated, jubilant, relieved, spent, as if a huge weight had been suddenly lifted from my shoulders. "It's as much you as it is me Honey. You've been my staunch supporter and confidant through all of this. When I've been down you've always believed in me. Supported me. Thank you, Hon."

"I can't believe it. What a final leave this has been. What a truly incredible leave this has been. Time for another script, sweetheart. Wonder how this next chapter will turn out?"

"Time will tell Hon. Time will tell. Hopefully I can now make a difference with Oregon Aero's support behind me. If I can save the lives of just one flight crew it'll all be worth it."

Kaye gave me another long hug.

"You will, Darling, I just know you will."

END

The following is a list of HEMS fatal accidents that occurred during the nine years I worked for Abu Dhabi Aviation.

(Source Air Medical Memorial Website
www.airmedicalmemorial.com)

2004		
Air Evac	Apache Junction, AZ	December 14, 2004
Med Flight	San Diego, CA	October 24, 2004
AIRHeart	Choctawhatchee Bay, FL	October 20, 2004
Access Air	Battle Mountain, NV	August 21, 2004
Regional One	Newberry, SC	July 13, 2004
MCH CareStar	Pyote, TX	March 21, 2004
EagleMed	Dodge City, KS	February 17, 2004
2005		
Life Star	Smethport, PA	October 7, 2005
Airlift Northwest	Edmonds, WA	September 29, 2005
Tri-State CareFlight	Mancos, CO	June 30, 2005
Yampa Valley Air Ambulance	Rawlins, WY	January 11, 2005
LifeEvac II	Oxon Hill, MD	January 10, 2005
North Mississippi Medical Center	Falkner, MS	January 5, 2005
2006		
FlightSource	Johnstown, PA	December 26, 2006
Mercy Air 2	Hesperia, CA	December 10, 2006
Eagle III	Green Bay, WI	April 13, 2006
Hawaii Air Ambulance	Kahului, HI	March 8, 2006
2007		
AirEvac Lifeteam	Colbert County, AL	December 30, 2007

LifeGuard Alaska	Prince William Sound, AK	December 3, 2007
Eagle Air Med	Charley's Peak, CO	October 4, 2007
Southwest Med Evac	Ruidoso, NM	August 5, 2007
U-M Survival Flight	Milwaukee, WI	June 4, 2007
Benefis Mercy	Belgrade, MT	February 6, 2007
2008		
Air Angels	Aurora, IL	October 15, 2008
Arizona DPS	Sedona, AZ	October 14, 2008
Maryland State Police	Forestville, MD	September 27, 2008
Air-Evac Lifeteam	Greensburg, IN	August 31, 2008
Classic Lifeguard, Guardian Air	Flagstaff, AZ	June 29, 2008
PHI Air Medical-PHI Med 12	Hunstville, TX	June 8, 2008
UW Med Flight	La Crosse, WI	May 10, 2008
Valley AirCare	Laguna Madre, TX	February 5, 2008
2009		
Mountain Lifeflight	Hallelujah Junction, CA	November 14, 2009
Carolina Lifecare	Georgetown, SC	September 25, 2009
2010		
MedFlight of Ohio	Wellston, OH	October 19, 2010
Air Evac Lifeteam	Scotland, AR	August 31, 2010
Air Methods LifeNet	Tucson, AZ	July 28, 2010
EagleMed	Kingfisher, OK	July 22, 2010
Air Ambulance Stat	Alpine, TX	July 4, 2010
CareFlite	Midlothian, TX	June 2, 2010
Hospital Wing	Brownsville, TN	March 25, 2010
Southwest Med Evac	Fort Bliss, TX	February 5, 2010

2011		
Mayo Clinic	Palatka, FL	December 26, 2011
Trans North Aviation	Riverwoods, IL	November 28, 2011
Air Methods LifeNet	Mosby, MO	August 26, 2011
2012		
REACT	Compton, IL	December 10, 2012
2013		
Mercy Air Med	Ventura, IA	January 2, 2013
Eagle Med	Oklahoma City, OK	February 22, 2013
Air Evac	Manchester, KT	June 6, 2013

Postscript

In the column I write every month in *Rotorcraft Pro Magazine* called, "My Two Cents Worth," I'd written a piece about the power of crew resource management in preventing accidents. I received an email from retired Continental Airlines pilot and former HEMS helicopter pilot, Mike Brezden, who'd read the article and wrote to me to comment. His observations are worth noting:

I, too, flew as a pilot in a helicopter EMS program early in my career (1982-1984). Sadly, not much has changed in the industry. I left that position, got my fixed-wing ratings, and went on to a 23-year career with Continental Airlines. I consider CRM training at Continental the single most important training I've ever received in aviation. It works.

It was my experience that the pilots who resisted CRM the most were the ones who needed it the most. It was the same with checklists; the ones that had the least checklist discipline were the ones that really needed a checklist.

I'm glad to hear that CRM training is now mandated in the helicopter EMS industry. Any additional awareness on the part of the flight crews will help, but unfortunately, until management is willing to spend the money to make twin engine, IFR the norm; I suspect the accident rate will remain high. Adding a second pilot would reduce the accident rate even further.

If I could offer any advice it would be to try to get the message across that CRM is a radical change in lifestyle. It's something that will take effort on the part of all involved and probably won't come naturally, especially in stressful situations. At Continental Airlines it was a central part of our recurrent ground training every year. Additionally, once we "got it," it was the only way we flew, both in the simulator and on the line. In training, there was no such thing as one pilot passing a checkride, and the other failing, as sometimes happened in the old days. You were now a team. We used to joke that there is no such thing as "Your side of our airplane is about to crash."

And most importantly, if someone speaks up, tell the people not to take it personally. There are some super-sensitive egos in this business, and they bruise easily. Team members must learn how to say things without sounding critical, and they also must learn how to accept and encourage such challenges. That's by far the toughest part of this whole CRM concept.

As far as your ideas about two-crew, IFR currency, and single engine VFR at night; I agree 110 percent. Last fall things worked out where I flew 16 hours in a Bell 407 with our mutual friend, Tom Einhorn. I really enjoyed that, and realized how much I missed it. I started asking around with some local EMS programs what jobs were available, and what the employment conditions were like. I was soon offered a job flying a single-engine helicopter.

I really wanted to get back into flying helicopters and was tempted to take the job, but declined the offer. A major factor in my decision being I considered it too dangerous to routinely fly a single-engine, single-pilot, VFR-equipped aircraft at night.

I'm a 21,000-hour pilot with ATPs (airline transport pilot) in both fixed and rotary-wing aircraft. I have instrument instructor certificates in both fixed and rotary-wing aircraft, and many, many hours of night and IFR flying; and yet, I thought that job presented too great a risk. I'm very confident in my skills as a pilot, but at this point in my life, I have nothing to prove to anyone.

I wish you the best of luck with your CRM training.
Mike Brezden
Continental Airlines, retired

Made in the USA
Middletown, DE
27 December 2022